12/10 (2) IAD 9/.

STATE OF EMERGENCY

STATE OF EMERGENCY

TRAVELS IN A
TROUBLED WORLD

NAVID KERMANI

TRANSLATED BY TONY CRAWFORD

polity

First published in German as *Ausnahmezustand: Reisen in eine beunruhigte Welt* © Verlag C. H. Beck ohG, Munich, 2016

This English edition © Polity Press, 2018

11 maps © Peter Palm, Berlin/Germany

The translation of this work was supported by a grant from the Goethe-Institut.

Polity Press
65 Bridge Street
Cambridge CB2 1UR, UK

Polity Press
101 Station Landing
Suite 300
Medford, MA 02155, USA

ISBN-13: 978-1-5095-1470-0
ISBN-13: 978-1-5095-1471-7 (pb)

A catalogue record for this book is available from the British Library.
Names: Kermani, Navid, 1967- author.
Title: State of emergency : travels in a troubled world / Navid Kermani.
Other titles: Ausnahmezustand. English
Description: Cambridge, UK : Polity Press, 2018. | Translation of: Ausnahmezustand : Reisen in eine beunruhigte Welt. | Includes bibliographical references and index.
Identifiers: LCCN 2017036533 (print) | LCCN 2017039888 (ebook) | ISBN 9781509514748 (Epub) | ISBN 9781509514700 | ISBN 9781509514700 (hardback) | ISBN 9781509514717(pbk.)
Subjects: LCSH: Kermani, Navid, 1967---Travel. | Middle East--Description and travel.
Classification: LCC DS49.7 (ebook) | LCC DS49.7 .K44513 2018 (print) | DDC 915.604--dc23
LC record available at https://lccn.loc.gov/2017036533

Typeset in 10.75 on 14pt Janson by Servis Filmsetting Ltd, Stockport, Cheshire
Printed and bound in the UK by CPI (UK) Ltd, Croydon

The publisher has used its best endeavours to ensure that the URLs for external websites referred to in this book are correct and active at the time of going to press. However, the publisher has no responsibility for the websites and can make no guarantee that a site will remain live or that the content is or will remain appropriate.

Every effort has been made to trace all copyright holders, but if any have been inadvertently overlooked the publisher will be pleased to include any necessary credits in any subsequent reprint or edition.

For further information on Polity, visit our website: politybooks.com

CONTENTS

WE TOO LOVE LIFE 261

LIFE AS WHAT IT IS 277

EDITORIAL NOTE

The reports in this book originally appeared, in much shorter versions, as newspaper and magazine articles in the *Neue Zürcher Zeitung* (Afghanistan I), the *Süddeutsche Zeitung* (Pakistan), *die tageszeitung* (Palestine), *Der Spiegel* (Iraq) and *Die Zeit* (all other chapters). I thank the editors and the archives of those publications, especially *Die Zeit*, and my editor Jan Ross, for their encouragement, support and advice. I would also like to thank the Goethe Institutes in Ramallah, Jerusalem, Karachi and Cairo, the Goethe Centre in Lahore and the Konrad Adenauer Foundation in Cairo, which invited me to give readings and lectures. All the other trips were taken on assignment for the publications named.

The travelogues written between 2006 and 2009 have become part of the novel *Dein Name* (published by Hanser, Munich, 2011).

I thank my editor Ulrich Nolte at C. H. Beck for his excellent collaboration over many years, most recently on this book.

CAIRO, DECEMBER 2006

The tea house where I was the youngest of the regulars, twenty years ago, has expanded but lost none of its charm. To be exact, a few more plastic chairs have been set out in the narrow alley between two sooty colonial buildings, nothing more; but, in this place, just moving some furniture is a cultural revolution. Because any natural sense of taste seems to have died out in Cairo three, four decades ago, progress mostly takes the definition Adorno gave it: preventing progress. Around one, two o'clock, the tiredest whores in Cairo are sure to turn up for a last cola or a first client, while Umm Kulthum sings, as every night, of 'those days'. The enchantment of the tea house, like that of every hostelry worthy of the name anywhere in the world, consists in the fact that nothing matches and therefore everything, as chance would have it, goes together: the furnishings and the decor, which must have been shabby already when the place opened; the cordial staff who nonetheless overcharge; the most artistic Arab orchestras from the most excruciating loudspeakers; the men regressing to little boys over card and board games; the women likewise acting as if they were still young; and, most of all, the laughter, the loud, chortling, jangling, squeaking, hoarse, malicious, self-effacing, gloating, roguish, jolly, forgiving laughter that is heard more often in Cairo than in any other city, and nowhere in Cairo more often than in the tea house in the evening, and, fortunately, still heard today, I must record, for I am always afraid until I return that the demon responsible for it all may have vanished. An entry in a travel guide could be the end of it, or a notice in the newspapers by one of the new zealots nostalgic for something that never existed – prostitution is among Cairo's traditions, but not puritanism. There is no way that a symphony like the tea house could be composed today. And of course it never was composed; it was simply there, already a relic on its opening day. All the guests gather and pose for a group portrait, together with the staff and the neighbourhood's shopkeepers, for a daughter eager to take a picture with her birthday present. Then the head waiter takes a picture of father and daughter that by itself is worth the twenty-year journey.

PARADISE IN A STATE OF EMERGENCY

KASHMIR, OCTOBER 2007

HOUSEBOAT 1

The Paris Photo Service, whose assortment features Kodak film, rows by. Although the sun is shining, the mountains look as if God had dipped them in milk and hung them up to dry. Next comes a shikara, as the gondolas are called in Kashmir, bringing groceries to the houseboat that was recommended to me by my local friends. And in fact it is clean and comfortable, in the British colonial style, like all of Srinagar's eight hundred floating guesthouses, with heavy, dark furniture, oriental rugs, massive armchairs, although it is oriented towards Indian rather than Western tourists because it is close to the city, where Dal Lake is no wider than a river. As a result, the promised experience of silence, space and snow-covered mountains mirrored in the water turns out to be rather less than majestic. I have a view of cars and rickshaws, multi-storey office buildings of bare concrete, and a hill with a television antenna on top. The Indians seem to find the hundred yards that separate us from the noise of the traffic more than enough. But I, against my best intentions, was slightly disappointed, especially since the evenings on the veranda of the houseboat are so cold that I crawl back indoors and under my blanket to write.

Nevertheless, I am gradually discovering more and more advantages of the situation I have landed in. The boat belongs to a family with deep local roots whose thirty-two members can always find exactly what I happen to need and can supply the full spectrum of opinions, demands and desires that Srinagar has to offer, in addition to a driver, a change of travel reservations, a SIM for my mobile phone. My Indian SIM doesn't work here for security reasons. To get a new prepaid SIM, you have to have a fixed abode and the approval of the army. Now the boat owner's niece will have to do without her phone for a few days. She doesn't seem to use it much anyway – there are no contacts stored on her SIM except the service numbers that came with it: Astro Tel, Dial a Cab, Dua (prayers), Flori Tel, Food Tel, Horoscope, Info Tel, Movie Tel, Music Online, Odd Jobs, Ringtones, Shop OnLine, Travel Tel, Weather. For a city at war, where hardly a street lamp is lit in the evening, the offerings are stupendous. After almost twenty years in a state of emergency, Kashmir has long since grown accustomed to it.

The division of the Indian subcontinent has torn open many wounds: a million people dead, 7 million driven from their homes. Kashmir is one of these wounds that never seems to heal: heavenly Kashmir of all places, whose glaciers, lakes and meadows enchanted more than just poets and voyagers, unfortunately. Foreign rulers had been conquering the valley since the fourteenth century, exploiting it, and often buying and selling it. After the withdrawal of the British in 1947, the larger part of the province fell to India, in spite of its predominantly Muslim population; the west fell to Pakistan; a strip in the northeast was later claimed by China. India promised the United Nations to hold a referendum in which the Kashmiris would decide their own fate. That has not yet come to pass; instead, three wars with Pakistan have. Delhi did accord the province a high degree of autonomy, but in 1989, after a series of patently fraudulent regional elections, an armed rebellion broke out which has since cost hundreds of thousands of people their lives – among a population of 5 million. The Indian army is said to have stationed some 600,000 soldiers in the province, most of them in the Kashmir Valley, which is barely twice the size of Luxembourg. There is no remotely comparable concentration of troops anywhere in the whole world. There are soldiers everywhere, in every city, in every village, on the main roads and the side roads, the high streets, the lanes and even the tracks between the fields, then in the fields themselves, and of course on the lakeshore across from me, one every fifty yards. To the Indians, it is a war against terror. To the local people, it is an occupation.

IN THE CITY

Dead zones interrupt all phone calls near a military facility – if you're driving, that happens every three minutes. Otherwise, except for the soldiers everywhere, you would never notice during the daytime that Srinagar is at war. But is this war? The army itself, which is not inclined to downplay the danger, sets the number of rebels remaining at about one thousand. The journalists I meet in Srinagar, Indians included, estimate there are a few dozen fighters – at most two, three hundred – plus an indeterminate number of men who work at their jobs in the daytime and at sabotage in the evening. About once a week on average, the newspapers report a skirmish or an attack, often foiled at the last minute. The news agencies issue reports from about eight dead upwards. They write the number of extremists killed, always extremists, whether it is Reuters, AP or CNN. If you read the local press, it is remarkable how many extremists carry address books with them neatly listing the names of their accomplices and ringleaders. A few days later, the same newspapers report a wave of arrests, saying the authorities have struck an important blow against terrorism.

The people, all the people I talk to without exception, are fed up with war. 'Fed up' is the expression I hear the most often by far. All right, to be honest I hear *salamualeikum*

more frequently, or *aleikum salam* whenever I surprise someone with the Islamic greeting. 'Peace be with you': that has
a very peculiar sound in Kashmir. As time goes on it sounds
like a supplication, and this is more than just my imagina-
tion; it is an inkling that each new person I talk to will tell
me once more they have had quite enough of war, they
are fed up: with the nocturnal searches, the ID checks; fed
up most of all with the arbitrary actions of these foreign
soldiers – foreign-looking, too, darker skin, foreign language, foreign religion, foreign food, foreign customs, and
looking as if they're guarding even the chicken coops with
their loaded machine guns. Even at the university, the heart
of the movement for independence a few years ago, I meet
no one who would still be willing to fight: fed up. Everyone
supports the demand for self-determination, I am assured by
a professor of English who looks about as old as the Indian
state, a professor emerita, that is – but what happens the day
after? she asks her students. We need to know that before-
hand: none of you has told me anything about that. Will
other powers intervene? Neighbouring countries, China,
the United States? Will this be another Afghanistan? What
about people of other religions? What about women? She
can't see a secular Kashmir. One look at the potential leaders
of a free Kashmir is enough for her: Islamists. The students
are silent. Some of them have founded a magazine, which
mainly limits itself to the problems on campus. The whole
resistance has shrunk to this, says one of the editors, to these
few stapled pages out of the photocopier. Graduating is
more important. See that you don't get involved in politics,
their parents warn them, many of whom fought themselves
for *azadi*, as the magic word was in Kashmir in 1989: for
freedom.

In 2002, regional elections were held that are said to have
been relatively honest. The coalition in Srinagar is at pains

to curb the human rights violations of the Indian army and demands that the soldiers return to barracks. The army has already withdrawn from the old city centre with its narrow lanes. I am so surprised to find no uniforms there that I find myself watching for them. And then I do spy the occasional soldier: machine guns slung on their backs, they stroll casually, shop, haggle over prices. The Indian tourists on the other hand don't seem to feel safe yet in the old centre, which is so picturesque with its stone and wood houses that one expects to see around every corner a troop of Japanese, a German in a sari or an American in shorts. Since the war, however, tea houses and squares where one lingers aimlessly are no longer a part of Kashmiri culture, but the mosques on the other hand are so well frequented as I have seen only in war zones.

HOUSEBOAT 2

Yes, the Indians are back, recognizable by their clothes, their cameras, their dark skin. On my houseboat too an Indian family has checked in, an engineer from Calcutta with his wife, sister and two children. The engineer and I discover we are the same age, almost to the day. Hey, we have to drink to that, he says, and regrets that the houseboats no longer serve alcohol. His views are just as moderate as those of our host – in other words, irreconcilable. To the engineer, Kashmir is a part of India, 'an integral part, of course,' he emphasizes. No, in the schoolbooks there is nothing about the founders of the Indian state promising to hold a referendum. So the soldiers know nothing about it? No, they don't know; you would have to go to university or otherwise concern yourself with history to find the Kashmiris' cause anything but absurd. India, he says, pumps enormous amounts of money into Kashmir. He pays twice as much for tomatoes in Calcutta as in Srinagar. Kashmiris want peace, every people wants peace – but the terrorism … if it weren't for the terrorism. The Indian family is going to spend the day in Gulmarg, a skiing town at 9,000 feet. See you this evening. Yes, see you this evening.

The boat owner, an educated man of about fifty, clean-shaven morning and evening, nods to indicate a white building on the bank, a former hotel that the Indian army has commandeered as a barracks. A few days ago two young people were shot there, officially two suicide bombers trying to get in. The boat owner says the young people were brought to Srinagar by the army and executed here. None of the houseboat residents or the local police witnessed anything to do with an alleged attack. In the photos in the newspapers that the boat owner shows me, the faces are disfigured, so they offer no clue as to whether they are Kashmiris or, as the army claims, foreigners. In any case, the boat owner is convinced they were not suicide bombers, but prisoners. The government of Kashmir, he says, is putting pressure on the army to give up the hotel and reduce its presence in the city. The army is presenting its kind of evidence that terrorism is still a threat to the state.

Between the guests and the hosts I am almost a kind of mediator, trying to elicit understanding sometimes for one position, sometimes for the other. They themselves have nothing more to say to each other – although no unfriendly tones are heard – except when the meals will be ready and where the remote control for the television set is: masters on the one side, not as Indians over Kashmiris, but as guests over the staff, free enough of prejudice to spend their holidays among the rebels; servants on the other side, glad that someone at least is staying on their houseboats again.

POLITICIANS 1-4

Kashmiri politicians who have not gone underground live in their own neighbourhood, separated from the population by roadblocks. If you want to visit the mansions in which the Indian state accommodates them, you first have to pass through several checkpoints. The best-known politicians at least seem to be assigned a whole company of soldiers who bivouac on their park-like grounds, using the garden pavilion as barracks, the tool shed as a field kitchen, the gatekeeper's lodge for the officers' quarters. As stylish as the mansions look from the outside, their interiors have all the charm of furnished flats. Of course, to the ordinary people, politicians belong to a caste of their own whose loyalty is richly rewarded by the Indian state. In the mansions themselves, the impression is different. Here the politicians look rather lost amid the furniture that doesn't belong to them, with soldiers outside their windows, their own city a territory in which they hardly ever set foot – they usually traverse it in a heavily armed convoy.

One politician especially, Yussof Tarigami, chairman of the Communist Party of Kashmir, which tolerates the governing coalition, is convincing in his uneasiness, sitting on the sofa as if he was his own guest, a melancholy man in his fifties with black hair, somewhat too long, parted on the side, who could pass for a police detective in an Italian film. I have no choice, he says. Two years ago he barely escaped an assassination attempt, not his first.

The politicians have little good to say about the state that guards their lives. In the mansions I heard the same accounts of arbitrary arrests, continual humiliation, alienation from India. Violence is on the wane, Tarigami feels, but not because the Kashmiris have reconciled themselves to the occupation: out of exhaustion rather. He himself considered armed resistance wrong from the beginning and decided to carry on the struggle through the institutions. His living in this mansion, yes, a captive, is of course the consequence of having stayed within the system. He too demands self-determination, but points out that the state consists not only of the Kashmir Valley, with its largely Muslim population, but also of Jammu, where the majority is Hindu, and Ladakh, with its many Buddhists. What would happen to them if Kashmir fell to Pakistan? Tarigami asks me, as the English professor asked her students the day before. Independence sounds good, yet a secular, multicultural state is perfectly unrealistic in view of the three giants it would have as neighbours, India, Pakistan, China, none of which would give up its share of Kashmir. There is no perfect solution, Tarigami sighs, and goes on to sketch a plan for a Kashmir that is largely autonomous, though not formally independent, with open borders to the Pakistani part and regional self-government in the three provinces Jammu, Kashmir and Ladakh. That is exactly what the Indian prime minister Atal Bihari Vajpayee and the Pakistani president Pervez Musharraf proposed back in 2003. Vajpayee's successor, Manmohan Singh, expressed something similar in 2005: not to eliminate the borders, but to make them irrelevant.

'All we can do is exert pressure, by peaceful means, so that India and Pakistan finally do what they have basically long since agreed on, Tarigami explains. We have to get public opinion in India and Pakistan on our side. We have to show that peace is possible!'

One of the paradoxes of Srinagar is that it is easier to meet with the leaders of the resistance than with political office-holders or with representatives of the military. You simply ring the bell, and sometimes it is the leader himself who opens the door of his house, which is modest, but at least belongs to him. What is still more perplexing, however, is that the resistance leaders are demanding the same thing in principle as the government politicians: autonomy, open borders, withdrawal of the army – the solution sketched out by Hojatoleslam Abbas Ansari is no different.

As a leader of the Shiite minority, the cleric Ansari is one of the spokesmen of the Hurriyat Conference, the umbrella organization of the various resistance groups. The English professor included politicians like him in her warning against Islamists yesterday; Ansari himself assures me he rejects theocracy. Sitting cross-legged, his heels pulled up close under him, an impish smile under his white turban, he moves his hands incessantly as if something suspenseful were about to begin, a match or a game, a coup or a revolution. Perhaps because our conversation is in Persian, he describes the disputes within the resistance with surprising candour. Everyone knows, he says, that the armed struggle is over. The opposition must negotiate in order to stand, perhaps not in the next elections, but in the elections after that. The extremists are not so extreme; they are only insulted that no one has invited them to the table. Make them ministers and you'll have them on your side.

'The people say their leaders have sold them out,' I observe, and I emphasize, '*all* their leaders.'

'The people are right,' Ansari answers.

'That means you have sold them out too.'

'Yes.'

'They say the leaders of the resistance have received money from both sides.'

'True. We leaders of Kashmir have failed, one and all.'

'You too?' I ask.

The cleric looks up at the ceiling, as if he would leave it to God to answer that.

If it is a slim majority in Palestine and Israel who know what peace would imply, in this conflict everyone involved knows it: the people, the politicians, the soldiers, the world community – yet for years nothing has happened; there are no more talks, no peace conferences and, since the new Indian-American cooperation, no more international pressure on Delhi and Islamabad. That was different in the 1990s, when the American president Bill Clinton called Kashmir the most dangerous conflict in the world because India and Pakistan both have the atomic bomb. Today India is too strong internationally to have to accept a compromise, and the Pakistani government is too weak domestically to be able to accept one. So peace is limited, for the time being, to a bus that runs once a week between the Indian and Pakistani parts of Kashmir.

Finally I meet a leader who still clings to armed struggle and the goal of an Islamic state. Coincidentally, or perhaps not, Syed Geelani is by far the most charismatic politician Kashmir has to offer, an elegant, older man with a snow-white beard, his cheeks and his upper lip shaven except for a thin moustache. His rectangular cloth cap makes his face look still narrower. Weary eyes, soft voice, good English, clear articulation. Two days before, he was prevented by force from leading Friday prayers – not by the army, but by Kashmiris, the adherents of a rival resistance group which has backed away from the demand for a referendum. Perhaps because he still feels the humiliation, he embraces me, a reporter still asking for his opinion, a few seconds longer than is customary, and silently. When he thinks he sees me shiver, he brings me, although he could just as easily call a servant, a heavy wool blanket from the next room, and one for himself too. Then we sit, bundled up, face to face.

I fully understand Syed Geelani's position, the wish for self-determination for which he argues persuasively, with unchanging composure and firmness. He describes in detail the atrocities of the Indian army, especially the rapes, a twelve-year-old before her mother's eyes, then the mother before the eyes of the twelve-year-old, and so on. The problem is that, unfortunately, he is not exaggerating; at most, he is neglecting to mention that the number of assaults seems to be declining. He dismisses as Indian propaganda the accounts which hold the rebels likewise responsible for abuses and murders. From what I know of Pakistan, I think his advocacy of the annexation of Kashmir by Pakistan is, with all due respect, not such a good idea, although I do not phrase it so directly. Geelani radiates such a dignity that one hesitates, as his junior, to contradict him openly. The Pakistanis themselves have dropped the demand for a referendum, I object at last. As if the Pakistanis had had anything to say in the matter, Geelani counters. Not the Pakistanis, but Pervez Musharraf dropped the demand for a referendum: Kashmir, he says, has been betrayed yet again.

A traitor? To the question whether she considers herself an Indian, Mehbooba Mufti answers without hesitation: 'Yes, of course I am Indian. I am Kashmiri and Indian.' Whenever a Western television team has found its way to Kashmir in recent years, it has been happy to portray Mehbooba Mufti as a figure of hope: a middle-aged woman, divorced, who, as chairman of the People's Democratic Party, calls on her people to put down their weapons and, at the same time, raises her voice against the crimes of the Indian army, a diplomatic, Muslim Joan of Arc, religious and feminist. She persuaded many Kashmiris to vote in the last elections and led her party from a standing start into the coalition government. When I visit her in her mansion, she is much more a politician than I had assumed from the reporting: her answers seem prepared in advance, not because they sound implausible, but because I'm unable to ask her any questions she hasn't already answered many times. That she is considering leaving the coalition because the state government is not putting enough pressure on the army and on the national government in Delhi is at least worth a mention in the local press, as I will later discover. It is striking, says Mehbooba Mufti, alluding to the 'faked encounters', that a terrorist attack always occurs exactly when calls to withdraw the soldiers get louder.

She takes me along the next day on a tour through the villages of her constituency in her Ambassador – the Indian saloon car we know from Agatha Christie films – and with an escort of fourteen military vehicles. Although she said yesterday that the Kashmiri police were easily able to ensure domestic security, today she admits that the Indian soldiers guarding her are necessary. The route, and especially the spontaneous detours and pauses she commands, are a nightmare for her bodyguards, whose faces show their frustration and tension. Is it a show she's putting on for the foreign reporter? She wins elections by financing a well here and a cemetery fence there, listening to the complaints about an arrested son, listening to the mistreated father, writing down names, promising to look into it. It occurs to me that, if all the members of the Establishment did their campaigning on the rural tracks, the country would at least have more wells and fewer torturers. The people along the roads and tracks welcome the official car.

'What has the whole uprising got us?' Mehbooba Mufti asks, showing signs of agitation: 'That we would be happy today to have the autonomy back that we had before the uprising.'

Kashmir teaches not only how far democracies can go. Perhaps more frighteningly, it also teaches what they can get away with once they declare a state of emergency. One soldier for every ten inhabitants and extreme harshness – that's enough to break the backbone of even the most rebellious population. When I get out halfway back to Srinagar to return with my own driver, Mehbooba Mufti points me the way to a nearby shrine, the tomb of a mystic.

'Shall I pray there for you?' I ask.

'No, pray for Kashmir.'

NIGHT

Because the city seems so normal by the light of day, it takes a few days before I understand why no one wants to meet with me in the evening. If you have a car, you can drive through the empty, unlighted streets to the house of an acquaintance or to one of the more elegant restaurants, which are open until nine or, at the latest, nine-thirty. Later than that, you could probably find a bar, if you are rich enough to afford the expensive drinks. But there are no taxis to be had after eight and not even a rickshaw after nine. Even my own driver, Faroq, who cherishes me like his own personal state visit, can't be persuaded to go out that late, not for double the fare. The only way I could move him would be to ask it as a favour, but then he wouldn't take money at all. Once, Faroq drops me off in the city at seven because I have arranged to visit someone. They'll bring me back to the houseboat, I reassure him. To deter my hosts from driving me home themselves, I tell them my driver is waiting outside. You always find a rickshaw or something, I say to myself. As I walk through the city for the next two hours, it feels as sinister as a minefield. There's not even a soldier to be seen, even at the checkpoints. At this hour only ghosts are abroad in the city, says the ferryman, who has waited nervously at the dock to take me across to the houseboat. Besides my jacket and sweater, I warm myself with the sweet jasmine tea that the boat owner brings in a thermos bottle, as every night, before bedtime.

HOUSEBOAT 3

Another Indian family arrived yesterday evening, of about the same composition as the engineer's family from Calcutta, to judge by the noise that kept me awake late: a man; some women; tired, crying children, or perhaps only one child. The man, who has just come on deck, spoke to me before in Hindi and was perplexed that I was not one of the staff. I can't tell whether he doesn't speak English or prefers not to talk to me. The engineer's wife, on the other hand, gives me a greeting. In general, middle-class Indian women do not seem to be in the habit of answering the greetings of male neighbours on the first day. Perhaps out of pity, she nodded to me for the first time when I sat alone at dinner before the tomato chicken – being alone seems to be something only holy men can be expected to bear – she even smiled, and this morning so did her older daughter, who is taller than I am and plump, and looks seventeen, which doesn't make life easier for a thirteen-year-old. When they come back to the boat, she turns on the television set before going to her room – usually quiz shows. Yesterday evening, as I sat freezing in my idyll on the Dal canal, I followed with one eye a TV series about a youth striving after a beautiful girl – in vain so far, but the next instalment is on today.

THE SHRINE

An excursion to Sokkur in western Kashmir, where Ahad Baba, one of Kashmir's highly revered mad holy men, whom

I wanted to visit, has just left for Srinagar. He had an inspira-
tion to go, they explain to me with a shrug, as if Ahad Baba
might be inspired tomorrow to fly to New York. Faroq, my
driver, offers to take me to the shrine of the medieval mystic
Baba Shakur-ud-Din, so that the two hours we have driven
will not be for nothing. If the Islamists have not prevailed,
it is not only because of the superiority and brutality of the
Indian army. It is also because most Kashmiris are dedicated
to their traditional faith with its mystical influences. In contrast to Afghanistan, Iran and parts of Pakistan, Sufism in
Kashmir has held its ground against the new ideology.

The shrine is on an isolated mountain, an outlier of
the Himalayas jutting into Wular Lake, the highest lake
in southern Asia. On the mountaintop, everything that
makes up Kashmir's culture and attraction comes together
in a powerful experience of nature and religion – the giant
expanse of water below the shrine like a blue-green oil
painting; the fecund meadows and forests in the valley, the
glaciers round about; emanating from the shrine the song of
an enchantingly mournful choir.

Following other visitors, I first enter a little mosque to
one side of the actual sanctuary. When I come back out after
prayers, the choir has stopped singing. I enter the shrine and
am amazed to find no group inside it that I could have heard
singing just now. Just one young man is reciting something
from a divan or a prayer book in a soft singsong voice. The
unornamented hall also contains mostly young people, the
boys with stylish haircuts, the girls in colourful saris, their
scarves pulled up over their heads, each one praying singly,
including children, a few old men and women in various
positions, some standing, some sitting, some crouching, two
in ritual prayer. Other voices are lifted and mix in with the
singsong in all corners of the room. And suddenly the choir
is there again.

HOUSEBOAT 4

The cordial warmth of all the Kashmiris I come in contact with, which is staggering even by Eastern standards, contrasts with the forbidding or at least sceptical looks I encounter in the street. Do the people take me for an Indian? Gazes do not grow more inviting in the mosque, perhaps because renegades are dreaded most of all. Kashmiris, the boat owner said this morning as he brought the jasmine tea, Kashmiris recognize each other wherever they meet, whether Hindus or Muslims, and when they meet far from home they weep in each other's arms.

Intimidated by the threats, arson and several hundred murders committed by Islamic extremists who gradually hijacked the originally national resistance, almost all the pandits, as the Kashmiri Hindus call themselves, have left the Kashmir Valley, about 600,000 people. The engineer from Calcutta thinks the pandits were driven to flee not by isolated fanatic groups but by the masses. The boat owner, on the other hand, asserts that the Indian army expressly permitted some terrorists to terrify the pandits so that people would think the Muslims were barbarians. The engineer would not deny what the boat owner says next: 'In the 1980s we not only lost hundreds of thousands of lives, not only ruined our economy and brought up a generation that knows nothing but war: we also lost our reputation, our dignity. The world thinks we are Taliban.'

'No, it's not as bad as all that,' I say, but I don't mention the reason: that the world doesn't think of Kashmir at all, or vaguely remembers at most the decapitation of a Western tourist.

'Then we rank just below the Taliban,' the boat owner says.

When the attacks were going on, he often slept at his Hindu friends' houses to protect them, and he wasn't the only one. Now he urges them on the telephone to come back. The pandits were generally better educated, says the boat owner; the Kashmiris need them, especially in the schools, where there is now a shortage of teachers. The engineer finds that the Kashmiris' urging is limited and points out that no Muslim leader has yet apologized publicly for the expulsion.

'That's true,' the boat owner replies to the objection when I raise it with him, 'but with 600,000 Indian soldiers who have broken every bone in our bodies it is perhaps too much to ask for us publicly to apologize and demonstrate for the pandits' return.'

The engineer, each time I mention the army's brutality, does not dispute it outright but refers to the expulsion of the pandits. At the same time, he affirms that there is really no hatred between Hindus and Muslims, between Indians and Kashmiris, and asks how it is in the Middle East. I answer that an Israeli cannot simply take a stroll through Hebron, nor a Palestinian through an Israeli settlement. And in Germany? Naturally the engineer knows the reports of foreigners being beaten up, including Indians. In Germany too there are places, I say, that a person with dark skin would do well to avoid. That is unimaginable in Kashmir, says the engineer in amazement. In Kashmir, any Indian can go wherever he wants without having the least difficulty or fearing for his safety. He himself has never experienced a friendlier reception anywhere.

The boat owner lends me the nineteenth-century account of an English traveller who describes the exploitation of the Muslims by the pandits and calls on the British colonial government to intervene: 'Everywhere the people are in the most abject condition.' It can't have been just a few militant groups who interpreted the Asian tradition of 'we are all brothers' as if it referred to Cain and Abel.

IN THE COUNTRYSIDE

In the air of the Martand Surya Temple there is peace, real peace: Sikhs playing cricket by the temple wall, old Muslims stretching out on the lawn, a few older pandits who offer me a chair. Neither the Indian government nor the state government in Kashmir does anything to bring back the expatriates, or even to compensate them, they complain, and, as per Asian custom, they will not hear a word against their Muslim neighbours. Of the two killed here in the village, one was a Muslim himself, say the pandits: the guardian of the temple, whom the outside militants took for a Hindu. I see two women playing with their hands in the big basin, the younger one a heavenly beauty of the kind told of in fairy tales: in love at first glance; her or death. I ask the two whether they live here – Yes – and how life is for them now – Good. Their answer sounds honest, and so I am glad that there are younger pandits in Kashmir too, until it transpires that the women are Muslims. The heavenly beauty pulls up her scarf over her head for the photo, as if she knew every trick from every fairy tale under the sun.

Out of five hundred Hindu families who once lived here, thirteen remain, and, of them, almost none but the old people are left. All around the temple are burnt-out houses, abandoned houses; on a riverbank are vendors' stands catering for visitors. The colours of the sweets, the colours of the autumn woods, the colours of the fields and meadows, the colours of the saris – you don't need to think about what colours you can see. You have to look long to figure out what colour the women avoid: only grey. Apart from that they wear every primary and every mixed colour in every combination imaginable, and occasionally black or white besides, and for all the variety the outfits are always harmonious, as if automatically.

I drive on eastwards, through villages with narrow lanes and stone houses that look more like Switzerland than southern Asia. The extreme poverty, ubiquitous in the rest of India, seems to be non-existent in Kashmir. The families own land. Because of its autonomy, Kashmir is the only state in India that was able to carry out a land reform after independence. Add to that the money India and Pakistan have pumped into Kashmir during the war to shore up or to buy off the leaders of the resistance. The new mansions are occupied by the old warlords.

In Mehbooba Mufti's electoral district, through which I rode the day before yesterday in her official car, I meet the people who would never wave to it: a talk with the manager of a bank's branch office, who inveighs against the Indians guarding his bank and longs for the Islamic caliphate; beside him his veilless employee, rolling her eyes. The struggle is not over by any means; it's just not armed now – but it won't be won at ballot boxes provided by the Indians, either. But in the end the bank manager would be content with the same thing as the English professor, the communist Tarigami, the resistance groups and almost every political party, not just in Kashmir, but in Pakistan and India too: autonomy and open borders. That is something I have observed on many journeys: conflicts that seem hopelessly complicated, like that between Israel and Palestine or that in Afghanistan, are the exception. Most conflicts, such as those in Aceh, in Chechnya and here in Kashmir, would be solvable; a willingness to compromise has long since been attained – only someone has to take the trouble to put pressure on the actors, as actually happened in Aceh after the tsunami, when peace negotiations were not only begun, but brought to a conclusion within months.

Samir and Riaz, both educated, in their mid-thirties and fathers, one a computer programmer, the other a white-collar worker, show me their town in which no house is without a burst of bullet holes in its façade. The epicentre of the uprising was in this area. We sit down on the grass on the edge of a football pitch. Samir used to play for Kashmir in the under-nineteen team. All the things the army did – searches, rapes, always the same stories; everyone here has a sister, a father, a son who fell into their hands. Samir shows me his scars. But it's true, the Indians are trying to regain trust now, even the army itself. The government has started a few development programmes, opened social welfare facilities, invested a little money in the schools. 'But when a person has lost three sons to the army's bullets, he will not trust the Indians again,' Samir says.

He has not given up hope of freedom, but, after all, you have to live, feed your children. In a town where all the young people worked for the resistance in the 1990s, only 5 per cent still do today. Samir's friend Riaz thinks even this figure is too high: 'A hundred per cent of the people here want nothing but peace.'

Perhaps the next generation will succeed in attaining freedom, Samir hopes, but Riaz asks, 'Do you want to see your son fighting?'

As dusk falls, Samir takes me along to his village, once a stronghold of the Islamists. A visit to the elder, an old man with a cloth cap and a big white beard, his cheeks and upper lip shaved like a Frisian fisherman's; he is as gentle as Father Christmas and the only person today who still advocates armed resistance. Caliphate and democracy is what he would like to see, something like Saudi Arabia.

'But there is no caliphate in Saudi Arabia, and certainly no democracy,' I observe.

'Yes, well, then not exactly like Saudi Arabia, but something similar.'

His idea of Islam calls for women to wear burqas, which no woman in his village does, nor even a headscarf – not even the women in his own household, who greet me with a friendly smile, unlike my Indian neighbours on the houseboat.

HOUSEBOAT 5

The two women next door are chattering away. I imagine they alternate taking breaths like a relay team passing the baton, so that one of them at least is always talking. In any case they don't take time to catch their breath between sentences. They are not loud, but not exactly melodious as a babbling brook either. What could they be talking about, I rant silently to myself, what could they have experienced today: an excursion with the children and the taciturn man to one of the Mughal gardens; a ride in a shikara. I would give a lot for five minutes of simultaneous interpreting.

THE MOTHER

On 18 August 1990, Javed Ahmad Ahanger, a schoolboy in year ten, stayed the night in the city at his cousin's, with whom he was studying for his final exams. About three in the morning, soldiers pounded on the door and called, 'Javed, is there a Javed here?' Javed's uncle opened the window; Javed Ahmad looked out too: 'I'm Javed.' Soldiers pulled him out of the window and beat him. The family swore in vain that the boy had nothing to do with the militant resistance, was much too young in any case, and was preparing for his exams. Later it transpired that a militant named Javed Ahmad Batt lived in the house next door. But Parveena Ahanger never saw her son again.

Together with her husband, a simple farmer, she went from barracks to police station, from police station to government office, from government office to ministry. At one point she was told Javed Ahmad had been arrested and was currently in a military hospital. Parveena Ahanger inquired at one hospital after another. In 1994 she joined with other families of missing sons to found a self-help group whose membership today numbers six hundred families. It's not a fancy NGO with computers and young English-speaking activists who know how to raise public awareness and funds – sometimes only funds. On the outskirts of Srinagar, just before the airport, in a room of 130 square feet off a dilapidated courtyard, the walls painted a bilious green an eternity ago, no furniture except a metal desk and a few chairs – here sits Parveena Ahanger; this is where she works, she says, twenty-four hours a day at finding her son and the other sons lost in the war, a woman as sad as she is determined, looking older under her yellow headscarf than her forty-five years. Once she was offered a million rupees, about €18,000, if she would give up her campaign, once 600,000 rupees plus a salaried job, once by the military, once by the state. Some families have taken the offers.

Does Parveena Ahanger see a difference between this government and its predecessors in Srinagar? No. Or, rather, yes: the new coalition has decided to perform DNA tests when body parts are found. Some bodies have been identified that way. She trusts in God that her son will not come back as a cadaver. The current chief minister of Kashmir may be right in his statement that no new missing persons have been reported this year, for the first time since the outbreak of the rebellion. The army, Parveena Ahanger says, doesn't want such cases any more. They have begun depositing the bodies in fields or at roadsides, with machine guns in their hands.

'So there are no more disappearances, only deaths?'

'Yes, we have no new members at present.'

What is Parveena Ahanger's hope for Kashmir?

'The army should withdraw!' she answers. 'I am not a political activist. I am not fighting for Kashmir's independence. When my son comes home, that will be my freedom.'

HOUSEBOAT 6

The first merchant of the day to board the houseboat goes right past me and extols the quality and the price of his collection of leather jackets to the Indians – in vain, although the jackets are double-sewn, as the merchant repeats several times. He seems to have counted me among the staff of the houseboat, doesn't even try his double-sewn jackets on me, only thanks me when I move my legs to clear the way back to his gondola. Now the Paris Photo Service comes by again; soon the supermarket will be along and, last, the gondolier, to ask whether I plan perhaps today to take the boat tour I have agreed to.

AHAD BABA

Because even the deceased Shukur-ud-Din delighted me, I set out at dawn on the two-hour drive to Sokkur, with still greater anticipation than a few days ago, to see a living saint before I leave, and I find him this time sitting on the lawn, a remarkably bright old man with long hair and a little round belly, naked as ever, stark naked, with an armchair behind him as blue as the ones from IKEA. While the pilgrims line the garden fence by the hundreds, a helper receives the things they have brought – letters, articles of clothing, photos – and rubs them on Ahad Baba's thigh as he moves his head and spits at intervals of perhaps ten seconds; he has long been beyond words. Someone taps my shoulder from behind me, leads me to the knee-high wooden gate that would not be out of place in a German allotment garden, and closes it again after me. I have no idea whether I am supposed, allowed, to approach Ahad Baba, or with what gestures, words, facial expressions; I know only that hundreds, perhaps a thousand eyes are on me. I am already walking towards Ahad Baba when it occurs to me that I am walking on the holy lawn with my shoes on; or, more accurately, it doesn't occur to me, but the grumbling of the crowd communicates to me my faux pas. If I go back to take off my shoes I'll draw still more attention, and leaving them in the middle of the sanctuary is equally out of the question, so I go on and hope for indulgence as an ignorant foreigner. First I bow while standing, then I kneel a yard away from Ahad Baba, who continues to spit, then I bow as I kneel, and because nothing happens I simply wait, without feeling any aura, much less a blessing – on the contrary: under the eyes of a faithful crowd who have already grumbled, and face to face with a stark-naked holy man who is ignoring me completely, I would much rather vanish into thin air. But not even that wonder takes place.

Suddenly Ahad Baba looks at me with impenetrable eyes. What happens now? I am still wondering, when I suddenly feel the spit on my nose. To my surprise, I am not in the least offended but accept the spit, which runs down my lip, as God-given, and even feel somewhat honoured to have been noticed at all. As if at the push of a button, the tension

has been released; I hear no more grumbling behind me, so
that I wait a few minutes with the spit on my face, dripping
on my shirt, to see what will happen next, when Ahad Baba,
just as suddenly as he spat on my nose, smiles at me. I bow
twice to take my leave, once kneeling, once standing, and
walk backwards, with my shoes on, through the garden gate.

IN KASHMIR, FAR AWAY
FROM KASHMIR

On the drive back, Faroq lets me out, with a sigh of relief
that he can finally show me a tourist attraction, at one of
the Mughal gardens, which overwhelms me – still more than
the holy man, to whom I set out with such high expectations
– probably because I did not expect much from the standard programme of Indian tourists, and then it turns out to
be that Paradise on Earth that never goes unmentioned
in reports about the war, the giant – no, gigantic – green
and red trees, the unbelievable order of the fountains and
streams, flowerbeds and cascades, the shimmering Dal Lake
before them with the shining black gabled roofs and cupolas
of Srinagar in the background, the brown mountains behind
us, the autumn colours no less bright than the colours of the
saris. Out of sheer delight I have Faroq drive me, in spite
of his warning that I might miss the flight to Delhi, back to
the houseboat so that I can take the gondola tour and tick
off item two of the standard programme. This is the place
to live on Earth, I understand, as I drift past the houseboats
on the farther shore of Dal Lake: in Kashmir, far away from
Kashmir.

If I come back – and I have promised Faroq, who will never
throw away the paper tissue I used in his car to wipe off the
spit, promised him I would bring my wife and children next

time, to tick off many more standard items – if I come back on holiday, that is, I would still find it hard not to stay on the houseboat near the road again, with the Paris Photo Service rowing by every morning, the floating supermarket, and the boat owner bringing all the news along with the sweet jasmine tea. It would be nice then to meet the engineer from Calcutta and his family again.

LANDLESS

BETWEEN AGRA AND DELHI, SEPTEMBER 2007

LUMPENPROLETARIAT
IN FORMATION

A picture that might have been projected in a play by
Brecht: Lumpenproletariat forming and rising up. Twenty-
five thousand people marching in three files, most of them
in rubber sandals, many barefoot, women in colourful saris
in the middle, the men on the outside in cream-coloured
shirts and matching dhotis, the rectangular cloth wrapped
around the legs. The men carry their plastic-covered bun-
dles on their shoulders; the women balance theirs on their
heads. Everyone has a long stick in one hand with the
green-and-white flag of Ekta Parishad, the Indian land
rights movement. Between the files there is space for the
marshals, musicians and singers, jeeps or other vehicles if
necessary. Every block of a thousand marchers is led by a
tractor pulling a water tank and followed by a bicycle rickshaw with two big metal loudspeakers, one aimed forwards,
the other backwards. It is as loud as almost everywhere in
India.

The expressions and colours of the faces are different in
every block, as are the patterns of the saris, the jewellery, the
women's reticence or confidence, and the language, because
the marchers are from all parts of India. Many of the landless are old, some of them ancient, leaving the younger ones
in their villages to work, although I will later discover that
the outcastes and the members of the lower castes and the
tribal peoples look as old at fifty as Europeans do at eighty.
For twelve days they have been marching; they have come a
hundred and fifty kilometres and have another two hundred
kilometres ahead of them before they reach the parliament
in Delhi if the authorities continue to clear their path, which
is not idyllic, but motorway, the main road from Bombay to

Delhi. Beyond the crash barrier the traffic backs up. Not all the motorists look delighted.

WHY COMPLAIN?

India is booming. Over 9 per cent economic growth annually, globally competitive in information technology, pharmacy, biotechnology, aerospace engineering, nuclear energy and, of course, the services sector, which is now siphoning off not only business from the West but also labour: the pay is not higher, but life is much cheaper, a German business magazine raves, pointing to 'the sensational leisure value' – Himalayas over Alps, Goa over the Costa Brava. As a proportion of its gross domestic product, the Indian state invests more money in research and development than Germany does. In the cities, where perhaps 200, perhaps 250 million people are at least indirectly involved, the signs of growing prosperity are unmistakable: mobile phones, high-rise buildings and shopping malls. The new private airlines offer better service and more modern aircraft than most European airlines. Naturally people book online and fly with e-tickets. Those who once belonged to the lower middle class now drive small cars and send their children to private schools. Those who earn more withdraw into one of the gated communities that are popping up everywhere. And for the wealthy there are no limits in India. The country is no longer a supplicant but a future superpower, as the international press explains forwards and backwards.

I climb over the crash barrier and thread my way between the cars. The traffic would probably be flowing in spite of the blocked carriageway if the drivers didn't insist on passing between the two remaining lanes, and always in both directions at the same time. As it is, the cars are wedged together

every hundred yards like rugby scrums. Some of the drivers
have got out and are staring in disbelief at the other carriageway. Japanese travellers take photographs from coach
windows. For people on unemployment and social welfare
benefits to block the motorway from Frankfurt to Cologne
even for one day would be unthinkable. In India, no government, in the states or in the capital, is interested in a
confrontation because the landless represent the lowest stratum of society, and hence the majority of the voters. The
minister of agriculture was expected yesterday. He cancelled
at short notice, pleading a cabinet meeting. Disappointment
mingled with the marchers' fatigue, which was heightened by
the cold of the nights they spend on the asphalt or in fields.
Prosperous Indians have donated blankets, a euro or two
apiece, but there are far too few of them, only five thousand
so far. Along the entire route, housewives distribute baked
goods, schoolchildren sing songs, and local politicians greet
the marchers with speeches. Occasionally an intellectual or
an actor drives up from Delhi or Bombay to march along for
an afternoon. A long-bearded, white-robed holy man who
joined the column has collected four thousand shoes so far,
smiling constantly. He himself walks barefoot.

There is a magazine lying on the asphalt. It seems to have
been dropped by a woman talking on the phone in the back
seat of a tiny Suzuki Tata. The wages in India are so low
that even compact cars have chauffeurs. As I walk on, I read
an interview with a television hostess who spent her holiday
with friends. I imagine a scene like a TV commercial, young
attractive people under palm trees, only not white, but
brown, light brown like almost all Indians who can afford
the Maldives. They had a bungalow with a view of the sea,
left and right and centre; the sea on three sides of the pool
too, which was set higher for a better view; a pool bar of
course, it's so nice to sleep late, no appointments, drinks, and

the best thing: no cars. 'Stuff in my shopping bag: Nothing!
I took a holiday not only from work but from shopping as
well. But, yes, I couldn't resist buying a bikini, a pair of
sunglasses, a sarong, a photo frame and a bright pink trol-
ley bag.' There is a more expensive category for politicians
and celebrities, of which she is not one apparently, for about
$900 a night. 'But why complain when I had a Jacuzzi in my
bathroom?'

THEY WANT LAND

Two hundred and fifty million consumers are a giant market
for global players but a comparatively small figure for India.
Seven hundred and fifty million Indians have little or no
share in economic growth. India therefore ranks 126th on
the United Nations Human Development Index, behind its
neighbour Sri Lanka and only slightly ahead of Bangladesh.
A large proportion of the rural population still have no
access to educational institutions or health care, and many
have no electricity or running water. Almost half of all children are underweight, a higher proportion than in Ethiopia.
Indian agriculture, which employs two-thirds of the working
population, has seen only minimal growth for years. Food
production is also stagnating, so that the average caloric
intake is actually declining, according to government statistics. Declining prices, declining subsidies for seed, fertilizer
and pesticides, and the reduction of tariffs on imports from
China, Pakistan and the United States have ruined many
farmers. Many of them cannot cope with the industrialization
of agriculture, advocated by agribusiness and accelerated by
price pressure. When they are unable to repay the loans they
have taken out for new machines or expensive, genetically
modified seed, they lose their land. The current suicide rate

is about 12,000 farmers annually, not counting unreported cases.

No one in India would dispute that unspeakable misery persists, least of all the Congress Party, governing in a coalition with left-wing partners who campaigned on promises of social justice. The parliament recently passed a law that guarantees every family a minimum of one hundred days of work a year. Another new law, the 'Right to Information Act', allows every citizen to address inquiries to government agencies for the equivalent of twenty cents: the authorities must answer within thirty days. The problems in the enforcement of these laws do not disprove the government's good intentions. The critical point is that the country's economic policy, and a large part of public opinion, assumes that the increasing wealth will trickle down. Thus the poorest are supposed to benefit indirectly from the free market through higher tax revenues, an expanding infrastructure, and new jobs – poorly paid ones, but better than unemployment. But will they really benefit? And, most of all, will the rural population? The state of Gujarat, where the economy is growing faster than in any other state in India, also has one of the highest rates of suicide among farmers.

Ordinarily, these spindly-legged men are only rarely visible, perhaps from the windows of the trains leaving the city, standing along the tracks or in the fields with bales of straw or brushwood on their backs. Their furrowed faces, the few wrinkle-free patches of skin tanned a dark brown, look dull like worn leather, teeth sticking out, teeth missing, teeth rotted, teeth all gone. And then the elegant gait of even the oldest women, especially in comparison with the two hundred supporters from Western countries who march along, each of them for a few days. Twenty-five thousand people under the sun make a seemingly endless procession, especially when you pass them walking quickly between two of the three files. Once when I had almost arrived at the front of the column, I rested at a petrol station. Until the time the jeep arrived that would bring me to the front again, I watched with the attendant, who offered me water and a chair, as the stream of people flowed past. 'Poor people,' says the attendant, whose parents worked in the fields.

He himself learned automotive mechanics and is glad to see the traffic growing heavier from year to year. Unfortunately, the cars are getting more and more complicated, with more and more electronics that only the authorized garages can repair. If his youngest daughter continues to work hard, she will be admitted to the English-language senior secondary school. Then one day perhaps she will fill up her tank at her father's petrol station.

'Very poor people,' I agree.

'What do they want?' the attendant asks.

'They want land,' I answer, 'they want land so they can live.'

EXPULSION AS INDUSTRIAL DEVELOPMENT POLICY

Make the landless into farmers, Mahatma Gandhi said when independence was won. Today the opposite is happening continually: farmers are being made landless. Anywhere mineral resources are discovered, factories built, multinational businesses located, or one of the many tax-free special business zones established, the inhabitants rarely have a chance. With the backing of politicians and civil servants who can count on revenue for the public coffers, and often for their private ones, private security services or sometimes the police move in to expel those farmers who are unwilling to sell their land for a few rupees. Sometimes even the pro forma offers to buy the land can be dispensed with. Many families have been cultivating their plot of land for generations without any documentation of their ownership on paper. Then one day a lawyer appears in front of their hovel with a bill of sale that his client has negotiated with the state. The 25,000 who are marching on the parliament in New Delhi are not a movement of solidarity: they are all personally affected.

Babam Saharia received a visit from the forester – from the Department of Forests, to be exact. As a member of a 'primitive tribe', he grew up in the forests, lived, like his ancestors, from everything that grows on and under the trees, fruits, nuts, lentils. No one had papers to show their ownership. A big landowner from the region bought the land that Babam Saharia and his neighbours lived on – bought it by bribing the officials, the wiry, almost white-haired forty-year-old is certain. Forest wardens stood in front of his cabin with weapons, police too. The farmers were rounded up along with their families, packed onto the bed of a truck and unloaded on the other side of the mountains. If you come back, they'll kill you, the wardens told them as they left.

'When did the expulsion happen?' I ask.

'1983.'

'1983? But you were only sixteen then.'

'I was already living with my wife. The children came later.'

'And your wife?'

'Died.'

Saharia became a labourer, but without giving up the hope of getting back his land. The soles of his feet flat on the ground, he sits on his haunches and takes from a polystyrene bag the letters he and his neighbours have sent since then. Some of the letters bear a handwritten note in English by an official, one even by the Minister of Forests. 'Forward for immediate action', they say, or simply 'Approved'. But nothing happened, Saharia says bitterly, simply nothing, although he demands only his right. Once he lay in ambush for the big landowner and attacked him, with his bare hands, he says emphatically. Twenty-two days Saharia spent in jail for that. A few years ago he joined the land rights movement, rather than throwing in his lot with the freebooters.

THE SKY AND THE GROUND

The organization and discipline are unbelievable. The jeep that clears a path to take me to the head of the march again glides as if through water, so fluidly the ranks open before it and close again behind its tailpipe. A truck for every block of marchers drives ahead to the camp sites. They fill up the water tanks free at the petrol stations. Very few of the marchers are accustomed to warm meals at home. In their villages there is a barrel that the neighbours have gradually filled with grain for the families of those who have been sent on the march. After the meal, a relaxed expansiveness unfolds. The people sit in groups on the road, as if at a happening. Then, as if by a signal, they are busy again, since everyone washes thoroughly before night falls, the women at the water trailers, the men mostly at hoses with which they take turns spraying each other, always with soap, which also serves as shampoo and as laundry detergent for the women's saris. Their dexterity in covering their private parts is surprising, as is the dignity they maintain even while soaping up, while the Westerners look rather bedraggled in their dusty short or long trousers and their sweaty T-shirts. Ditches have been dug beside the road, wooden boards laid across them. Sticks have been planted in the ground and a blue-and-white plastic sheet woven around them to form cabins for the five hundred latrines.

The central demand of the landless marchers is surprisingly moderate. No redistribution, no expropriation, not even new legislation; they only want the government to carry out the land reform that is already enshrined in the constitution and to distribute public land to the landless. They also demand the establishment of an agency or a commission to which every Indian who has been illegally driven from his land can appeal. Up to now, the farmers complain, their legitimate claims get referred by the districts to the states, by the states to Delhi – and by Delhi back to the districts.

'We rely on dialogue with the politicians, not on confrontation,' says the leader of the land rights movement, whom everyone calls simply Rajagopal, a gentle man of almost sixty with a black moustache and a boyish haircut.

His movement, Ekta Parishad, is committed to Gandhi's ideals, in contrast to the Naxalites, the Maoist resistance group that now controls whole swathes of the countryside in northeastern India. Of course, they are campaigning for more than just a new government agency. They want to raise awareness: 'It's the Indian middle class that we want to reach. They have to realize that the poverty that is spreading threatens their own prosperity, their own safety.'

The farmers who have lost the basis of their subsistence, Rajagopal says, inevitably end up in the slums of the big cities.

'No one likes having slums at their door,' says Rajagopal at a frugal evening meal in a primary school, where he is camping for the night in the schoolyard along with the other urban supporters – professors, journalists, students – while the farmers sleep in the field beside the motorway or on the asphalt. 'The middle class see slums as dirty, a source of disease, violence and crime. So we say, Stop producing more and more new slums.'

If the poverty continues to grow while the wealth becomes

more and more visible through television and cinema, Rajagopal continues, there will inevitably be conflict, if not a social explosion. But the Indian middle class stare as if hypnotized at the heavens of globalization, blinded by their own economic advancement and the blessings of consumerism: 'It will take some time before they notice that the ground is giving way under their feet.'

RAM PAYDIRI DOESN'T UNDERSTAND

Ram Paydiri from the village of Kali Pari in Shivpuri District, Madhya Pradesh, wants to kiss my feet when she learns that I am going to report on the march abroad. She is a widow, fifty, snow-white hair, expelled long ago from her two and a half acres of land, she too beaten and forbidden to go near her land, her four children moved to the city. On a good day she picks up a job, in the fields or some kind of handiwork, 50 rupees for who knows how many hours, the equivalent of a euro. She lives in a straw hut. Why is she here?

'We are willing to die to get our land back.'

What will she do when she returns?

'Go on working.'

And when she is old and frail?

'Work, as long as I have legs and hands.'

But if one day she can no longer work? She is all alone.

Ram Paydiri doesn't understand the question.

THE LABORATORY

GUJARAT, OCTOBER 2007

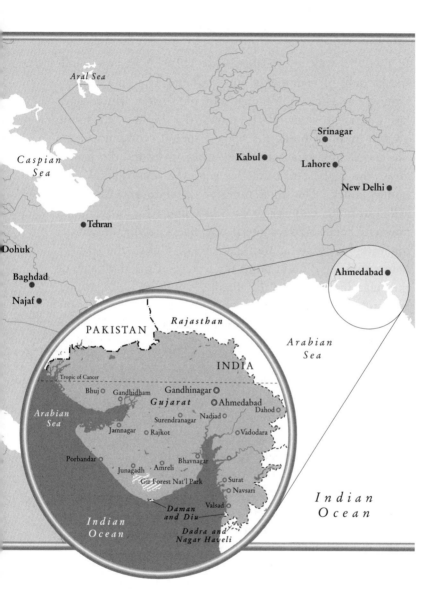

AN IDOL

Is this the way a fundamentalist talks? Narendra Modi speaks only of technology and business. The data he presents are excellent: the Indian state of Gujarat, which Modi has governed since 2001, shows the highest economic growth in all of India, the biggest special economic zones, the fastest industrialization, the most investors, the lowest taxes, the highest research budgets, the most liberal economic policy. The chief minister, as state governors are called in India, emphasizes each new figure by throwing his powerful hands forward alternately, like a conductor thrashing with his baton at the final chord. Unlike the speaker before him, he did not go to the lectern at the right side of the stage but stands in the middle, where he looks smaller and still more rotund than on his posters. He wears rimless designer glasses above his white, shorn beard. His white ankle-length robe is short-sleeved, after the current fashion, like a business shirt.

Modi inserts long pauses between his sentences, as if he wanted to let his arguments reverberate as well as his deep, raucous voice. His intonation is not emotional, or even entreating. The chief minister presents himself as rationality personified. After half an hour, I no longer listen to the interpreter beside me, only to the English words that occur in every sentence: development, capacity, management, computer, technology, software, screening, engineering, industry, advanced, laser printers and even metro. What? They want to build a metro? I ask, startled. No, no, the interpreter explains, 'metro' is Gujarati for 'friends': beginning with his opening greeting, Modi is signalling to his adherents that he is one of them.

To most of the ten thousand students assembled this

afternoon on the campus of the Ahmedabad technical college, Modi is an idol, efficient, hard-working and, most importantly, not corrupt. 'We thank our C. M.', say the posters, or, in anticipation, 'Lots of Congratulations'. If Modi is re-elected in early December, most of the commentators predict, he will reach for the chair of his party, the Hindunationalistic BJP – with the goal of becoming India's future head of government. Gujarat, his supporters have announced time and again, is merely the 'laboratory' of a radically new, religiously grounded political movement. For the many losers of Gujarat's unbridled market economy, however, and still more for secular Indians and for India's 130 million Muslims, the state is more like a witches' den. To them, Gujarat does not 'vibrate', as the BJP slogan announces; it stinks to high heaven.

ON THE RUBBISH TIP

No, Bibi Khatun and her sisters-in-law have not grown used to the stench, you can't get used to that. They have electricity, praise be to God, two little rooms in which the five of them live, even a fan. Five nails to hang their clothes on, two energy-saving light bulbs; for their furniture two couches, a table, two plastic chairs; tin pots on the bare concrete floor. Sure, it's cramped, but next door there are eight in the same space. The problem is the water. Although there are wells in the Shah Alam Relief Camp, in which some two hundred families live, someone is always sick because the rubbish tip contaminates the soil. The nearest doctor is five kilometres away, and where there might be a school no one knows. The table is piled high with blue jeans in which they sew white patterns, two rupees a pair, the equivalent of four euro cents. Three of them sewing manage forty pairs a day.

Bibi Khatun's son enters the room. He is no more than five. Fortunately, I think to myself.

Five and a half years ago, on 28 February 2002, the rampage against Muslims began in Gujarat. The day before, fifty-seven Hindu pilgrims had died when their train caught fire. Although a state commission has determined in the meanwhile that the fire probably broke out inside the train, Hindu nationalists continue to call the disaster a terrorist attack that led to a spontaneous outpouring of emotion. There are doubts, however, as to the spontaneity. According to human rights organizations, the attackers who arrived in the morning in trucks in the state capital Ahmedabad were well organized. In addition to knives, the tridents traditionally associated with the god Vishnu, fuel and explosives, they also had with them lists of the addresses of Muslim households and businesses. Their brutality is documented in horrible detail. In many places, the police not only watched the massacres without intervening but drove Muslims trying to flee their neighbourhoods back into the mob. State parliament members of the governing Hindu nationalist party, and even cabinet members, gave instructions by mobile phone saying which Muslim neighbourhood was to be attacked next. The central state, then also governed by the BJP, let three days pass before sending the army – and forbade the soldiers to shoot. About two thousand Muslims died. Hundreds of thousands were driven from their homes.

Several months later, Narendra Modi campaigned for re-election. In his speeches, he did not limit himself to technology and business. As the forceful documentary *Final Solution* by the Indian filmmaker Rakesh Sharma shows, the government openly incited hatred against Muslims and, time and again, indirectly excused acts of violence while consistently denying their magnitude. When Modi got up in front of the audience, his voice broke. In those days he talked like a fundamentalist. To the refugees in the Shah Alam Relief Camp, he still is one.

I ask Bibi Khatun whether all the members of her family were at home on 28 February 2002.

'The government had declared a curfew,' she reminds me.

About ten thirty, the noise: she looked out of the window. The attackers were already storming into the alley in her neighbourhood, Naroda Patiya, all wearing the same clothes, brown shorts, orange headbands; called all the inhabitants outside, where the jerrycans of petrol stood ready; then the fire, so fast that the bravest and the most timid were burnt to death. Miraculously, Bibi Khatun lost none of her family. Her neighbour Koussar Banu was eight months pregnant; the attackers cut the foetus out of her belly. Yes, Bibi Khatun saw it herself. One of her sisters-in-law nods; the other gets out a photo. The attackers did it so that everyone would see. She herself counted twenty-five severed body parts. There is supposed to be compensation, the equivalent of a €100 for an injury, €300 for the loss of a leg, but the state won't pay, although they have many organizations on their side, lawyers too, good lawyers who represent them free of charge. Here are the papers, look, we even have a positive decision from Delhi, look here in the newspaper, it even says so in the newspaper. Yes, they had time to count the severed limbs; the police blocked the exit to the main road. The attackers had time too, raped one woman after another. You too? I don't dare ask. From time to time someone comes by and asks the same questions, but nothing ever changes.

'I can't change anything,' I admit, 'I can only help make sure you are not forgotten.' After me will come someone else to remember 28 February 2002, and another and another, hopefully, and someday something will surely change – yet they are grateful for the visit nonetheless; the women are anything but intimidated; no headscarves, graceful features and

slender bodies; they show a good deal of skin and still more
self-assurance, even though most of what little support they
have received came from Islamic organizations – Islamists,
the interpreter later confirms. As everywhere in the world,
the expellees had never had problems with their neighbours.
As everywhere in the world, it wasn't their neighbours who
did it. As everywhere in the world, the neighbours pointed
out the houses for the attackers to set on fire.

INTO THE CENTRE

Inspired by European fascism and especially by racial doctrine, Hindu nationalism developed in the 1920s and
1930s and crystallized in the RSS, the 'National Volunteer
Organization'. Today the RSS still forms a kind of umbrella
organization for a number of groups, some social, some
militant, and for the BJP. The central concept of Hindu
nationalism, *Hindutva*, calls for the harmonious unity of all
Hindus within the hierarchical structure of the caste system.
The RSS advocated militancy over Gandhi's pacifism, saying
Hinduism must overcome its natural gentleness in the face
of the Islamic and Christian conquerors. And the nationalists
defined India, against the secular ideals of the independence
movement, as *Hindu Rashtra*, the nation of the Hindus. By
definition, Christians and Muslims could only be guests,
'illegitimate' citizens; hence the Indian Muslims are still
called Pakistanis by Hindu nationalists today.

For a long time, *Hindutva* was a postulate mainly of
the upper castes, who have a natural interest in preserving
the social hierarchy. Only in the past two decades have the
nationalists been able to obscure the tensions in the caste
system, which are still much more commonplace to most
Indians, by invoking an existential conflict with members of

other religions. The events of late 1992 in Ayodha, where 300,000 Hindu pilgrims destroyed the Babri Masjid to build in its stead a temple marking the birthplace of the god Rama, were a signal of the new direction. Politicians like the 57-year-old Narendra Modi have been able to expand the potential electorate of the BJP significantly because they come from a lower caste themselves. Abetted by the corruption in the Congress Party, which had governed India since independence, the BJP grew within a few years from a splinter party into the strongest faction in the Indian parliament, supplying the head of government between 1998 and 2002. Yet in Delhi it was bound up in the constraints of a coalition government, and its nominee for the office of prime minister, Atal Bihari Vajpayee, was not called a religious zealot even by his political opponents. In Gujarat, however, the BJP governed alone, and under Narendra Modi it won more than two-thirds of the seats in the state parliament in 2003. The party won the highest proportion of votes in precisely those districts where the violence against Muslims had occurred.

In Gujarat you can find Hindu hate-mongers who would like to take away Muslims' right to vote and sterilize them by force, who would prohibit interreligious marriages, or who demand jail sentences for apostate Hindus. Just a few weeks ago, in early September 2007, the magazine *Tehelka* presented videos in which radical Hindu activists such as Babu Bajrangi boasted of the numbers of Muslims they had raped during the rampage. With a suitable montage – images of the massacre juxtaposed, the refugee camps, excerpts of Modi's earlier speeches – it would be easy to convey the impression that the state was ruled by a Hindu Taliban. But that doesn't describe the situation in Gujarat. The resentment against Muslims erupted in the special situation of 2002 after a series of Islamist attacks in India, after battles with Pakistani irregulars in the mountains of the Kargil district,

and after 11 September 2001, which the Hindu nationalists thoroughly exploited. The horror that set in throughout
India after the massacres led to a collective feeling of defi-
ance in Gujarat, which Narendra Modi made the most of.
He recast the criticism of the massacres as a defamation of
peace-loving Gujaratis: 'So you are supposed to be the rapists that all India is talking about,' he grinned at his audiences
at campaign events. But, in the long run, hate-mongering
extremists cannot command a majority, not in India and now
not even in Gujarat. Most Gujaratis may not denounce the
2002 massacres, but they find the memory rather embarrass-
ing. Accordingly, Narendra Modi now avoids any allusion
to the events. Instead of talking about the peril of Islam, he
prefers to speak of technology and business. This draws criticism from extremists. But it could bring him into the centre
of Indian society.

SOCIAL PRAXIS

The four friendly students I accost in the university cafeteria
the day after the chief minister's speech have to think a long
time to remember what happened in 2002. When I prompt
them with the word 'disturbances', their first thought is of the
earthquake six years ago. Oh, the rampage against Muslims.
Naturally they're against it, against violence in general. 'But
it was a reaction; you have to see that side of it too.'

I mention the state commission's report on the cause of
the train disaster: the students have never heard of it.

'The Muslims', one continues, 'have committed so many
other attacks. Sooner or later there is a reaction.'

'Not all Muslims are terrorists,' another says, repeating an
argument that is also heard in other parts of the world, 'but
all terrorists happen to be Muslims.'

Again, they are against violence, they affirm, and have
nothing against Islam. They practically never discuss politics,
for that matter. The chief minister supports the universities;
that is important to them. No, they personally don't know
any Muslims. Not even from the university? Yes, of course,
there are one or two students, but they don't know them.
Only one or two students in the whole university? Yes. And
from school? There were no Muslims in their classes.

No wonder Modi is popular on the campus of a technical
college: under his leadership, Gujarat has invested enormous amounts in education and technology. And, oddly, the
authoritarian and xenophobic ideology of Hindu nationalism
dovetails well with his extremely liberal economic policy. It
is striking that the violence affected mainly newer neighbourhoods which had recently developed from slums into
lower-middle-class residential areas. Even before that, there
had been Muslim streets and Hindu streets in these quarters.
In the old centre of Ahmedabad, however, where Hindus
and Muslims are poorer and have always lived next door to
one another, there were only isolated abuses.

As in so many countries, especially the Islamic ones, it
is primarily the middle classes in India, paradoxically – the
people whose lives are most swept up in globalization – who
are rekindling their cultural identity. Suddenly, television
stations are careful that their programming is religiously
inoffensive, and self-contained housing estates advertise a
return to 'harmonious living as prescribed in the Vedas and
Vedanta'. The attitude expressed in such advertisements is
not one of hatred – which would hardly be compatible with
the idealizing images that the modern advertising industry
produces – but one of self-assurance, traditional values and
piety. More and more Indians oppose the emphatic secularity
on which the Indian state was founded and the subcontinent's primordial multiculturalism, which Europe could

learn from even today, and yearn for a dominant Hindu culture in which, although no one would prevent Muslims and Christians from becoming movie stars or even holding political office, those movie stars and political office-holders would not practise their religions publicly, even if Hindu celebrities jump on every pilgrimage train that happens to have a television camera pointed at it.

Law enforcement, too, which has maintained a remarkable independence for decades, seems to be susceptible to the virus of dividing the society into a Hindu 'we' and a non-Hindu 'they'. While Hindu extremists are rarely charged, a mere suspicion is often enough to get Muslims arrested as possible terrorists. The scandal over the alleged planners of the attack on the Indian parliament, who were held for months in 2001 without access to lawyers, and tortured, only to prove themselves innocent in the end – except for one – is just the best known of many recent examples. One might say the suspects were freed in the end, the many protests helped justice triumph, civil society stood the test. But the tests grow tougher – and the society doesn't always master them: it is for this development, a much less conspicuous one, that Gujarat has become a laboratory, not for obtuse religious hatred. Nowhere else is the discovery and construction of what is declared 'ours' carried over so distinctly into social praxis.

Alone at a long table in the university cafeteria sits an older gentleman, recognizable by his cap and his beard as a Muslim. When I go to sit by him he stands up to take his tray back. True, his plate is empty; perhaps he was really about to leave, but his haste is jarring nonetheless. I decide to leave my plate unfinished and follow the gentleman. He is a professor, it turns out when I catch up to him in the yard, one of the few Muslims who still teach at the college, but now he really must go; no, no, everything is fine, he just has an urgent appointment; no, everything is fine, praise be to God. The fear in his eyes awakens memories of dictatorships, of meetings with people who flinch.

'Peace be with you,' I say, taking leave with the Islamic greeting.

'And with you, peace,' the professor replies.

As he turns to go, he mutters to me that there is no future for the Muslims in Gujarat. 'That fellow' – and he glances over towards the stage where the chief minister spoke yesterday about 'development' and 'capacity' – 'that fellow is very clever.'

INDIA'S FUTURE

Sixty thousand Muslims are still living in improvised camps, dependent on aid from Islamic organizations, not all of which propound the mystical Islam that is still typical of Muslims in Gujarat. The trials of the leaders behind the massacres come to nothing. There are hardly any Muslims working in state institutions or holding political office any more; they have next to no chance of getting the new jobs created in the universities or public facilities. Those schools that are not completely segregated by religion have divided internally into H-classes for Hindus and M-classes for Muslims. Films and documentaries that discuss Hindu nationalism critically are shown everywhere in India – except in Gujarat. Handbills urge Hindus not to eat at Muslim restaurants, not to hire Muslims, and to boycott films with Muslim actors. Churches too are considered centres of enemy proselytism and are set on fire again and again. Some Muslim entrepreneurs have made their peace with Modi and appear with him on camera. Others, especially the young men in the refugee camps, prove susceptible to the tirades of Islamist preachers who have swarmed out in Gujarat since the massacre. The majority of Muslims, especially the people from the lower and lower-middle classes, have withdrawn into their own residential quarters, often separated by fences from their Hindu former neighbours. Is this what India's future looks like?

'No,' says Marendra Singh, 'definitely not.'

In his early forties, Singh is one of the younger members of the Indian parliament. In his bookcase is the canon of the global civil society, from Orhan Pamuk to *No Logo*; on the walls are posters, flags and newspaper clippings about Liverpool FC. I ask whether he went to university in England. No, in America; he has been a Liverpool FC fan since his boyhood in India. Singh read Middle East Studies and considers the Quran a remarkable book, 'truly humanistic for its time'. The Muslims, as I probably know, came to India not with sword in hand but as merchants and Sufis.

'But many schoolbooks today say the opposite,' I interject.

'The schoolbooks were changed under the Congress Party government. Now we're suffering the consequences. A whole generation has grown up with this propaganda.'

Marendra Singh is no left-wing activist. He is a member of the BJP. But he has little time for Narendra Modi. I tell him my impressions of the ghettos and the refugee camps, the creeping Hinduization of the universities and the administration. Singh knows all that. 'I've seen the camps myself. I know the situation is horrible.'

Singh makes no effort to gloss over the conditions in Gujarat. He speaks critically of Hindu nationalism. The BJP must distance itself more clearly, he says, from the umbrella organization RSS. He candidly admits that his party failed in 2002, the whole party. But Gujarat is not India, he says, and Modi is not representative of his party. When the BJP formed the government in Delhi, relations with the Muslims were better than under the Congress Party. Vajpayee sought a settlement with Pakistan and agitated for peace in Kashmir. Marendra Singh himself earned more Muslim votes in his district than any other candidate. Never would an election in India be won with a fundamentalist platform.

'Perhaps not parliamentary elections – but what will you do if the Modi wing takes control in the BJP? Will it still be your party?'

'It will not happen.'

In fact, it is difficult to imagine for the time being that Hindu fascism, as many intellectuals and journalists call the nationalists' ideology, could dominate Indian politics. But the radical wing that Narendra Modi still represents in the BJP seems not quite as weak as Marendra Singh paints it, and no doubt wishes it. If Modi wins the elections in Gujarat, he might succeed in bringing the BJP around to his line. Even the other parties would then give more consideration to the Hindu leaders' sensitivities. That would be the end of the already minimal pressure on the government of Gujarat, a state with more than 60 million inhabitants, to reverse the ghettoization of its almost 6 million Muslims and call the perpetrators of violence to account. But exerting influence is one thing; threatening the secular state by winning absolute majorities is another – and at present only Narendra Modi's most loyal supporters think him capable of that. The country is too diverse for that, and the liberal and leftist forces too strong. As much as Modi would like to let bygones be bygones, his political opponents never tire of reminding him of the 'holocaust', as Prime Minister Singh recently called the events of 2002. That the United States has denied Modi entry up to now is a clear signal from India's new ally. The poorer Indians – and hence the majority of the voters – have other things to worry about than the fight against other religions. Their fight is for sheer survival.

They voted the BJP into government in 1998, not because of its Hinduist ideology, but in spite of it. And they voted the BJP back out because they found it had redeemed none of its promises of social policy.

WHERE EVEN THE ATHEISTS PRAY

On the way to Chisti's mosque, the driver suddenly stops by the side of the thoroughfare.

'That is where the famous shrine of Wali Gujarati stood,' say my companions, pointing to the middle of the road.

'Where?' I ask.

'There.'

'I don't see anything.'

'Exactly.'

I follow my companions to the broad dividing strip. In the dark I spy the outlines of the tarmac that was laid later than the rest of the roadway. Wali Gujarati was the first poet of Gujarat to write his verses in local Urdu instead of Persian. His tomb was a site of pilgrimage for literature lovers and mystics, for Muslims and Hindus. It was reduced to rubble in a single evening. Within a week the debris had been cleared away and the site tarred over, as if every remembrance of the largely peaceful shared history of Hindus and Muslims on the Indian subcontinent was to be blotted out. History as it is taught by fundamentalists the world over knows only their own as victims and the others as perpetrators. The websites portraying the daily attacks of the respective others the world over work according to the same pattern and with the same phrases: no tolerance for intolerance, because all of them the world over consider themselves tolerant. Like the Jewish-Muslim roots of the Enlightenment in Europe or the Jewish and Christian heritage of the Orient in the Middle East, the interconnection of the religious traditions which fused indistinguishably in mysticism is denied in India. As late as the census of 1911, 200,000 Indians identified themselves as Hindu-Mohammedans. The 'pure' Hinduism championed by the nationalists, on the other hand, is a thoroughly modern phenomenon.

The coexistence and commingling of many different doctrines and practices which was first named Hinduism by the British colonists becomes under the Hindu ideology a doctrine with an unambiguous answer to every question and a clear definition of belief and unbelief. But, even today, many Indians find the boundary lines between the religions much more permeable than religious leaders in Cairo or Rome could ever imagine.

In Chisti's mosque, which stands in all its beauty a little way further towards the city limits, Hindus and Muslims continue to pray together, men alongside women, children alongside greybeards rapt in devotion before the tombstones.

'In our sect, even the atheists pray,' Rashid Baba Nasir ud-Din Chisti laughs. He is the eldest descendant of the saint and the head of the family, a statuesque man with a white beard sitting in the garden of the shrine with friends and relatives.

The gathering is educated, wealthy and, as one of the gentlemen stresses, anti-fundamentalist. Although most of the people around here voted for the Hindu party, they have never had problems with their neighbours – how could they, when the neighbours come here to pray? The mob – ah, it's easy to get up a mob anywhere with money and alcohol; there is an outbreak of violence somewhere in India almost every week; just read the newspapers. Only, in Gujarat, the mob is organized by the state, not the neighbours – that's the difference. For their part, they were lucky; the police station next door protected the shrine. They talk about the impending elections, in perfect English, and about the strategy of the Congress Party, which shows little interest in the Muslims and instead strikes religious tones itself. The Muslims, they estimate, will vote for Congress regardless. Rashid Baba is pragmatic: in Gujarat the Congress Party must win over the moderate fundamentalists to prevent the victory of the Hindu party. Other gentlemen refute him vigorously, saying there is no moderate fundamentalism. The gathering is unanimous that a re-election of the chief minister would also leave their order in difficult straits, although it has been here forever, ever since the city was founded five hundred years ago. As I go to leave, Rashid Baba accompanies me out of the gate, casually receiving the kisses of the faithful on his hand.

'Good luck for the next five hundred years,' I say.

THE PIT

Bibi Khatun can't imagine ever living next door to Hindus again. Although she doesn't blame all the neighbours, God knows, and certainly not all Hindus, the very thought induces panic; she still has nightmares. Other families have returned to Naroda Patiya. My first thought is that the houses don't look much better here than in the camp. Then I realize that these are shacks provided by the Islamic charity. A hundred yards away are the first houses of the Hindus, two storeys with verandas and trees, far from luxurious, yet there are mopeds leaning on many walls and satellite dishes on the roofs. At the back of the estate, where the mob assembled back then, cows graze in a meadow that might appear idyllic but for the neighbouring factory with its barbed-wire fences. In the middle of the grass is a ring of concrete eight feet across, a pit, it turns out, perhaps twenty-five feet deep, with the same rubbish and stench around it and in it as on the rubbish tip that Bibi Khatun lives beside today; the inside is black with soot. On the ground lies an old school bag. I have read about this concrete funnel. On 28 February 2002, dozens of bodies were set on fire in it as the day went on. 'We believe in setting them on fire because these bastards say they don't want to be cremated,' Babu Bajrangi explained in the interview in *Tehelka*.

On the other side of the estate, at the exit to the road that the police blocked that day, a new mosque has recently been built, not particularly pretty, not particularly big. The old mosque was levelled by Babu Bajrangi's men. Hindus helped collect donations for the new building.

A VISIT TO
THE SUFIS

PAKISTAN, FEBRUARY 2012

RHYTHM OF GOD

What is that rhythm? As hard as I concentrate, while tapping on my thighs, I hear sequences of sometimes nine, sometimes eleven, sometimes sixteen quick beats, if I'm not miscounting, but I surely am miscounting because the very impenetrability is what draws me, the outsider, into the music, so that my thoughts cease for seconds or minutes and I am no longer aware of the cemetery at the shrine of Shah Jamal in Lahore, although my eyes must be open, since I see the two tremendous drums that the Sain brothers have hung around their necks, and their four arms, although I can't see the four drumsticks: they are whirling too fast. This rhythm is much too complex to invite any clapping, tapping, humming along, and yet the perhaps two hundred, perhaps three hundred listeners are swaying as they sit closely packed under the trees or on the steps of the tombs, many with their eyes closed, some with their heads circling. Most of them are people from the lower classes, recognizable by their cheap garments, in many cases by the dark hair colour too, some Malangs among them, wandering dervishes who look like aging hippies, long hair and beards, bracelets, necklaces, earrings and deeply furrowed faces; clean-shaven men in simple but more genteel clothes smiling pensively; and also younger people in Western clothes, students no doubt, ethnologists or artists interested, with a digital camera or an iPhone in their raised hands, in the rich traditions of their own country.

Again and again one of the brothers leaves the common rhythm, builds up to a breathless solo, breaks off and merges back in. *Mast Qalandar*, croaks the older brother, Gunga Sain, who owes his fame in Pakistani Sufi circles to his outstanding art, but also no doubt to his appearance, as burly as an adventure film hero, giant black eyes, striking cheekbones, long black curls, black beard and many-coloured necklaces over his snow-white robe. To add to the legend, Gunga is practically deaf and dumb; he doesn't hear the drumbeats but feels them as vibrations in his body; he doesn't speak but only brings shreds of sound from his throat, and the invocation of the holy Lal Shahbaz Qalandar, who lived in the thirteenth century, 'O ecstatic Qalandar'. *Jhule lal*, the listeners respond in chorus, 'Red dancer'. *Shah jamal*, Gunga calls, another nickname of the saint, 'king of beauty', whereupon from all the other throats *Jhule lal* resounds again. In the rising responsorial, some cry out loud in rapture. A Malang produces tremendous tones from a little horn.

Later the music quiets down again, and Gunga, waving his arm, signals the listeners in the front rows to move to the back, which makes the crowd between the graves still denser. In the space made free, the dancers come forth one by one, in red, white, multicoloured or patchwork clothes, their faces marked by asceticism and contemplation, by experiences in a different world from this one. Each of them has his own way of yielding to the music, surrendering to ecstasy, shaking his head wildly or spinning rapidly, stamping on the ground or jumping in the air – a hard rock concert is an orderly affair in comparison. But what looks wild at first glance requires long practice, a skill that is nothing less than artistic. One, for example, the smallest of the dancers, whirls in place so fast, with his arms outstretched and his long, flowing hair, that it makes me dizzy just to watch him. How does he do that with his feet? I wonder, as I wondered in the beginning at the rhythm. Young people try a few times to join in among the dancers. They are immediately pushed to one side, at first with paternal gentleness, but then sternly and firmly if necessary. This is no entertainment; it is a worship service, performed only by those who have mastered the ceremonial acts, not just the rhythm and the steps but also the prayers and the succession of internal states.

WAR AGAINST THEMSELVES

Pakistan, which is better known today for its extremist movements, for Talibanization, terrorism and discrimination – Pakistan of all countries is one of the few in the Islamic world in which mysticism is still the predominant form of religious practice. Seventy to eighty per cent of all Pakistanis, the scholarly literature relates, feel themselves to be in a broad sense part of the culture of the shrines, which is steeped in Sufism; those who are not themselves members of an order visit the tombs of mystical saints and poets; they give alms to wandering dervishes; they follow a *pir*, a Sufi guide; they love the various kinds of religious music; they take part in the ecstatic rituals. Mysticism, an individualistic form of devotion oriented towards a personal, inner experience, rejecting violence, setting an example of tolerance and emphasizing divine compassion and beauty among all the attributes of God, has always been the opposite pole among Muslims to the legal scholars' literalist piety and the scholastic theologians' towering edifices of ideas.

For a long time the Sufis were largely left in peace and occupied a huge parallel universe within Islam, but in the course of the twentieth century they became a target of the new fundamentalist movements, which not only looked down on them as the orthodoxy did but fought them, by words and, more recently, by increasingly frequent actions. In Saudi Arabia, for example, the Wahhabis systematically destroyed all the shrines decades ago, even those of companions and relatives of the Prophet, to suppress the mystical cults, and in the theocratic Islamic Republic of Iran the Sufis were subject to massive persecution particularly under the presidency of Ahmadinejad: dervish convents were razed, the leaders of the mystical orders arrested, tortured, or shorn and driven through the streets.

In Pakistan too, the mystics have been targeted by the fundamentalists. In recent years there have been numerous attacks on shrines, such as that of June 2010 against the greatest holy site in Pakistan, the shrine of Data Ganj Bakhsh in the centre of Lahore, in which forty-five people died. But that was only the bloodiest attack, and one that was reported in the international media. Hardly a month goes by in Pakistan without a bomb exploding in a shrine or the custodian of a shrine being murdered. Compared with the previous years, there are few spectacular attacks among them; most such attacks kill only two, three, occasionally ten people at most. Rarely does anyone claim responsibility; the war being waged here is generally undeclared. Only who it is being waged against is public knowledge: not against the West; not even against the state or the government. This war is being fought against the heart of the Pakistanis' own culture. The intention seems to be to keep people away from the shrines by the very regularity of the violence.

The state tries to protect the Sufis by securing their sanctuaries with soldiers, barricades and checkpoints like those at airports. At the same time, however, it radically restricts the practice of mysticism. The Sain brothers have long since been barred from performing in the shrine of Shah Jamal itself; they can only play in the small adjoining cemetery, and even there only for two hours a week. Could be worse, I think the following evening, as I enter the shrine of Madhu Lal Hussain.

THE LOVERS' TOMB

Shah Hussain was a Sufi saint whose love for his Hindu disciple Madhu Lal overcame the boundaries of religion, class and convention. As a sign of their unity, the saint took the name of his beloved, calling himself Madhu Lal Hussain. Their common grave became a place of pilgrimage for worshippers and lovers of both religions. When I visited Lahore for the first time twelve years ago, the shrine was filled throughout the day with men and women, with old and young people, with middle-class and Malang visitors, and every evening several groups played qawwali, the mystical love poetry accompanied by harmonium, drums and chorus, made famous in the West as well as the East by the late Nusrat Fateh Ali Khan. This time, I arrive at nightfall, but there seems to be no one there, not the many devotees, not the music, no light burning; the security checkpoint is abandoned; the gate is locked.

Behind the fence I see a young, thin man crossing the yard, and I call him over. When he hears that I have travelled from another country and would be so glad to pray at the tomb of the two lovers, he lets me enter. After my prayers I ask him about the silence, which I find dismaying. After the attack on Data Ganj Bakhsh, the provincial government not only set up barricades and established security checks: they also banned the music. But if no one sings at the shrine any more, most of the devotees will stay away, or will just say their prayers and leave. No one spends their evenings any more with Madhu Lal and Shah Hussain.

'Shouldn't we be glad that the state at least tries to protect the Sufis?' I ask.

'Really?' the custodian answers, and points out that the Muslim League of the former prime minister Nawaz Sharif, the governing party of Punjab province, is aligned with Saudi Arabia. 'Their concern for safety is only a pretext to dry up the bloodstream of our religion.'

The young custodian takes me into his nearby room to offer me a cup of tea. In the dark, which usually prevails indoors too in the poorer quarters of Lahore because the power goes off in the evening more often than elsewhere, I sit down on the blanket that the custodian spreads out as a bed at night. He brings tea, sweets and a torch and then begins to tell his story: he was a musician, a drummer in one of the most famous groups in the city, and used to perform in the evenings. Their group was even invited to India, to a festival in Agra, he says proudly, and holds up to the torch a certificate in a wooden frame that attests to the drummers' fabulous success with the Indian audience. He personally was lucky: when the music was prohibited at the shrine of Madhu Lal Hussain, he was offered the job of custodian, so at least he is still close to the lovers. The other drummers have cast off their colourful robes and earn their living as tradesmen or labourers. They are not the only ones; most of the musicians in Lahore share the same fate, at least the religious musicians. Sometimes they play at weddings or saints' festivals, but that's all, and it's not enough to live on. The custodian of the two lovers writes down a link where I can hear the music on YouTube.

O PAPA, PROTECT ME

On the following evenings I visit the shrines of Lahore that were once famous for their musicians, dancers, wandering dervishes, their colourful crowds in general. At the biggest shrine, Data Ganj Bakhsh, where Ali al-Hujwiri, one of the most important theoreticians of Sufism, lies buried, I have to pass an obstacle course of gates and be patted down for weapons four times before I am allowed to enter the court-yard, which looks deserted in comparison with the Friday evening crowds that were once customary. No traces of the 2010 attack are visible, but the qawwali that Pakistan's best groups recently played here is not heard either. Yet hardly anyone has described, analysed and praised *samaa*, listening to ritual music to attain ecstasy, as thoroughly as al-Hujwiri did in the eleventh century. Only his grave is surrounded by devotees who seem to be immersed in tête-à-têtes with the saint.

At the shrine of Misri Shah, the *pir*, a tall and powerfully built gentleman with a red beard and a red cap, recommends I come back on Saturday after the night prayers: then the festival of Mir Hossein begins, and they will play music no matter what the police say. The faithful do not kiss the hand of the tall, broad-shouldered *pir*, as I have seen done in other countries, but press themselves against his body, which must be the source of a special blessing. Gladdened by my interest in Muslim tradition, he calls the other elders to pose with him for a group photo. In parting, he gives me a paternal hug.

Before the shrine of Bibi Pak Daman, the police officers on duty fish the camera out of my bag and hand it to their commander, who is sitting behind a desk playing with her phone. I have to check it here for the duration of my visit, she says with a stern look. I promise not to take any photos, I reply, smiling innocently.

'You really promise?' she asks, giving me back the camera.

A few yards away from the shrine of Mian Mir, in which silence has likewise fallen, an old, very lean man sits cross-legged on a cheap blanket and sings a sad song to the passers-by and the vendors. On his head he wears a black cap; in his face, white stubble; over his long robe, a fleece jacket; and over that, a grey, oversized sports jacket. He spreads his right hand behind his ear as he sings and raises his left in lamentation.

'O Papa,' he sings to the saint Mian Mir, 'O Papa, your feast is destroyed, O Papa, only you know my pain. O Papa, the gardeners in your garden, they are all new. But what are they doing, O Papa? The new gardeners are tearing out all the flowers. O Papa, take me in your arms, O Papa, protect me.'

IN THE MANSION DISTRICT

I accepted the lady's offer to take me to a gathering of Sufis, not least to find out what the term means in her circles. She is fortyish, I estimate, wears an elegant sari and her long hair naturally loose; perfect English, self-assured conversational tone, so attractive and worldly in her appearance that I can more easily imagine her at a gallery opening or a luxury hotel than among wandering dervishes. As we climb into her SUV, I wonder where the driver is going to take us – with his long white beard and his knee-length robe he looks like a Sufi himself.

It was not in Pakistan that the lady first entered the mystic path, but in New York. At the workshop of a *pir*, a Turkish Cypriot master, she discovered the wisdom of her own religion, Islam, and was so moved that she followed the *pir* to Cyprus and soon became a novice in his order. Once she had learned the fundamentals of Sufism, the *pir* referred her to his Pakistani disciple, who has since been her guide on the path. One or two times a year the *pir* also comes to Pakistan himself and gathers the members of his order together. They are many, says the lady, many more than I can imagine, I who hadn't even imagined a mystic like herself in Pakistan.

She observes the commandments of Islam strictly, prays five times a day, drinks no alcohol. Although in Sufism what matters is the inner experience, one must still observe the external duties, she says, distancing herself from esoteric fads. I ask if she has anything in common with believers among the simple people who visit the shrines and the saints' festivals.

'I still belong to my class, of course,' the lady says, making no bones about her social status, 'and as you can see I have not become an ascetic, renouncing everything secular.'

Her Pakistani mentor has instructed her, however, to visit the saints' tombs because they are a source of blessings, and so she goes every Friday to meditate at the shrine of Bibi Pak Daman in one of the poor neighbourhoods of Lahore. I ask whether she doesn't stand out there, by which I really mean, doesn't she sometimes experience unpleasant situations as a woman from well-to-do circles at a shrine?

'I am always there very early when it's relatively quiet.'

When we climb out of the SUV, we haven't left the mansion district. The gate is opened here by guards who naturally have machine guns slung over their shoulders. The courtyard is adorned with flowers in terracotta pots; the house is simply and tastefully furnished, with few but precious rugs on the stone floor, indirect lighting and grey, possibly Italian sofas. The gathering we enter is cultivated and wealthy and includes a filmmaker and a writer, a physician and a lawyer. Only the disciple of the Cypriot *pir*, who is a mentor to the other guests as well, stands out. Not only because he wears the robe, the white cap and the long beard of the theologians, but also because he is noticeably younger than the other Sufis, in his early thirties I would say – and yet he is always asked for the final word in the discussions. His accent betrays the fact that, unlike the other guests, he has not been speaking English from his earliest schooldays.

The topic to which the talk returns again and again is the murder of Salmaan Taseer, the governor of Punjab, a year ago. Taseer had demanded the repeal of Pakistan's blasphemy law after a Christian had been sentenced to death for allegedly insulting the Prophet. Now there are so many assassinations in Pakistan that I have only to open the daily newspaper to judge the level of political violence: a suicide bomber killing twenty-nine Shiites in a mosque near Islamabad doesn't even make the front page any more; the story appears the next morning on page twelve. And yet the assassination of Salmaan Taseer is widely perceived as something new, especially among artists, intellectuals and the secularly oriented upper class in general. For the assassin, Mumtaz Qadri, one of Taseer's bodyguards, is not a member of a Wahhabi terror organization, and his crime had no ethnic, criminal or sectarian background; the assassin was a Barelvi, an adherent of the theological movement that represents the majority form of Islam in Pakistan. It is not identical with Sufism but, nonetheless, supports the culture of shrines, supplies a dogmatic foundation for the mystic rituals and is widely considered 'moderate'. After the attack on the shrine of Data Ganj Bakhsh in June of 2010, it was Barelvis who held mass demonstrations calling for resistance against extremism. The militant arm of the Barelvi movement, Tehrik-e Sunna, was financed in part by the American government as a bulwark against the Taliban. And now it was an adherent of precisely this school with its mystical influences who murdered a secular politician, and five hundred leading theologians of the Barelvi movement explicitly approved of the murder in a joint declaration. Tehrik-e Sunna honoured Mumtaz Qadri as a hero, rewarded his family with a great deal of money, and threatened to kill Taseer's daughter. In the parliament, numerous politicians refused to join in a prayer for the murdered governor.

'We are no longer talking about a few marginal groups,' the mentor says, dismissing any tempting illusions. 'The virus of fanaticism has infected the middle of our society.'

He points out that few scholars and statesmen have had the courage to condemn the murder publicly. And those who did express criticism were threatened with death or, like the minister of minorities affairs, Shahbaz Bhatti, actually killed. Thus the murderer achieved his goal: hardly anyone dared to question the blasphemy law; the discussion about it was practically smothered, the death sentence against the Christian still not reversed. Hardly anyone dares to express solidarity with the minorities, as Salmaan Taseer did, with the Ahmadis, the Shiites, the Christians, who are bullied, threatened or killed.

'The moderate forces are totally intimidated,' an older gentleman concurs, whose family manages one of Pakistan's largest shrines.

I ask whether those people who still make pilgrimages to the shrines, the so-called simple people, have also turned radical. The gathering is not entirely unanimous, but everyone present agrees that the changes among the simple people are in any case much less serious than those in the middle class and among the theological elite. Those who make pilgrimages to the shrines are immediately endangered, they say; they may be intimidated by the attacks but are certainly not driven into the hands of the extremists. The problem in Pakistan is not a fundamentalist mass movement – after all, the Islamists always do poorly in the elections; there is no comparison with the Muslim Brotherhood in Egypt, for example. The problem in Pakistan is the lawlessness.

It is well known that the military supports terror groups, has even founded some to deploy for its own purposes in Kashmir and Afghanistan. Many of these fighters have returned to Pakistan and regrouped. Are they the genie that won't go back in the bottle, or are they an instrument to keep the country in a permanent state of emergency, perpetuating the ascendancy of the military? In any case, what is clear is that terror can be perpetrated in Pakistan practically with impunity, especially against 'soft' targets such as shrines, mosques and schools, which cannot be effectively protected even with a few police officers. Although there are so many attacks, an attacker is almost never arrested, and those who are usually have to be acquitted for lack of evidence because the underfunded and overburdened police investigate so sloppily. The courts are one of the few institutions that still function halfway normally.

'And the government?'

In this group it goes without saying that the Bhutto family's PPP, currently the governing party in Islamabad, is just as corrupt as all the other parties. But it is almost equally accepted in the mansions of the upper class, those where whisky is served as well as those where meditation is practised, that the PPP is to be preferred as the lesser evil, the party which has its base in the rural population, at the opposite end of the economic scale. The strange alliance of the poorest and the richest is the result of the government's support for popular piety; the prime minister himself is descended from a respected family of Sufis. Not the townspeople, but the farmers, not the engineers, but the tradesmen are the pillars of a secular state in Pakistan – secularism is not a modernization, but the tradition.

'It is not as if only Sufism was under threat,' the lady sighs when we have regained the back seat of her SUV. 'Everything is threatened that is in any way deviant: minorities, transsexuals, artists, women.'

Lahore was once a city of culture, a beautiful city, as colourful and diverse and crazy as New York, with theatre festivals, readings, wonderful cinemas and classical concerts, with bars, revues and red-light districts. Now, when there are public events at all, they are not advertised, out of fear. Sometimes she daydreams of cycling through Lahore, and then it occurs to her that it's not a dream but a memory: when she was a child it was perfectly normal, even for her as a young girl, to play in the street, to stroll around town, and to ride a bicycle.

THE POOR PEOPLE'S PEACE

At the shrine of Baba Farid in Pakpattan, about four hours by car from Lahore in the south of Punjab province, a bomb exploded a year ago and six people died, but now the place looks almost as it did before. Only the gateway where the bomb went off is walled shut, and at the main entrance the security checks have been tightened. Although it is only noon on an ordinary working day, the faithful almost fill the huge marble-tiled courtyard, sitting on the steps and in the niches, under trees or in the mild winter sun, meditating, talking, reciting the Quran or sleeping. Children frolicking here, cool teenagers walking up and down with their earphones there; young women giggling here, mothers supervising there. The qawwali, so ecstatic at night, now sounds like the idyllic score of a pastoral film; musicians are playing in front of two different walls of the rambling courtyard, the audiences in semicircles around them, not quite getting into the performance. It is too early yet, a Malang explains. I would have to come back at night, or on the saint's birthday.

I ask whether the government hasn't prohibited the music. Oh yes, says the Malang, that was the first thing the government did after the bombing, prohibited the music and locked up the shrine at night. But the people protested so vehemently that the orders had to be rescinded. Here in the

countryside, he says, you can't suppress Sufism by decree.
But what does he mean by countryside? What may have
been a village at one time has long since become as loud,
noisy, hectic and polluted with exhaust fumes as most cities
in the subcontinent.

You have to have spent a day entirely on the streets, or
in a motor rickshaw, without your own chauffeured car, to
have any idea of the permanent sensory stress the people
must feel, regardless of how accustomed to it they may be,
especially the noise, the dust and the exhaust, the shrill colours of the billboards, the cinema posters and the painted
buses in the treeless greyish-brown of the streets. When
you step from that into a temple, a mosque or a shrine,
the world seems to transform between one step and the next.
Movements grow calm, voices grow soft, the colours and
the shapes harmonize, the great courtyard offers sweeping
vistas, music accompanies the scenery, even the twittering
of the birds is audible. Perhaps it is an exaggeration to say
that the shrines resemble the Catholic churches of Central
America that Graham Greene described in *The Lawless Roads*
as the only man-made work of beauty that most inhabitants
ever see. Be that as it may, however, there are not many
places for the poorer citizens of a Pakistani city, and fewer
still for the poorer women, that invite them to idle moments,
to aesthetic enjoyment, to encounters with the opposite
sex and, at certain times, on special days, to experiences of
aesthetic extremes. Thus the shrines fulfil more than just
a religious function: they permit experiences that, in other
societies, are divided among many different places, cafés and
parks, playgrounds and sports clubs, museums and concert
halls, churches and nightclubs. If the people were kept away
from the shrines, or restricted there to silent prayer, as the
regulations attempt to do in the major cities – what escape
into beauty, into freedom, would be left them to offset the

tribulations of their day-to-day lives? When I ask the people themselves, they often say, almost always in fact, that in the shrines they find *sokun*, inner peace.

The very thing that makes the shrine culture so attractive, however, is politically two-edged in its effects: it calms the people, but it can also numb them. The reason for the wrath of the Taliban and other radical groups against Sufism is not only the religious practices they consider un-Islamic. Sufism is also a pillar of the dominant social order and closely connected through key figures with all the major parties, especially with the governing PPP. The president, the prime minister and numerous cabinet members are descended from families of *pirs*. And almost all the shrines in the country are managed by large landowners, who derive great religious prestige from them in addition to economic power. They have a natural interest in preserving the status quo that privileges them in this way but keeps a large part of the population poor, dependent and illiterate. This is illustrated by two statistics: Pakistan's rate of charitable donations, at 5 per cent of the gross domestic product, is one of the highest in the world, and one reason for this is certainly mysticism, which constantly emphasizes God's mercy and teaches charity. But at the same time Pakistan has one of the lowest tax rates outside of Africa: only 2 per cent of Pakistanis pay taxes at all. These two figures go together. Without a doubt, individual charity alleviates misery, but the glaring lack of a sense of commonwealth leads to the impoverishment of public institutions such as schools and hospitals. Sufism in Pakistan is thus a bulwark not only against fundamentalism but also against any change, and especially against upheaval and revolution. And thus the Barelvi theologians combat political Islam, not out of a liberal mentality, but out of a deeply conservative if not reactionary one, legitimizing by religious arguments the prevailing order with all of its blatant economic injustice.

Although the Qalandariyya is considered the most ecstatic of Pakistan's Sufi orders, the Malang with whom I have struck up a conversation, for all his anarchic appearance, his long, shaggy hair, his wild beard and his purple and green ski jacket over a bright red robe, belongs in a sense to the dominant social order; the Malang has a membership card, a mobile phone and even a business card so that people can ask him for prayers. It is not he who decides what shrine he frequents and where he begs, but his order. For twelve years he wandered, the Malang recounts, but then three years ago he saw Paradise in a dream. Shortly thereafter, the order notified him that his mother was sick and instructed him to care for her. Since then he has lived with her. Then he understood his dream: for did not the Prophet say that Paradise lies at our mother's feet?

Of course there are independents among the Malangs, he explains, but among the independents there are also many charlatans, unfortunately, who get high on drugs, not on God, and only simulate poverty to beg alms. Not everyone can become an officially registered Malang; there is a waiting list, then an admission test, a training course and, finally, the initiation, during which the novice, head shorn, takes an oath of poverty. For that, after all, is the essential work of the Sufi path: to kill one's desires, not to succumb to them.

'And what is the essence of Islam?' I ask.

'Love,' answers the Malang without hesitation. 'Islam is love, nothing else, love of God and love for people.'

The Wahhabis, on the other hand – by which he seems to mean all puritanical movements, including the Taliban – the Wahhabis see only God, not people; they think only of following the law and don't understand that love is the prerequisite for following the commandments, that the inside is what matters, not the outward form of the faith. Besides, they have lots of money, and the Sufis do not, that's another difference; they have influence with the authorities, he says, with the police.

Has he heard of the assassination of Governor Salmaan Taseer?

Yes, he has; the Wahhabis kill so many people.

'But Salmaan Taseer was killed by a Barelvi,' I interject.

'By a Barelvi?' The Malang is surprised. 'Hmph! The Barelvis too are only interested in the outward forms.'

'And the people,' I ask, 'have the people changed?'

Yes, he says, the Wahhabis have gained great influence, especially with the young people. Some people don't even shake his hand any more. To this Malang, the Wahhabis are at war with Islam. Nonetheless, he is optimistic: 'The Wahhabis have lost since they began attacking the shrines.'

I ask him how he can tell.

'I can tell by the fact that the whole world is waging war against the Wahhabis, first in Afghanistan, then in Swat or here in Punjab. It's not America, and it's not our army. It's our saints who have called out the armies.'

'So you think it's good that America is fighting the Taliban?' I ask.

'The Taliban are an American creation!' the Malang cries, demonstrating the paradoxical thinking typical of Sufism.

QUIET, CLEANLINESS AND ORDER

In a dusty outer district of Lahore, along a six-lane arterial road, the headquarters of Jamaat-e-Islami, the 'Islamic Community', the most important of the parties that represent political Islam in Pakistan, is unmarked on the outside. When the gate opens, you drive onto an estate that was probably built in the colonial period or not much later, the buildings of red brick, the pavements lined with tall trees. There are schools, leisure facilities, a guest house, neither traditionalist nor ostentatiously modern in the Saudi style, but substantial and more middle class. In a different way from the mystics' shrines, the 'Islamic Community' is also an alternative world to the noise and chaos that ordinarily characterize the Pakistani street scene, to the clashes of colours, ethnicities and social classes. As if the party were trying to present a model of a future Pakistan, the scene is dominated by quiet, cleanliness and order. All the men are bearded, the white caps on their heads and their knee-length robes nearly uniform, the women of course in headscarves. No one seems to dawdle in the grounds; no one's appearance stands out.

Because I have arrived earlier than expected, three staff members sit down with me, one after another, at the conference table in the open-plan office of the international section to keep me company over tea until their supervisor, Abdul Ghaffar Aziz, can see me. First a young man who has just returned from a visit to Tehran kills time with me. Naturally he likes the Islamic Republic, although he wouldn't want Pakistan to adopt its theocratic system. Next an older gentleman who travelled through Europe forty years ago speaks to me in German. He was young, he says, curious about the world; actually didn't want to stay so long, but then he liked Germany so much, especially the friendly people, but also the fairness and efficiency, that he wanted to learn the language. The third person to take time for me is a university lecturer in his day job.

'What subject?' I ask.

'English, unfortunately,' he answers, with no indication of irony.

I ask the lecturer about his party's vision for Pakistan. A just, Islamic, progressive, developed country in which the

state offers its citizens the basic social services. Based on
sharia? Of course. What if someone doesn't want to keep
the Islamic commandments? No one will force him. And
the religious minorities? They'll manage their own religious
affairs. A democracy? No, a *shura*. What's the difference?
In a democracy, 51 per cent of the people rule over 49
per cent; in a *shura*, they all strive for consensus. And if
the *shura* cannot agree? Then the leader decides. Who
chooses the leader? He is elected, of course. And what if he
is elected by only 51 per cent of the people? I believe Mr
Aziz is here.

Only Mr Aziz is not there; first it is time for prayers. The
question whether I want to wait in the office or come along
to the mosque is asked in the most casual way imaginable.

Abdul Ghaffar Aziz, tall and broad-shouldered as a
hammer thrower, has a big map of America under the glass
plate covering his conference table.

'Why America specifically?' I ask after prayers.

Oh, no reason, Mr Aziz answers, and points to the wall,
where a map of the world hangs. Before we sit down, he asks
about my driver.

'The driver?' I ask, surprised. Throughout my whole trip,
this is the first time a host has expressed any concern for my
driver.

He doesn't have to wait in the car, Mr Aziz says, and steps
out to have someone fetch him.

We get along splendidly, Mr Aziz and I; he has a searching and very earnest expression, but at the same time a sense
of irony, and it doesn't take much to make him smile gently
into his beard. If he were a hothead, of course, the Islamic
Community would hardly have put him in charge of its
international section. Asked to describe my impressions up
to now, I admit candidly that what has impressed me most
about Pakistan is the diversity, the close juxtaposition of

apparently incompatible opposites. New York also houses many different worlds, but in a city like Lahore I would find them all in one place; I could walk fifty yards in the old centre and see women with their faces veiled and transsexuals in makeup, barefoot fools with shaggy long hair beside businessmen in suits, a Quran school next door to a beauty salon. Where else but in Pakistan could I walk across the street from a shrine full of ecstatic Sufis, whose predecessors go back to the ninth century, to a shopping mall with glass lifts and all the current brands of global capitalism? And then the many peoples, with their different languages, customs and clothes, the many religions, the diversity of denominations even just within Islam – Sunni and Shiite, Sufi and orthodox, Islamist and laicist – what richness!

Mr Aziz hadn't looked at it like that before, it seems to me; in any case he is silent and seems to be thinking. Perhaps he is only waiting to see what I'm driving at. I wonder, I continue, whether such a contradictory society, but a society that tolerates contradictions, is compatible with the life model advocated by Jamaat-e-Islami. What happens to the many who do not conform to the ideals of equality, modesty and discipline that the Community sets as models?

'We believe that what our society has in common is greater than the differences,' Mr Aziz says, leading into a long explanation of why his party in particular supports tolerance and equal rights. He mentions Christians and Hindus who have run for office as candidates of the party, points to the many women who are active in the party, tells of the Shiite brother who prayed with them in the mosque just yesterday. Mr Aziz speaks, without having to be asked, of the religious minorities who suffer the most severe discrimination: 'We can also have a dialogue with the Ahmadis and find solutions together.'

'And what about the Sufis?'

As if he had been waiting for that question, Mr Aziz now presents the evidence of his party's respect for mystical Islam: here a classical Sufi treatise that has been translated into Urdu by a leader of the party; there a member of the party leadership who comes from a respected Sufi family.

'But, dear Mr Aziz,' I say, 'surely you don't expect to convince me that your party supports Sufism.'

The only thing the Islamic Community criticizes, he replies, is the practices at the shrines, where enterprising dervishes exploit the ignorance of the simple people, where drugs are consumed and, in many places, even prostitution flourishes. And I know myself, he tells me, that Sufi preachers are an obstacle to all development, especially in the countryside, that they do nothing against the poverty that cries to Heaven, and they prohibit the building of new schools for example.

'And the ecstatic music,' I ask, 'the dances, men and women praying together, what about that?'

Oh, those are secondary aspects, he says, minor symptoms that will go away by themselves once the fundamental illnesses of the society are cured.

'The fundamental illnesses?'

To Mr Aziz, they are injustice, corruption, the poverty he mentioned and, in connection with it, the feudal order, which, incidentally, he also blames for the poor electoral results of the Islamist parties, since loyalty in Pakistan springs not from faith and convictions but from economic dependency.

'But if the society has so much in common and the differences are so minor, why then is there so much aggression between the different groups, religions, denominations?'

Mr Aziz blames the state for the violence: the state foments the ethnic and religious conflicts in order to secure its own legitimacy – after all, weren't the attacks on churches in Egypt planned by the Mubarak regime's secret police? And if the state is not directly involved in the terrorism in Pakistan, surely it has the means to bring the terrorists to justice. 'We, in any case,' Mr Aziz affirms, 'are categorically opposed to violence and respect the rights of those who hold different opinions or a different faith than we do.'

I ask Mr Aziz about Salmaan Taseer, the governor of Punjab province who was assassinated because he wanted to abolish the blasphemy law.

'We called on both sides to engage in dialogue,' Mr Aziz answers, 'both Salmaan Taseer and his accusers.' Vigilante justice is not permitted in an Islamic society, he says; at the same time, Salmaan Taseer offended the religious sensibilities of many people. The Islamic Community therefore demanded legal action. Besides, the blasphemy law protects the religious feelings of all people, including the Christians, Sikhs and Hindus.

'But if Jamaat rejects vigilante law – does it then condemn the murder of Salmaan Taseer?' I ask.

'We called on both sides to exercise moderation,' Mr Aziz reiterates.

'Yes, very well, but now one side has evidently not exercised moderation, but killed their opponent instead,' I insist. 'Do you think that's all right?'

'We called on both sides to exercise moderation,' Mr Aziz repeats.

'But the murder, do you condemn it?'

'We called on both sides to exercise moderation.'

'Yes, but my question was ...'

'... And that was my answer,' he says, shrugging his broad shoulders with a gentle smile.

When I take leave of Mr Aziz and his staff, my driver also thanks him for the tea and the pleasant company.

THE FEAST

At the shrine of Misri Shah in Lahore, there are countless people after night prayers – in the shrine, in the courtyard, and in the surrounding streets – but it doesn't look like the wild celebration I was told to expect: no music to be heard, no one dancing, no one getting into a frenzy. Most of all, though, it is strangely dark, even inside the shrine, although its ceilings are colourfully hung with tinsel. The sparse lamps create a dusky light that heightens the reverential atmosphere. Many people are praying, repeating ritual formulas as they immerse themselves in the contemplation of God, or softly reciting the Quran; others seem simply to wait or to wander between the columns; hardly a word is spoken.

I wonder whether it is always like that, or whether it is just a power failure, and I look around for a free patch of carpet to sit on. It was a power cut, it turns out twenty minutes later, when the shrine suddenly becomes as bright as day. The cry goes up immediately that God is greater, along with praises of the saint whose feast can now begin. While silent worship continues inside the shrine, a rising hubbub of voices comes in from the courtyard, talking, giggling, laughing. Not two minutes later, the qawwali is heard, the singing of the Pakistani mystics accompanied by harmonium and drums.

I step outside, where strings of lights and coloured flags are hung between the trees, and make my way through the dense crowd towards the musicians, who seem to be gaining momentum all the faster for the long wait. The first heads begin to rotate among the listeners, then the first bodies. Beside me stands a young Malang with an orange turban over his long hair, a black fleece jacket and a face as gentle as an angel's. With a gesture I ask whether I can take a photograph of him, and afterwards I show him my camera's display: he lays his hand on my head, laughing, a friendly mockery or a precious blessing. The music has just left a first climax behind when, a few yards away, a drum and brass ensemble begins clanging. The qawwal singer looks up in annoyance, then raises his voice again to drown them out, but he soon realizes that he hasn't a chance against this unfair competition. He tries again with a few tremolos for three or four minutes before giving his accompanists a sign to take a break.

There is nothing mystical whatsoever about the drummers and brass players, and they are not particularly talented either; they are more interested, it seems, in drawing a maximum of attention by maximum loudness. A man with dreadlocks nonetheless goes into a trance, a middle-aged woman dancing around him, her headscarf covering her hair but not her suggestive looks, gestures and swinging hips. Not just her, but all the people in the courtyard of the shrine – so many eccentrics, freaks and no doubt saints too among the ordinary people – where do they hide during the day, I wonder, all the wild haircuts, motley rags, extravagant rings, voluminous necklaces, but most of all the furrowed, ecstatic, transported faces that seem to be living in a different time and place? Here an old man is dancing with a plastic basket on his henna-coloured hair, eyes closed; there a youth cries aloud for love of God.

It is long past midnight when I leave the shrine, two or three o'clock, and only then do I notice that the whole neighbourhood is in a festival mood, the dusty alleys hung with garlands, lit up, and filled with the aroma of freshly cooked sweets, the humble street restaurants and tea houses packed, the merchants in front of their shops calmly watching the festivities, many with children or grandchildren on their laps, clusters of women strolling around, led by the matrons, processions coming, drumming and singing, from every direction, marching towards the shrine, carrying over their heads a long, finely embroidered cloth to lay on the tomb of the saint. The Sain brothers too I meet again, the two famous drummers whose concert I attended at the cemetery of Shah Jamal at the beginning of my journey; this time Gunga and Mithu are standing on a proper stage, a great crowd of listeners in front of them, abandoned to the complicated rhythms that I still cannot decipher.

On flat-bed trucks with giant loudspeakers, the major parties advertise themselves by distributing free food and turning up the qawwali as loud as it goes, as if they needed not just to outvote their competitors but to drown them out too. The biggest truck bed and the loudest music are those of the Muslim League, although they are allegedly financed by Saudi Arabia. Elsewhere young men dance in ever-changing formations, not enraptured, not artistic, but rather unbridled to the point of obscenity. The smell of marijuana is unmistakable, and the young and the not so young women discreetly eyeing you up don't look as if they are about to go home to their parents any more than do the flamboyantly made-up transsexuals.

The scriptural scholars were right, it occurs to me: this no longer has much to do with the content of the Quran, with Sufism as it is taught by the classical treatises, but more with a fair or the cathartic transformation of a carnival, except that this party is celebrated on the birthday of a saint, at the gates or in the courtyard of a mosque in which at the same time other believers are meditating on God or reciting the Quran, in spite of the noise. And at the same time it is that very ability to tolerate contradictions, the most diametrical opposites in one and the same place – indeed, to consider them perfectly natural – that the complex philosophy of the mystics, conversant with paradox, ambiguity, riddles, has been perfecting on the Indian subcontinent for centuries. That is why the compulsion towards homogeneity, towards crystal-clear definitions of the permissible and the proscribed, the Islamic and the un-Islamic, engenders such a particularly violent commotion in Pakistan, because here traditional lives still harbour so many ambiguities. Mithu Sain for example, the younger of the two drummers, can't even give a simple answer to the question whether he is a Sunni or a Shiite; somehow he is both, he says – and that in a country where violence between Sunnis and Shiites has become almost a daily occurrence.

THE COSMIC ORDER

I visit Mithu the day after the festival. He lives with his wife and three children in two tiny rooms in a poor neighbour-hood in Lahore, the double bed serving as dining room table and living room sofa. Under a shimmering purple robe he wears jeans at home, a stocking cap on his curly head. He didn't get home until seven in the morning, and his eyes show it. Mithu's father was a drummer, and his grandfather too. When his brother Gunga was born deaf, his father, sad that the chain seemed to have broken, took him to his *pir*. After all kinds of rituals and magical invocations, the *pir* solemnly prophesied that Gunga Sain would be a great drummer – and not only that: Gunga would fly. When they were invited to a festival in Europe a few years ago, the brothers knew the *pir* had been right.

'It was quite a celebration,' I say, whereupon Mithu says that, ten years ago, the *urs*, the saints' feast days, were bigger and much wilder.

Today many people are afraid a bomb will go off, he says, and, besides, the economic situation has got worse for the poorer people. And, yes, many people have given up the culture of the shrines. Sometimes when they play at a festival he hears someone shout, 'Sin!' That never used to happen; the same people used to revere the brothers as saints, almost. Which they aren't, of course, but they are *faqirs*, literally 'poor people', striving for nothing but the love of God and love for people.

The prohibition against drumming at night in the shrine of Shah Jamal, as they used to do, has nothing to do with the fear of terrorists, as I had assumed. The prohibition, Mithu enlightens me, was issued two years before the devastating attack on Data Ganj Bakhsh, Lahore's biggest shrine. Allegedly the neighbours around Shah Jamal had complained about the disturbance, but in fact there was a dispute about land, and then the plaintiffs went and got a fatwa from a fundamentalist mullah who declared the drumming un-Islamic. But that was really only a pretext. And the officials in the Ministry of Religion, which issued the prohibition, were on bad terms with the musicians since they had tried to hire them for a wedding and they had refused to lower their fee. The policeman who barricaded the shrine to prevent anyone from drumming or dancing went blind shortly afterwards, incidentally. For Mithu, that is the punishment sent by the saint who is also called Jhule Lal, 'Red Dancer'.

'And since when are you allowed to play in the cemetery next to the shrine?' I ask.

The ministry soon noticed that hardly anyone visited the shrine any more, and accordingly the alms boxes, which the ministry manages, were empty. So they allowed the music again, although only once a week. The officials are only interested in money, nothing else; they are all corrupt. No one in the Ministry of Religion has any idea of *ruhāniyat*, spirituality.

'And the rhythm?' I ask at last.

They ordinarily begin with classical rhythms, Mithu Sain explains, and taps his fingers on his thighs to illustrate, fives and sixes, and then they expand these rhythms, counting seven, eight, nine, eleven or eleven and a half, and often they play two different rhythms at the same time, that's why it sounds so complicated, and, yes, in the first part they do want to impress the listeners; the first part is rather for art's sake. Then, when the dancers perform, they change to the dhammal rhythm, which then simply repeats with variations so that the dancers, and the drummers themselves, go into a trance. This is where the connection to the holy arises; that is why they never play the dhammal rhythm on secular occasions, at weddings or other feasts. When he plays it, he is *mast*, 'inebriated', and one with all living things, yet at the same time more than awake, perceiving in the instant every movement, every variation of the rhythm, every nuance that his brother Gunga plays. Only when he is inebriated is he truly present; then it is not he who is drumming, someone else is drumming through him.

Some people would accuse the Sufis of being too passive, Mithu Sain knows, of not standing up against the fundamentalists, not getting active in politics, not organizing protests; after all, the majority of Pakistanis are still adherents of mystical Islam. But they are not passive, he affirms; they are just working in a different system, in the inner system: 'We are striving more for the cosmic order.'

In the other of the two rooms, as every afternoon, the drummer's students are waiting.

BLEAK NORMALITY

AFGHANISTAN I, DECEMBER 2006

PEOPLE DON'T CHANGE MUCH

'It is still a privilege to visit Afghanistan,' wrote the author and photographer Nicolas Bouvier, who drove his Fiat Topolino from Switzerland via Kabul to Bombay in 1953. 'Not so long ago, it was an adventure. Unable to hold the country, the British army in India hermetically sealed off access in the east and south. For their part, the Afghans had sworn to keep their country from all Europeans. They almost kept their word, and were all the better for it.' Since 1922, barely a dozen Western daredevils have managed to visit Afghanistan, Bouvier writes. The scholars were less lucky. While the Orientalist James Darmesteter had to settle for information from Afghans in Pakistani prisons because he couldn't get across the Khyber Pass, the archaeologist Aurel Steiner waited twenty years for his visa, and received it just in time to die in Kabul. 'Today, you can do it with a little tact and patience; when we presented ourselves at nightfall at the border village of Laskur-Dong on the Quetta–Kandahar road, armed with the precious visa, there was no one to show it to. No office, no barrier, no control of any sort; just the white span of the track between the mud houses and the wide open countryside.'

While his travelling companion searches for the customs officer in the village, Bouvier, with an injured hand, falls asleep in the car.

> The sound of the door made me jump: an old man was pushing a lantern under my nose and exhorting me vehemently in Persian. He wore a white turban, a white robe, a well-trimmed beard and, round his neck, a silver seal as large as a fist. It took me a moment to realize that this was the customs officer. He had come along simply in order to wish us a good trip and to give me the address of a doctor

in Kandahar. His dress, his presence and the welcoming note he brought to his job made him such a sympathetic figure that I stupidly pointed out – to prevent his getting into trouble – that our visas had expired six weeks previously. He had already noticed, and wasn't bothered. In Asia people don't keep to timetables, and, anyway, why refuse us in August the passage that would have been allowed in June? People don't change much in two months.

REALLY CRAZY

The visitor arriving in Afghanistan at Kabul Airport in late November 2006 puts on a military protective vest and a helmet. British soldiers drive me in a convoy of armoured Land Rovers to the headquarters of ISAF, the foreign troops who are supposed to provide military security for the country's reconstruction. My view of the city is through a thinner slit than the window of the burqas that very few women are still wearing in Kabul. When, after the third PowerPoint presentation that started with the obligatory battle cry 'Winning hearts and minds', the soldiers drive me to an Afghan army training centre, I at least receive permission to put my head out of the roof hatch like a lookout. 'Alamo' is the name of the camp of containers, prefab houses and tents that houses the American instructors.

'Don't you find it a pity that you see nothing at all of the city?' I ask the friendly officer who leads me around.

'Oh, that's no problem,' First Sergeant Weber answers. 'When I want to go out, I ask three colleagues and we go to headquarters or to visit our boys in Bagram.'

He needs three colleagues because the foreign troops are only allowed to drive through the city in convoys of at least two armoured cars with two soldiers each. Some of the

soldiers themselves think it strange that they approach the
people they want to help only with protective vests, helmets
and loaded machine guns. But that's how it is; it's necessary for security reasons. Of course I understand that. On
each day of my journey, a suicide bomber blows himself up
somewhere. No one quite understands how they manage to
recruit them, since suicide is not only against the Quran but
also against the strict code of honour of the Pashtuns. They
must be foreigners, many people say – Pakistanis, Arabs.
But they can't all be foreigners: there are too many. I meet
a group of soldiers whose comrades were killed yesterday. I
also understand the disinfectant in front of every mess tent,
at every washbasin, in every toilet stall, as if Afghanistan was
poisonous. It is necessary for hygiene reasons. I understand
that the mess kitchens use no local foods and literally every
grain of rice and every drop of water is flown in. That is necessary, not, as I suspected, for reasons of security but because
otherwise the prices in the local markets would skyrocket,
explains the chef de cuisine of the German-Swiss company
that is the world leader in catering in crisis zones. Meanwhile
it is not for reasons of hygiene but for security that Afghans
never come into contact with the foods and, in the kitchens, are only allowed to do the washing up, while most of
the staff working for the foreign troops – even the security
guards who protect the soldiers! – come from countries such
as Nepal or India. Of course he would love to hire Afghans,
says the chef. They're cheaper, and they're really friendly.
But he is not allowed to do so, that's expressly forbidden by
his contract, and that is understandable. Yes, of course, I say.
But in this conversation too, as in so many, I quickly reach a
point that exceeds both parties' understanding.

'So, sometimes when I think about everything, I am surprised,' says the chef when I sit down after dinner with him
and his Nepalese and Indian employees.

'About what?'

'About everything, the way things work. We're here in Afghanistan, but all this has nothing to do with Afghanistan – the fruit from South America, the cutlets from Germany, the water from the Persian Gulf, the cooks from Nepal.'

'I suppose you're right.'

'But where it's really crazy is in Bagram at the American base.'

'Why is that?'

'They go so far as to fly in lobster from Cuba. From Cuba! Just imagine that.'

Then the chef, who would be happy to employ more Afghans and who is really not the reason why the country isn't getting anywhere, shrugs his shoulders sorrowfully. But what is the reason?

TWO BRITISH COMMANDERS

The British commanders, Brigadier Nugee and Colonel Moss, have an impressive manner: humorous, polite, direct, disarmingly candid – disarming in the sense that they take all your arguments away by acknowledging them. The Afghan police who are being trained by the Americans and Germans? Not very efficient, poorly led, corrupt, and a pyramid upside down: more officers than constables. The high rate of resignations? No wonder, when a policeman trained by ISAF earns more by mopping floors for ISAF. The warlords that Prime Minister Karzai is employing as security forces in the provinces? Gangsters. The corruption? We wonder ourselves, frankly, why the prime minister's brother is so rich. The Americans? Well, their police training, unlike that of the Germans, is really good. The Germans, you know – and the colonel begins to snicker – the Germans are very, very thorough, and that is a good thing; he respects that, but in Afghanistan they are not training inspectors for mid-level civil service in a provincial town in Germany. The Americans' police training, on the other hand, was perhaps a bit superficial, so now they are trying to steer a middle course.

'Well and good, but the contradiction between the Americans' mission and NATO's mission, between the war on terror and reconstruction?'

'Hm, good question.'

'The south, what about the south, the skirmishes, the many civilian casualties, four thousand dead this year? Why are the Taliban so strong, still or again, after five years?'

'Certainly there are reasons', says Brigadier Nugee, 'why the Taliban had regained broad support in southern Afghanistan when command was passed from the Americans to NATO.'

'What reasons?'

'You see, when we took command, we were surprised ourselves at the situation we found. The Americans had their bases, from which they hunted terrorists. As NATO, we wanted to spread out so that the country can develop.'

'Why was so little development work done in the five years before that?'

'The Americans had a different mission in the south; they were primarily concerned not with rebuilding the country but with fighting the enemy. When we wanted to begin rebuilding, we noticed that there was no security at all. We were attacked, and we were not prepared for it. There were enemies everywhere. We had problems; there were many civilian casualties, too many civilian casualties; our own losses were high. That was the news of this summer, the reports of fighting, of war, when the West was talking about the Iraqization of Afghanistan. But: we won the battle.

The Taliban had to withdraw. Since October, the numbers of casualties have decreased significantly. It is quieter. We are trying to persuade the aid organizations to start work at last in the south. We're starting with zones in which security is assured, and then we will expand them step by step. NATO has realized it must do more for reconstruction. We have to show the Afghans that they are better off without the Taliban. That's a better strategy than war.'

I ask whether the problem is not in the structure of the reconstruction: that most of the aid money doesn't reach the Afghans.

'Yes,' Brigadier Nugee admits.

'And the PowerPoint presentations?'

'TV adverts,' Colonel Moss says dismissively.

'The many civilian casualties – aren't they undermining the goal of winning the hearts and minds of the Afghans?'

'We know that every civilian killed creates a hundred new enemies,' says Brigadier Nugee, and continues with a tinge of agitation: 'We make mistakes. We know perfectly well Afghanistan cannot be won militarily. We need more resources, not necessarily for the military, but for civilian projects. Security is the prerequisite for reconstruction. It's a fair question to ask why so little was invested in reconstruction in the years before we had serious security problems in the south.'

'Where would Afghanistan be if there was no war in Iraq?'

'Well,' it is Colonel Moss's turn to sigh, 'what shall I say? Whether the Iraq war was right is a separate discussion, but in regard to Afghanistan I can say this much: we would be further ahead, of course. I can't quantify it, but we would be further. Anyway, this is not Iraq – this war is winnable.'

'The biggest worry,' Brigadier Nugee continues, 'the

biggest worry we have is that something could happen that
draws the attention of the international community, and
Afghanistan would be forgotten again.'

Our talk takes longer than planned.

'It's been very interesting talking with you.'

'Perhaps we'll run into each other again over a drink at the
officers' club.'

HUMANITARIAN MISSION

On this trip I am a guest of NATO, which commands the
foreign troops in Afghanistan, 32,500 soldiers at present. I
see the country from their perspective. That is new for me,
but customary for journalism – although it is not customary
to mention the fact. Afghanistan is not Iraq. I could have
come in on a civilian flight and travelled freely as a foreigner
throughout most of the country. The security situation is
not so precarious that a civilian would have to wear a kit that
looks from the outside like an astronaut's suit, and feels from
the inside just as heavy. A friendly reception by Afghans
should be the general rule still – or again. But if one wants
to observe how the self-image of the Western empire has
changed since the collapse of the Soviet Union, one should
not just look from the outside at the armoured vehicles in
which the West drives around in a growing number of countries to keep or to restore order. 'ISAF' is written on the
soldiers' uniforms, 'International Security Assistance Force',
with a motto in Arabic letters below it in the local language,
Dari: *komak o hamkāri* – 'Help and Cooperation'.

Travelling with NATO in Afghanistan does not oblige one
to be less critical of NATO's concept of treating humanitarian help as part of the military strategy aimed at assuring a
safe environment for the troops and gathering information.

One can still mistrust the term 'humanitarian', which has suffered from inflation (to the point that one NATO spokesman saw 'humanitarian bombs' fall on Kosovo). But, on the personal level, one develops such an understanding, and here and there even an admiration, as I would not have thought possible before this trip. I am not limited to official interviews and 'briefings'. Most of the time I am simply an observer, in military aircraft, in armoured vehicles, in mess tents and temporary bars, behind the soldiers on road patrols, in tents and in waiting rooms. Waiting not least: travelling with the military is probably a better way to learn patience than any meditation seminar. And nowhere do I get to know the soldiers better than when I wait with them for hours, or for days.

There must be soldiers who match the Rambo stereotype, but I don't meet any. Instead I meet young German recruits whose statement of their personal mission to help the people in Afghanistan is more clear, thoughtful and credible than any Bundeswehr PR film could have managed. I meet no officer who needs my explanation to know that you don't win the hearts and minds of a population by releasing bombs over their heads. Instead I hear everywhere criticism of the Americans, whose searches, bombardments and apparently arbitrary arrests are endangering the reputation, and hence the safety, of the other soldiers. And yet the Americans, too, affirm in conversations with me that they only want to help.

The first time he was sent to Afghanistan, says First Sergeant Weber, who seems sincerely pleased to see me again in the mess at headquarters, he thought he had come for a military operation. But soon he realized the civilian activities were much more important. The success or failure of their mission would be decided in the humanitarian sector. That was the reason why he was glad to have a second tour of duty in Afghanistan: because it is fulfilling to see concretely how he can help. It goes without saying that human beings would rather help than fight.

First Sergeant Weber has no martial air about him. His bright face, in which tiny red veins stand out, always has a good-humoured smile below his blond moustache, and when he takes his helmet off he puts on a slouch hat. The sergeant's eyes suddenly light up as he tells of Afghan villages where his company provided medical aid, of talks with the village elders, of the laughing women and children. But he also tells of the mullah who was hanged by the Taliban a few days after their visit. After that, the women in the village didn't visit their doctors any more.

I interject that the Afghans' perception of the Americans' demeanour seems to be growing more negative, and ask him whether he can understand their annoyance.

'Yes,' says First Sergeant Weber. 'When we're travelling in our cars, we always have to drive very fast, and inconsiderately, for security reasons. As an Afghan, I'd be mad about that too.'

I say I was thinking not of their driving style but of the many civilian casualties; does that bother his conscience as a soldier?

'My ultimate nightmare is a kid pointing a toy gun at me. I don't think I would shoot a child.'

'But the air strikes,' I press him. 'Bombing a village from above is something completely different from standing in front of someone who's pointing a weapon at you.'

The American air force has flown more missions from June to September 2006 than ever before in Afghanistan, 2,095 air strikes. For comparison, 88 air strikes took place in Iraq in the same period.

'Believe me, ordering an air strike is an infinitely difficult decision every time,' the sergeant assures me.

'And what goes on in your mind if the decision turns out to be wrong?'

'I don't know how you can justify that,' the sergeant answers.

But, after a brief silence, First Sergeant Weber attributes the air strikes too to a self-defence situation. They'd been attacked.

'As a soldier I know that there can be situations in which my company might abandon me if rescuing me was too dangerous. There are situations in which you have to sacrifice a few people to save many.'

IN KABUL

With a handshake I take leave of the two press officers who have accompanied me to the gate of the military camp. They are worried because they're responsible for my safety, and at the same time they are curious to hear what I will have to say when I return to the spaceship that is their headquarters, which they and all the other members of the International Security Assistance Force are allowed to leave only in military convoys. To avoid being mistaken for a NATO employee, I walk two hundred yards from the base before hailing a taxi. I want to get the soldiers' personal stories out of my head. I believe them when they say they mean well. But I want to understand why it's not going well.

My first impression is one of bleak normality: traffic jams, rubble, crude concrete barricades instead of buildings, poverty. No trees, no cafés, no laughter. The only people who linger in Kabul are cripples and the apparently inevitable children holding glue under their noses. But there are also many women in the streets, without burqas, schoolchildren, girls and boys. Yes, they do laugh, the schoolchildren. You

have to keep your eyes on the schoolchildren to avoid slipping into depression. But if you've read old travel accounts
about how Kabul looked five hundred, fifty or just twenty-
five years ago, even that won't help. Kabul was once a
garden. Grapes, pomegranates, apricots, apples, quince,
pears, peaches, plums and almonds flourished here, as the
emperor Babur noted in his memoirs in 1501. All the splendour of India, his conquest, was not worth the thirty-three
varieties of wild tulips that bloomed in Kabul. There were
nuts in abundance, and the wine was heady. Even Bouvier in
1954 found a Kabul that came close to 'the delightful portrait
drawn by Babur'. And the 1974 Polyglott guide promises
the traveller 'unique impressions that no other country can
convey in such richness'. Well-developed roads and a dense
network of domestic flights facilitated travel. The new era
was evident in modern marble and concrete buildings with
glass fronts. It was only regrettable, the Polyglott guide
laments, that Kabul had become an El Dorado for drug
addicts who seriously damaged the reputation of Europeans.

Hippies are no longer a problem in Afghanistan today.
On the contrary: Afghanistan now exports its problems. Five
years after the fall of the Taliban, United Nations experts
reported that nowhere near as many poppies had ever been
grown as under the eyes of NATO: 92 per cent of the world's
opium. Very little of the economic growth that is visible in
Afghanistan is due to reconstruction; most of the new villas,
office buildings and shopping centres that can be seen in
Kabul are financed out of drug money. And the militia leader
who is responsible for combating drugs in Afghanistan is
himself considered one of the country's biggest drug lords.

I accompany the young writer Massoud Hassanzadeh to
the parliament. A journalist for Voice of America in his day
job, he has an appointment to interview a member of the
so-called reform faction, the Shiite cleric Ahmad Ali Jebraili.

The cleric demands the rule of law and the protection of minorities. To provide these, the constitution does not need to be changed; it needs only to be applied.

'At this moment, as I am speaking to you,' the cleric says to the writer, looking him in the eye with consternation, '80 per cent of this state's business is ruled by personal connections, not by the law.'

Afghanistan is an Islamic state, he says, but its model is not the theocracy in Iran. Asked whether the parliament represents the Afghan people, the cleric answers that not everything that happened in the election was correct, but the result expresses the basic will of the people.

'We oppose the blanket criticism of the parliament,' the cleric objects to the accusations voiced by the Taliban. 'The destruction of the parliament benefits only the enemies of Afghanistan at home and abroad.'

What the cleric says sounds reasonable. But I haven't heard anything in his talk to indicate where he stands politically, whether in the national or the religious camp, in the opposition or with the government. No wonder, says the writer Massoud Hassanzadeh after the interview: all the factions preach the same thing. All of them are for reforms, the technocrats who make up the government, the 'democrats', as the former communists call themselves, and the old Islamists, who were the first to claim the name of 'reformers'. Yesterday he interviewed an ex-communist, Massoud tells me, whose statements were identical with those of the Islamist, absolutely identical: for the rule of law, against corruption, for democracy, against nepotism. But the ex-communist would never make common cause with the cleric – not because he holds different views, but because he belongs to a different camp. No one cares about substance.

I ask Massoud whether the difficulties he observes in the parliament aren't natural after almost three decades of war.

At least now there is a parliament to have difficulties. The writer agrees in principle but brings up the growing influence of the Islamists and the helplessness of the national government vis-à-vis the provincial lords and the Western generals. Besides, in any other country, war criminals would be put on trial, but in Afghanistan, he says, they sit in parliament, and, when asked about the thousandfold murders of which they are accused, they say no one hands out sweets in a war.

'But isn't it progress if now they all at least declare their support for democracy?' I ask again. 'Surely that says something about the Afghan reality if suddenly everybody is talking about peace and human rights to win elections. And maybe in the long term the slogans will influence the politics.'

'Possibly, but in the very long term,' Massoud Hassanzadeh says.

'Is there any alternative?'

'No. There is no choice. Either this corrupt government survives, thanks to the support of the West, or we have Taliban and war.'

WHERE IS THE PROGRESS?

The problem in Afghanistan is not the West's presence per se but its unwillingness to be as present as it would have to be to rebuild a country the size of Afghanistan. James Dobbins, the special envoy for Afghanistan under President George W. Bush, drew the bitter summary that, 'in manpower and money,' Afghanistan is 'the least resourced American nation-building effort in our history'. In proportion to the population, the White House appropriated one-fifth as many troops and one-twenty-fifth as much money as for the mission in Bosnia. A large part of the money promised was never disbursed. 'The main lesson of Afghanistan is: low input, low output.' But it is not just a shortage of money that is keeping a country like Afghanistan from becoming governable again. The goals pursued by the intervening powers in Afghanistan are so contradictory that, even five years after the Bonn Agreement, they do not add up to a strategy, and the different actors often get in each other's way. But, most of all, the distribution of funds contradicts all the concepts I read in preparation for the trip and all the insights presented to me during my travels with NATO: the $85 billion that the international community is spending on the military mission in Afghanistan towers over the $7 billion for civilian development.

And yet there is progress. Even the writer Massoud Hassanzadeh would not refute the statement that the existence of a parliament represents progress, in spite of all its shortcomings. Over a quarter of all Afghans, according to American data, have access to 'qualified medical care'. A hundred thousand teachers have been trained in the past five years and 40 million schoolbooks printed. There were 900,000 children going to school in 2001: now, five years later, there are 5 million. These figures are hardly verifiable, and the number of schoolchildren is lower than the figure given by ISAF while the number of teachers is much higher, yet there are other observations that don't require any statistics. At least in the big cities, the women can go out again without wearing burqas. Many Afghans are glad of the new television stations, which broadcast open discussions and critical reporting in addition to Afghan entertainment programmes. Especially important for the country's future independence is the development of the national army. According to most reports, interviews, and my own observations, what has been accomplished so far in this area is by all means satisfactory. It stands to reason that NATO would be most successful at setting up in Afghanistan what it does best itself: 35,000 Afghan soldiers are already on duty, and they enjoy a better reputation than the police. Almost all the army's instructors are now Afghans. Most foreign officers function only as tutors alongside them on the training grounds near Kabul. By 2008 the Afghan army is expected to have reached its planned size of 70,000 soldiers. Since their pay was recently raised, so that the soldiers now earn more than some doctors, the troops' morale seems to be relatively good. I heard no serious complaints, in any case, when I went walking through the camp alone to ask around in Persian among the soldiers. One is a Tajik, another a Pashtun, a third an Uzbek, and a fourth a Hazara Shiite. The army is the only national institution that seems to be largely free of ethnic tensions. Some of the officers used to fight for the communists, others for the Mujahedin; others still were Taliban. Some were first one, then the other, or all three. The atmosphere in the pauses from training is relaxed; there is plenty of laughter, more than in town.

Nobody has to teach the Afghans how to shoot, explains a Canadian instructor, Officer Feick. Tactical thinking, intelligence and perception are no problem; if there is one, it's topography, map-reading – which is no wonder if 80 per cent of the young recruits are illiterate. Most of all, though, the Afghans have a different concept of discipline and time. Brevity is not exactly their strong point. 'When you order an Afghan to do something, the first thing he does is ask why. That is a likeable trait, but not particularly helpful in the military.'

'Will the young men you're training here be able to fight someday?'

'Yes, I think so. And do you know why? Because they're here voluntarily. Because they hear everywhere – at home, in the street, on television – that the country needs peace, and peace requires a national army.'

A layman like myself is hardly able to judge the success of an army training programme. The friendly instructors and the jovial recruits are nice to see, but they don't prove anything. The field exercise with live ammunition on the mountain plateau 1 Charlie North/1 Delta North is no more informative to me, ignorant as I am of military procedures, than the place name itself. So I go to look for progress where I am better equipped to judge it: in traditional Afghan art.

MASTER TAMIM

Master Tamim began working as a miniature painter at the age of seven. At sixteen he became an *ostad*, a master. At the time the war began, his drawings brought him enough money to feed the whole family. Then the Taliban took power, and Master Tamim had to hide his pictures. Once a Talib stopped him in the street, a milksop of barely sixteen or eighteen who spoke only Pashto, the language of the Pashtuns. What did he have there? the Talib hissed, pointing his whip at the roll of paper the master had in his hand. Rolled up between sheets of newspaper, documents and harmless calligraphies, the Talib found a representation of a human being. He struck the master with his whip as hard as he could on the knee, making his legs buckle under him.

'After that, I fell into a depression,' says Master Tamim. It wasn't the physical pain. It was the humiliation.

Master Tamim announced to his family that he was going to leave the country. An artist could no longer live in Afghanistan. He took a few brushes with him, rolled up in blankets. When he arrived in Peshawar, Pakistan, he rented a room. A friend helped him. Master Tamim began painting again. After a few months he had sold enough pictures to fetch his family, his parents. In Peshawar he also found an institute where he could teach other Afghan miniature painters. When Kabul was liberated from the Taliban, Master Tamim returned. Now he teaches at a school for traditional Afghan painting that is supported by an English organization. 'The Turquoise Mountain Foundation' is its name, and it was founded by the young ex-diplomat Rory Stewart, who walked several years ago from Turkey to Nepal and wrote a wondrous, highly celebrated book about it, *The Places in Between*.

'I personally have freedom now. No one tells me any more what I can paint and what I can't.'

I wonder how old Master Tamim is. With his experience and his artistic mastery, he could be seventy. From his looks, I would say he is forty, forty-five.

'I'm twenty-eight,' Master Tamim laughs. 'It still happens that someone comes to the institute and asks me where the master is.'

Massoud Hassanzadeh, the young journalist and writer, also thinks the Afghans are content where they see at least a hint of progress. In Herat, for example, his home town in western Afghanistan, the situation is better than that in Kabul; there is something resembling normal life, and social structures are still more or less intact. But Herat was always different, and it survived the war halfway unscathed thanks to the governor, Ishmael Khan. Most Afghans were not inimical to the foreign soldiers and didn't demand their withdrawal. They are just desperate, Massoud says, purely and simply desperate. In Kandahar or Helmand, though, in the south, where almost all the reports of bombings and battles come from, the mood has tipped. In view of mass unemployment – the rate, according to Western researchers' estimates, is up to 90 per cent in some cities – it is not hard to persuade a young man to join the Taliban. There he would have at least food, clothes, shelter and perhaps a few afghanis left over for his family. Yes, there is development, says Massoud, returning to my initial question. But, in relation to the money that has been poured into the country, the net results are disastrous. 'Just thinking about it will drive you mad.'

'Here in this extraordinary piece of desert is where the fate of world security in the early twenty-first century is going to be played out,' said the British prime minister Tony Blair, visiting the troops just this week. So there is reason to be worried about world security as well.

THE NEW MOTORWAY

Why Afghanistan is not making progress, or is doing so only torturously slowly, is illustrated especially vividly where the pace should be the fastest: on the brand-new motorway from Sar-e Pol to Sheberghan in the north of the country. Campaigning for election in the northern provinces, Hamid Karzai had promised the population to build a clearway ten metres wide. He was accompanied by the American ambassador, Zalmay Khalilzad, whom many observers blamed for the southern tribes pulling away from the peace process. On 10 June 2002, behind the closed doors of the loya jirga, he had pushed through the withdrawal of the former king, Zahir, and then announced it to the public himself, for the sake of simplicity. Zahir Shah was the only Afghan politician who had the trust of all Afghanistan's ethnic groups, including the Pashtun south, but he had criticized the American air strikes.

Khalilzad promised that his government would finance the motorway if the Afghans elected Karzai prime minister. Karzai won the election, and the state aid organization

USAID allocated $15 million to build the road. The money was transferred to an agency of the United Nations, which hired the American company Berger as consultants. The actual building contract went to the Turkish company Limak, which in turn hired the Afghan-American ARC Construction Co. as a subcontractor. Each of these companies collected a healthy commission. According to the Berger company, just housing the foreign employees and importing the technical equipment cost $4 million. There wasn't much money left for the actual construction. Wages for the Afghan construction workers, at $90 a month, for ten hours a day, seven days a week with no holidays, hardly mattered. Nor were there any costs for health insurance or other provisions, and, when the labourer Mohammad Nassim was killed in a worksite accident, it was up to his colleagues to collect donations of money and food for the family that had lost its breadwinner.

But that didn't upset anyone very much in Afghanistan. When the inhabitants first drove on the new motorway, they were stunned. From the day of the opening ceremony, there were so many cracks and potholes in the road that its surface was more gravel than asphalt. Everywhere there are cars blocking traffic with a flat tyre or a broken windscreen. Because the underfunded roadbed was laid two metres narrower, it has no hard shoulder. Nor did any of the foreign engineers think of emergency laybys. The many cyclists who used to ride on the shoulders must now either stay home or squeeze between the cars. For them it's a consolation that the cars don't drive much faster on the motorway than they did on the old dirt road. If road users complain, the provincial government refers them to Washington. The province itself had no say at all in the road's construction and does not feel itself responsible for its repair.

But, wait, it gets even more absurd: some time after the motorway was 'finished', people living adjacent to it dug a ditch right across the road. They needed to establish a drainage channel before the rainy season. They were arrested for damaging public property. The elder of the village defended the suspects. The inhabitants had been glad about the new road, he said, but not about the fact that their houses would be flooded in winter. He called for the installation of a drainage pipe. The building firm pointed to an obscure, rarely applied paragraph in the Afghan traffic code which prohibited buildings less than thirty metres from a motorway. But the houses were there before the road, the villagers objected. When they realized that logic wasn't helping, they dug a ditch across the road two months later.

The American organization CorpWatch, which has documented the building of the Sheberghan motorway, notes that the reconstruction of Afghanistan has produced much bigger scandals. At least roads like the Sheberghan or the Kandahar motorway are drivable. Elsewhere, the shoddy work cost lives. 'But the Sheberghan highway is a cautionary tale about the pitfalls of privatizing reconstruction: wasted money, empty political promises, lack of central or local government control, and basic cultural and business misunderstandings that win resentment instead of hearts and minds.'

In 1978, before the Soviet invasion, Afghanistan was poor, but its people were able to feed themselves. Eighty per cent of its exports and half of its gross domestic product came from agriculture. Today the country is dependent on the benevolence of the international community. According to the figures of the minister of the economy, Mohammad Amin Farhang, 99 per cent of all merchandise on the market in Afghanistan comes from abroad. The World Bank, the International Monetary Fund, the development programmes of the United Nations and the American government have more control over the Afghan economy through their advisors and more influence on policy than the Afghan government. The donor nations and the financial institutions justify their power by saying they would be paving the way for corruption and mismanagement if they left it to Afghan institutions to administer the billions of dollars in aid. But the World Bank itself contradicts this logic in a report published in late 2005: 'Experience demonstrates that channelling aid through government is more cost-effective,' the World Bank's country director for Afghanistan, Alastair McKechnie, is quoted as saying. Western companies are often still more susceptible to corruption because they are only in the country temporarily, and their activity there is subject to practically no oversight and no jurisdiction. The worst sanction they risk is being flown by helicopter to Kabul and from there back to their home countries – as an employee of the security company USPI discovered after shooting an Afghan interpreter in a dispute. The employee of another security company took the liberty of slapping an Afghan government minister in public.

AMERICAN HEADQUARTERS

When the Swiss photographer Daniel Schwartz, who is accompanying me on this trip, is finally allowed to get out of the car on his drive around Bagram with four press officers to take photos of the desert in which the fate of world security in the twenty-first century will be played out, he triggers an alarm siren. A voice like that of God Almighty instructs the driver to stop the engine, but, instead of an angel, a guard armed with two machine guns is suddenly standing in front of the armoured car, as if to prevent an escape. He's a bassist, he says cheerfully, more jazz than classical, and glad that he'll be studying music when he gets home. Unlike the American press officer, who in all seriousness rummages through her papers for the name, the guard has heard of Alexander the Great. But he is surprised to learn that the conqueror came this far: 'Alexander the Great was in Afghanistan?'

'Yes,' Daniel informs him, 'and he had his headquarters right here where Bagram is today.'

'And?' the guard asks.

'He was utterly defeated – like every conqueror before him.'

The press officer, unable to find Alexander the Great in her papers, wants to know why Daniel set off the alarm siren: surely there's nothing wrong with looking at the scenery.

'No idea,' says the guard, who would rather go on talking about ancient history with Daniel.

Half an hour later, another armoured car drives up. The black officer who gets out has no machine gun, but half a cookie in his hand. Other people smoke cigarettes, he eats cookies, he explains, starting on his third. No, he doesn't know the reason for the alarm either, but he advises everyone to keep away from cigarettes.

Another hour later, a third armoured car arrives in the desert in which the fate of world security in the twenty-first century will be played out. The tall blonde woman who gets out is wearing dark sunglasses, jeans, trainers, a white shirt exposing her cleavage, and a leather jacket. She stands in front of the group, feet apart, hands on her hips, as if she were addressing a band of naughty children. Ah, I think, a Rambo after all. The mood changes.

'Which one is the guy?' she barks at her compatriots. Like schoolyard snitches, they point at Daniel, and she gives him thirty seconds to hand over his film.

'It's not the moment for a discussion,' the German press officer murmurs in his native language.

Before we can continue our tour, all the visitors' papers

are checked and their names written down, including those of the four press officers and the six British supervisors who have come with us from headquarters to Bagram, where three thousand American soldiers, five thousand civilians and two thousand Afghan labourers live, forming something like a Midwestern American small town, but one that could just as well be located in the Balkans, in Africa or in Iraq: a shopping mall with all the blessings of the American market, post office, bank, gym, hair stylists, beauty shop and spa, adult education classes, a shop specializing in Persian rugs, the usual hamburger, pizza and coffee chains, even bus stops – except that the pedestrians greet each other in passing with military salutes. That looks funny, almost like a cartoon, at busy hours: hand up, down, up, down, up. Odder still are the joggers in sports kit who still have their machine guns slung on their backs and salute just as assiduously. An encounter with Afghanistan is provided in the 'yurta tent', where two Kirghiz women sell souvenirs made in China: 'We give a percentage of our annual sales directly to foundations that inspire messages of hope for our continued freedom.'

VISIT TO THE PASSPORT OFFICE

On the way back, the little convoy stops at the passport office in Kabul because Daniel wants to extend his stay. Perhaps the press officers approved the detour to show that the North Atlantic Treaty Organization and the Afghans get along quite normally, and it's no problem to pop by the immigration office. But there is nothing normal about the procedure. Two press officers and two soldiers in their astronaut suits leave the capsule to accompany Daniel, who also has to wear a helmet and protective vest. A restlessness immediately breaks out among the Afghans in front of the passport office.

Not that they are aggressive – on the contrary, they seem to be anxious, noticeably keeping their distance and stepping quickly away from the door to which the astronauts, calling salam, salam, are heading to ask which room they need to go to. It really isn't a very rewarding task for a group of heavily armed young Europeans in battle dress, with headsets, helmets, sunglasses and body armour, to look friendly to the locals. The soldiers make an earnest effort, I can see that from the armoured car, which I am not allowed to get out of; they give a strained smile, demonstratively toss their machine guns behind their backs, soothingly hold their palms downward; the boldest even take their helmets off, calling salam, salam. And, in fact, a little cluster of Afghans forms, trying to find out what they can do for the astronauts, who have forgotten to bring one thing: an interpreter. After all, the detour to the passport office was not on the agenda today.

I see that I'm needed and get out of the car without asking the remaining press officer for permission. As I approach the astronauts and the Afghans, I realize that I too have forgotten something: the protective vest and the helmet. I find it so unpleasant suddenly to walk the streets of Kabul in military gear, where the day before I encountered nothing but hospitality, that I immediately turn around and hand my vest and helmet back into the armoured car. Then I finally rescue the other astronauts, who are exceedingly grateful, and the Afghans explain to me that we have stopped in front of the wrong office building. *Khodā hāfez*, the Afghans call after us: May God protect you.

COLA IN THE DARK

On the last evening, I go to visit Farid, who works as a recorder in the Afghan parliament but earns his living with a laundry in the Soviet district of Kabul. What remains of the middle class lives here in prefab estates. The taxi driver has trouble finding the address because there is no lighting at all: no street lamps, no advertising, not even lights on in the buildings, apart from a few kerosene lamps flickering here and there; nothing else but the headlights of the cars. But there are few cars about at this time, nine o'clock in the evening – where would they go anyway if there's no electricity and hence no public life? Five years after the overthrow of the Taliban, the metropolis Kabul still has electricity for only three to four hours a day. The water supply is pitiful, the sewer system a cesspit. Again and again I have heard NATO officers say that the victory or defeat of their mission is decided not on the battlefield but in the humanitarian sector. In that case, good night, I think, as I drive through the deserted streets of Kabul, through potholes as big as ponds, while speeding four-wheel-drives with Western passengers overtake me, past giant, pitch-dark tent cities in which refugees are camping for the fifth year running, past French restaurants and brand-new mansions in which foreigners and nouveau-riche Afghans get electricity and hot water from private generator systems and are connected with the world twenty-four hours a day by dedicated satellite lines.

In principle, nation-building would be a great idea. In practice, it means reconstruction strengthens the economies of the donor countries. The United States, for example, awards contracts to major American companies that excel not by the most advantageous offers but by the best lobbyists, the closest contacts and the highest campaign contributions. These businesses then engage subcontractors, which in turn hire sub-subcontractors. Most of the money ends up in the profit margins between one company and the next. The contractors don't have to show progress – only photos of progress that can be projected in front of legislative committees or reporters. Yet the shortfalls are well documented, not only in the reports of Afghan and Western NGOs. Thus the American Government Accountability Office has shown that the state aid organization contracts for projects in places that none of its employees have ever visited, such as roads in remote mountain areas, straight across cemeteries, or through flood plains. Some of the projects audited couldn't even be located at first, and, when the places were finally found, they turned out to be too remote or too dangerous to stay in for long. The GAO also criticized the fact that, due to a lack of internal communication, certain projects were awarded and funded twice.

Of the money that does make it to Afghanistan, furthermore, a large part flows back into the economies of the donor countries. Meals, management, engineers, equipment, housing, security guards, even the building materials and often the labour are flown in from abroad, just like most of the food and of course the conveniences such as satellite TV, air conditioning, armoured SUVs and generators that have to be provided to persuade a Western engineer to take a job in Afghanistan. The single private company that has contracted to train police officers has a fleet of three hundred armoured Land Cruisers, each worth $150,000. One foreign advisor costs $500,000 on average: $150,000 in salary, the rest for his security and living expenses and the margin earned by the contractor that employs him. The imported water he drinks costs more than an Afghan physician earns: $3 a day on average.

Like reconstruction after natural disasters, nation-building has developed into a whole industry, a gold mine with the corresponding gold-digger's mentality: go to the country, make your profit, tax-free of course, and get out. The results, in many places: hospitals where the only thing that isn't broken, from the very first day, is the façade; schools that collapse under the first snow; motorways whose asphalt surfaces don't last more than a few weeks after the ribbon-cutting; industrialized agricultural operations in which many farmers haven't been trained and don't know what to do, so that they are more desperate than before. There are individual projects that are more or less successful; besides profiteers there are many Afghans and foreigners who work for reconstruction to the point of physical exhaustion day after day, but there are also severe deficits in the general infrastructure. The result is that under the Taliban there was electricity, and under the Americans there is none.

Finally I find the right house number, tap on the window, and, behold, Farid opens the door of his laundry, a kerosene lamp in his hand. He fetches Coca-Cola from the shop next door. Tea would be my preference, and much cheaper, but – oh, right – to make tea you need electricity.

'How do you work the laundry, Farid? With three hours of electricity?'

'Well, the shop is open all day,' Farid explains, 'but I have to hurry to get everything washed in the three hours. Only sometimes the power goes off completely, then the laundry piles up.'

I ask Farid about his work in the parliament. He likes it. He studied political science at the University of Kabul, where American advisors are also at work now. The course was good, says Farid; they learned a lot from the advisors.

'And the parliament?' I ask. 'Do they debate in earnest, or is it just meant to look like a democracy?' Farid thinks a moment. No, he says, the debates are in earnest, it's not just a show. And, besides the corrupt members, there are many who are there as honest representatives and sacrificing themselves for Afghanistan.

'That means you are happy on the whole that the Taliban are gone?'

Farid looks at me and holds his hand flat below his chest. I don't understand. 'My beard was this long,' Farid laughs, 'this long – can you imagine it?'

I look around the circle, where more relatives have joined us since my arrival, his brother, his cousin, two nephews. As if on cue, all of them hold their hands below their chests and chortle along with Farid. Of course I've heard about the chest-length beards that every man had to wear under the Taliban, but only when you look at a gathering of amiable, clean-shaven gentlemen do you realize what that means. In the dim light of the kerosene lamp, with their scarves, coats and caps, which you don't take off even at home in Kabul in autumn, they look almost like a group of mountain climbers gathered in the refuge in the evening after a strenuous ascent. Then Farid lists the punishments that the Taliban handed out: the number of days people spent in prison for listening to music, the number of lashes they received for lacking a beard, the number of executions for premarital sex.

Later I ask Farid about the hole in his shop window, closed up with a makeshift plastic patch. Someone broke in a few days ago, he explains. Under the Taliban, he could have left the shop open all night; no one would have stolen anything. Now there isn't even anyone you can report a crime to.

'And the police?'

The group start snickering again.

THE LIMITS OF REPORTING

REPORTING

AFGHANISTAN II,
SEPTEMBER 2011

CEMETERY 1

In the early morning hours of 11 September 2011, I visit
the cemetery of Kabul, which is a refreshing place when
you arrive from the dusty hubbub of the city, with its constantly overcrowded streets. Almost immeasurable in their
dimensions, the grounds run up a hillside on the edge of the
city, above the cloud of exhaust fumes. Trees offer shade
here and there, incredibly, since the garden that was once
Kabul is never seen today except in photos that are decades
old. Stranger still is the silence: not a single car anywhere;
only the cries of two donkeys can be heard in the distance.
I have begun to fear I won't meet a soul whom I could ask
about the victims of the ten years' and the more than thirty
years' war, when my gaze falls on the first, then the second
and soon the many sheets that are stretched between the
fences of the family plots. Families are living under some of
them, it turns out, but most of the inhabitants of the Kabul
cemetery are old men, some of them very old, apparently
alone.

I strike up a conversation with one of them, who has carefully furnished his home: rugs on the ground; pots, pitchers
and a cassette radio on a board. Chickens are running around
in front of the tent, and a shorn sheep rubs up against the leg
of Nur Agha, as everyone used to call him – Master Light. I
guess his age as sixty, sixty-five at most, only streaks of white
in his beard, no furrows in his high forehead, his black hair
down to his shoulders. He's actually 81 years old, Nur Agha
estimates, smiling slyly.

'What have you done to stay so young?' I wonder.

'I was careful,' Nur Agha explains, pointing to his chest,
'not to let sorrow tie knots in my heart.'

Then he answers my question about his share of the

estimated 3 million dead that the war has claimed, one in ten of the 30 million Afghans: 'I have given seven martyrs.'

Twenty years ago, when the war overflowed into the streets of Kabul – fighting for every house and rockets from the mountains – he went ahead to Jalalabad to organize a refuge for his family. When he returned to Kabul to fetch them, a bomb had destroyed his house; his wife, all his five children and one sister dead. It was two weeks before all seven of them were buried – no, not here in the cemetery, but wherever there was a safe patch of ground. No one dared set foot in the cemetery in those days: snipers everywhere.

'Since then I have been all alone,' says Nur Agha, patting his sheep, as if to drive the loneliness from his mind.

When the people began burying their dead in the cemetery again, he set up a little tea stand here. Good location, he thought: after all, the war is still going on. He had no house any more, and no strength to start over again. So he stayed at the cemetery overnight: that was twenty years ago. Are things better today, I ask, or under the Taliban?

'Of course it's better today,' Nur Agha answers. Today people can visit the graves of their loved ones again, the women and the young people too. The women weren't allowed to leave the city before, and the young people avoided the road because there was always a Talib around to find fault with their appearance or to make them join in group prayers.

'So the Taliban were an economic problem for you?'

'No, no,' Nur Agha answers, 'I made more money under the Taliban.'

'Why?'

'Because the Taliban distributed alms. Nowadays there are nights even during Ramadan when I'm too hungry to sleep.'

'So why is it better today?' I ask.

'Because now we are free,' Nur Agha says, surprising me

with an argument like those in the PowerPoint presentations. 'No one tells me what to do, what to say, how to wear
my beard.'

'Oh, and 11 September 2001' – I remember my duty as
a Western reporter, ten years later to the day – where does
he stand on that? Nur Agha doesn't know what I mean. The
attacks in America, the airplanes that flew into the skyscrap-
ers? Nur Agha shakes his head. There was no television
then, he says, begging forgiveness for his ignorance, and no
one was allowed to turn on the radio.

We continue with the topics that are more pressing, in the
cemetery of Kabul, than 11 September 2001, such as the big
samovar with no fire under it. He doesn't sell tea any more;
he's too old and can't be bothered. He keeps his head more
or less above water with the money that the mourners give
him, but his life is destroyed anyway, wife and children dead,
all alone except for a sheep.

'If people want to help me stay alive, I gladly accept, but,
if someday no one helps any more, I am just as glad to die.'

WALLS IN FRONT OF WALLS

Back in Kabul five years later, the first thing I notice is the
new wall *in front of* the front wall of every building that represents state, capital, or a foreign country, and in front of
the new wall a third wall of cement sacks and guards with
machine guns. After a first appraisal, I am led through a
steel door and examined again through a grille. When the
door opens, I step into a passageway in which people search
my bag, check my ID and pat down my body. Finally one
of them, the only man not carrying a machine gun, knocks
on another steel door. Again a sliding window opens, a
quick look, and then I am allowed to enter, and find myself

– standing in front of the original façade of the building. This has become the regular procedure in the better hotels, restaurants, banks and shopping malls in Kabul, the three-stage process probably standardized, except that, in front of embassies and government ministries, the whole street is blocked off. Accordingly, the hotels and restaurants have no neon signs or other advertisements; they are recognizable from outside only by the metal roof jutting out and the barbed wire on top of the outer sandbag wall.

Has life in Kabul grown still more dangerous? No, everyone answers, or at least all the ordinary people in Kabul who are not representatives of the state, capital or foreign countries, in the street, in shops or among my acquaintances: no; the situation is not good, but it's better than it was, obviously. On the one hand, it would go against the duty of politeness to complain in front of guests, especially foreign guests; but, on the other, no driver, merchant or acquaintance mentioned any such improvement five years ago. What strikes me at first glance is that the poverty is no longer as obvious, at least in the city centre: no more begging women in burqas every few yards, no gangs of children getting high on glue; but in their place countless kebab stands, many more shops, urban life of a sort at last, rubbish collection for example, wonder of wonders, and two, three parks that look like nice spots to take a break. In the evening, the surprise that there is electricity – no street lamps yet, so that Kabul still lies in darkness, but some shops are lit by bare white tubes, and in the windows of the residential buildings I discern the wan light of energy-saving bulbs.

Light! The last time I was in Kabul, there were only three hours of electricity a day, and only during daylight hours. Five years of reconstruction had already passed at that time, sumptuous donor conferences had been held and aid promised in such amounts that, mathematically, no Afghan would have to live below the poverty line any more. Today Afghanistan still ranks 172nd among the 182 countries listed in the Human Development Index, and yet the change wrought by supplying a metropolis with electric power around the clock could not be more tangible. The state also seems to be providing a minimum of order in the form of soldiers and police standing on every corner. Crime is now practically non-existent, say the Kabulis, which we may take to mean you no longer have to stand watch in shifts guarding the doors and windows of your own home at night.

There are dangers, yes, but they have become more con-crete, and at the same time more abstract: concrete because the safety of every individual Kabuli is no longer threatened by general chaos and lawlessness; the violence is now aimed directly at the representatives, beneficiaries and guarantors of the ruling order – hence the protective walls in front of all buildings of symbolic importance; abstract because no one knows who will perpetrate the next attack when or where, or whether perhaps someone with a machine gun in his hand will simply snap. The Western military force has disappeared from the streets; no more speeding columns of armoured cars raising dust over two blocks on either side; Afghan security forces now man the checkpoints and, unlike the NATO soldiers, they do not look like astronauts in their protective gear. The Afghan recruit is occasionally seen in trainers rather than combat boots. The Kabulis I talk to are happy that the occupation appears to be declining, and at the same time they wonder what will happen if the foreign soldiers really do leave the country in 2014, stressing the 'if' with conspicuous frequency. They couldn't even be sure of visiting their relatives who live thirty kilometres away: too dangerous.

That is a problem for reporting too: large parts of the rugged territory are practically no longer accessible, not to the Afghans themselves and much less to foreign visitors. Most of the cities may be safe, but the roads are not. Thus a reporter can go almost nowhere except to the places reachable by air and, at most, the villages that surround them. That means that any appraisal of the country is necessarily one-sided, and first-hand reporting can cover only those areas in which there have been at least elementary advances: safe movement, open schools, electricity, some kind of public administration, police in the streets. The alternative would be to travel 'embedded' again, as a NATO-accredited reporter. Then I would be wearing one of those astronaut suits with helmet and protective vest, would be travelling outside Kabul in military aircraft and armoured cars, surrounded by soldiers any time I talked with villagers, and housed in maximum-security compounds. In other words, my view would be no less limited. It seems impossible at the moment – or impossible for me in any case – to see the war from both sides of the front on the same trip. If I wanted to see the Taliban's perspective – or more of it than interviews with their official spokesmen would show, which I can read anyway – I would do better to put my ear to the ground in northwestern Pakistan. But a foreign reporter can no longer go there either without the permission of the Pakistani authorities, not even to the major cities such as Peshawar and Quetta, which used to be regular matchmaking agencies for getting in touch with the Taliban. And the risk of marching with a band of fighters over the mountains into southern Afghanistan is too high at present even for journalists more intrepid than I am.

NORTHWARD

The link between Kabul and Mazar-e Sharif is considered the only safe transport artery in the country, nearly five hundred kilometres long, most of it through picturesque mountains and gentle green valleys. Newly improved at the beginning, the road soon changes into a dusty track on which, ten years after the beginning of a reconstruction programme which included billions for improving the road network, the tar forms islands of varying sizes. The surface is completely worn away in the many tunnels that date from the government of Mohammed Daoud Khan in the 1970s. Because the lighting that must once have been there is missing, you drive into a black dust cloud in which the headlights of oncoming vehicles flash suddenly and disappear.

My driver has a clear, uniform opinion on everything: it's always the Americans' fault.

'Would you rather have the Taliban?' I ask.

'The Taliban are America's slaves,' my driver answers.

'But then why are they fighting against America?'

'Didn't the CIA train the Taliban?'

'That was before the 9/11 attacks.'

'And who do you think supports the Taliban today?'

'Pakistan, they say.'

'And whose vassal is Pakistan?'

'The Pakistani government is dependent on America,' I admit.

'There we have it,' says my driver triumphantly.

Few if any of the villages on the mountainsides left and right of the road have electricity and running water. And this is not a remote wilderness, remember, but the most travelled region in the country. It is useless to ask about schools here. But there is an answer on the other hand to the question what happens to commercial vehicles when they are retired from the road in Germany: from the coach in the livery of a holiday tour operator to the lorry advertising a plumbing company in Bochum; from the University of Marburg to the transport firm of Willy Betz – they're all here. The whole fleet of the Afghan transport industry seems to have been bought second-hand in Germany.

MAZAR-E SHARIF

Unlike Kabul, Mazar-e Sharif was never a beauty: hastily erected concrete buildings on streets drawn with a ruler, its only attraction the shrine in which Imam Ali, the fourth caliph, is said to rest. But the bazaar is bursting with merchandise from Central Asia, Iran, Turkey and China; the streets are clean; the traffic is regulated by lights, whereas in the capital the flow of traffic is still largely unimpeded and hence comes to a standstill at junctions. It is late Thursday afternoon, and half of Mazar-e Sharif seems to be visiting the shrine. Although the cult of the dead is a thorn in the flesh of the puritanical Taliban, and although a single suicide bomber would kill dozens if not hundreds of people, there are no security checks at any of the four entrances that lead to the park-like grounds where the blue mosque stands.

Behind a door that is ajar, Sufis have gathered, Islamic mystics, densely packed on the floor covered with rugs. After the sermon preached by their leader, a white-bearded old man who speaks of earthly and heavenly love, the singer raises his voice in *zikr*, the musical contemplation of God. The other Sufis accompany his ecstatic singing with their breath, aspirating rhythmically in chorus. Gradually their heads begin to move, then their upper bodies sway in an ellipse. A second, younger singer joins in, the rhythm picks up, the singing grows louder. Now the Sufis, perhaps thirty in number, stand up, their torsos rotating ecstatically. The territory of modern-day Afghanistan is one of the cradles of Islamic mysticism; many saints and some of the greatest poets of Sufism are buried here. People knew during the

war, and even under the Taliban, who criminalized all musical rites, that mystical orders must have existed in secret.
But the Sufis gathering again today in public places for *zikr*,
before evening prayers at the shrine of Imam Ali, without
security checks, with the door ajar, are a stronger refutation
of the pessimistic view of Afghanistan than all of NATO's
bulletins.

THE BEST PLACE IN TOWN

Next to the brightly lit mosque is the bottle shop where you
can get spirits to take with you to the restaurant over the
road, since it doesn't serve any. The guests sit on rugs that
are spread on wooden frames. This is no sleazy den but the
best place in town, with a well-equipped playground, a family
area and two banqueting halls for weddings, big enough to
hold a thousand, two thousand guests, and always packed on
weekends; they are perhaps not the centre of the society, but
its upper quintile. The men sitting on the next rug think it
a far-fetched idea that the Taliban could return and impose
their strict Pashtun mores again on the Tajiks, Uzbeks,
Hazaras and other peoples of the north. I question them further, of course, and I hear about the arbitrary officials, the
obscene wealth of the erstwhile warlords and present entrepreneurs, the hollow promises of the government, the still
massive gaps in the infrastructure, such as the shortage of
doctors or of clean drinking water. But go back?

I ask whether the foreign troops should leave Afghanistan
in 2014.

'Absolutely!' The group on the next rug is unanimous.

'But then you would be depending on your own army.'

'Well, the foreign troops don't necessarily have to leave
on schedule.'

IN THE COUNTRYSIDE

I drive west out of the city to get as far from town as safety will permit. After about twenty minutes, the car passes the 'war fortress', Qala-i Jangi, where the dreaded General Dostum led a massacre after Taliban prisoners had attempted a revolt: 230 prisoners died, and the rest were loaded into container trucks under the eyes of the CIA, 250 or more in each of the thirty containers, the prisoners' knees pressed against their chests, some of them on top of each other, the only ventilation through bullet holes. Only a handful of Taliban in each container survived the drive to Sheberghan, Dostum's home town. All the others were taken out to the desert of Dasht-e Leili and buried in mass graves. Such a past is one reason why compromise is so difficult today; on both sides of the front are people who, while they may not be plotting revenge, have no reason ever to trust their opponents.

The driver turns off the asphalt road. In a village named Dehbadi we pass two German armoured cars coming the other way, the only foreign troops I will see on the drive through the countryside around Mazar-e Sharif. In the seven of Afghanistan's thirty-four provinces in which 'security responsibility' has been transferred to the Afghan army, the forces intend to demonstrate visibly that the withdrawal is feasible. None of the people by the roadside seems to pay any mind to the Germans, who, in turn, look just as impassively out of little windows.

I ask the men of various ages standing in the doorway of a house what they think of the soldiers who have just driven by. Polite people, the Germans, says one, but not fighters; all they ever do is drive around in their armoured cars, and if they ever had to get out they would be so afraid they would hardly be able to breathe. Nothing wrong with that, says another; after all, the war is over. Has peace already come, then? I ask, surprised. Yes, they all sigh with relief, it's peace now. For that reason the men find it right that the foreign troops want to leave the country.

'And perhaps they are tired of us,' one mutters sympathetically.

'And the Taliban?'

'When they came the first time, we didn't know them; they weren't from here. But now we know that their business is murder and terrorizing the people. They won't dare come again.'

Unlike Iraq, which under Saddam Hussein was a brutal dictatorship, yet at the same time a functioning state, Afghanistan had hardly known anything before the invasion of the West but oppression, bitter poverty, war. The Afghans are still not free, in spite of elections, nor prosperous – but the people in Dehbadi are grateful nonetheless that they now live in safety, and grateful to the foreign soldiers.

'I used to think health was the most important thing,' a retired teacher recalls, making tea, biscuits and nuts appear on his carpet in seconds; 'but then I saw that it's no use being healthy if there is no peace: what is there to live for in war?'

The analyses that predict chaos, war and relapse give too little attention to the fact that the people in Afghanistan will have a say in the matter. When the Taliban conquered the country from the south in 1996, it was in the throes of civil war. Even in the regions that were not inhabited by Pashtuns, the prevailing sentiment was relief that someone at least was imposing order. Today, the people would rebel against the Taliban, at least in the north, because they have had a taste of peace. Near Kunduz a girls' school was closed because of pressure from the Taliban, newspapers all over the world reported. No one in the world read that the school was soon reopened because of pressure from the parents.

'We don't have enough classrooms!' complains the deputy head of a village school, a robust Uzbek woman with gold teeth.

'Be careful,' the head whispers, 'the gentleman writes for a foreign paper; we should show ourselves content.'

'Nonsense!' the deputy head cries, and leads me to the overfilled classrooms in which the children are taught in three shifts from morning till evening, girls on the left, boys on the right. They are the first generation that has not known war.

'What would you like to be when you grow up?' I ask the six- to ten-year-old children.

It takes a moment before anyone has the courage to answer, but, once the first girl has started, her classmates cannot be stopped. The only strange thing is that they all have the same professional goal: doctor.

'They want to heal,' the deputy head explains.

'Doesn't anyone want to be something else?' I ask the children, and after a few seconds of silence I hear a girl in the last row whisper something.

'What did you say?' the deputy head asks.

'I'm going to be a pilot,' the girl declares in a firm voice.

IN THE PANJSHIR VALLEY

As if he were to watch over his people even in death, Shah Massoud's grave is on an outcrop of a mountain that offers the most majestic views of the Panjshir Valley on three sides, with the steep white peaks above, the white foaming river and the light green trees and meadows, sprinkled with clay villages whose deep brown echoes the colour of the mountains. A steady stream of people approaches the simple black stone, covered with sand, bearing a glass plate with the name. They pray, take pictures, deposit flowers; a few recite from the Quran. Engraved in the collective memory of the Afghans as the day that changed the world is not 9/11, but 9 September 2001, when Shah Massoud was blown up by two suicide bombers. Today we know that the two attackers, who pretended to be Belgian journalists, belonged to the al-Qaeda network, and that the murder was in preparation for the attacks in the United States. The plan was to neutralize the last opponents in Afghanistan before the anticipated American counter-attack and extend the Taliban's rule over the whole country.

I spend the night with former Mujahedin who fought for Shah Massoud in the best days and the worst, strong, bearded men with black-and-white kerchiefs around their necks. There is no electricity in the mountain village, no plumbing, but campfires, spring water and, as the sole luxury, a battery-powered radio. The slopes are so fertile that the people can feed themselves – that always ensured the independence of the Panjshir Valley, whose narrow entrance the leader blocked in the worst days with explosives.

If one person on Earth knew what it would mean for Afghanistan to fall into the hands of the Taliban – what it would mean to the world – Shah Massoud knew.

Did he not warn the world against the terror of al-Qaeda? He didn't even ask for support; he only demanded that Pakistan stop supplying the Taliban with weapons and money. But no one listened to him, not the United States, not Europe, not Iran; no one was interested in Afghanistan at all in the late 1990s except the multinational energy companies.

'This man blew up the Berlin Wall,' says one of the men, alluding to the decline that Shah Massoud inflicted on the Soviet Union in the 1980s.

It doesn't sound pathetic; it sounds like a simple statement.

But the world left Shah Massoud in the lurch for a few oil and gas pipelines.

Where are Shah Massoud's comrades today? I ask. They've become politicians, say the men, very astute politicians who have ministries and palaces, but haven't managed in ten years to build a decent tombstone for Shah Massoud. The memorial here was financed by a foundation and by Shah Massoud's own family. What else could you expect, they say; over and over again in history, the comrades in arms of great leaders turn out to be mediocre; charisma and greatness of heart, vision and humility are not contagious, unfortunately. No one in Afghanistan has trod the path of Shah Massoud.

'How do you see Afghanistan's future?' I ask.

'If the worst comes to the worst,' one answers, 'we'll dynamite the entrance to the valley again.'

IN THE SOUTH

Kandahar marks the absolute edge of the territory that is accessible to independent reporters. You can fly to Kandahar, stay in one of the two high-security bed-and-breakfasts, and drive a car from interview to interview. But, if you're light-skinned, you shouldn't go strolling through the bazaars, local friends advise. Kidnapped, a foreigner brings in a lot of money; killed, another point for the propaganda. Even the locals are careful where they go, with whom, and especially at what time of day. The last restaurants close at nine at the latest, and the taxi drivers hurry home.

Because there is no other way to travel from the northern to the southern part of the country, I return to Kabul to take the plane. In just the few days I was away, the feeling of security that the inhabitants had so carefully cultivated is gone. At noon the Taliban set off several bombs in different

places simultaneously and occupied an unfinished high-rise
at the edge of the diplomatic quarter. In the evening the city
is still holding its breath because the attackers are constantly
shooting from the high-rise. The streets are deserted three
kilometres from the scene; the taxi fares have quintupled. It
is not the number and not the rank or the background of the
victims that the Taliban will claim as their success tomorrow
– they haven't blown up a minister, a foreigner, or even a wall
in front of walls. It is the mistrust. Everyone in Kabul has
heard something different; no one believes the terse commu-
niqués that are read on state television. It is the impression
of being at the mercy of such attacks if the state can't even
protect itself. How is it possible, everyone wonders, for the
Taliban to pass all the checkpoints with kilos of explosives,
dozens of rifles and a whole carload of ammunition, and to
take up a position, just like that, near the American embassy?
Who helped them?

Indian MTV on the television set in the austere depar-
tures lounge, a milky spot over the miniskirt and the thighs
of the singer, like those on the faces of anonymous witnesses
in TV documentaries. The milky spot travels; it jumps onto
a car; eight men toss it in the air. Look, censorship! one
might cry, dismissing claims of new freedom, or one might
marvel at the permissive dance videos on Afghan state television ten years after the fall of the Taliban, to which none
of the travellers to Kandahar pay any attention, neither the
young people in jeans and T-shirts with big headphones
over their ears nor the old people in their tribal garb and
chest-length beards; neither the women under their burqas
nor two Afghan development workers in their cargo trousers
and trekking shoes. And all these people belong to the same
country, and the same time! We should probably envision
the future in Afghanistan only in the plural: the future of the
north, the future of the south, the west, the east; the future

of the cities and the future of the rural areas. In any case, in view of the means available to the central government and the funds that the international community is willing to invest, large and growing parts of the country are going to remain ungovernable in the foreseeable future. In Europe too it took longer than the Thirty Years' War before peace took shape. When the video shows several dancers at once, the application of the Islamic norms of propriety becomes altogether grotesque: lots of moving white spots on the screen, and in some shots even a milky strip covering half – no, covering three-quarters of the screen now, because the dancers have one shoulder free after the Indian fashion.

PEACE CONFERENCE

'When heaven is split open, / When the stars are scattered,' the Quran reciter begins at the peace conference of the province of Kandahar, which has opened two hours late, under even stricter security precautions than usual, 'When the seas swarm over, / When the tombs are overthrown, / Then a soul shall know its deeds and its omissions.' In rows of close-set chairs, several hundred men in traditional garb have gathered in Kandahar for a regional peace conference; half a dozen female delegates in headscarves to one side; behind them a whole contingent of press officers of ISAF, the international peacekeeping force, some with still cameras, others shooting video; embedded between them a few journalists who have taken off their helmets and protective vests; on the stage, the Afghan officials and Western generals in deep armchairs. Only the Taliban, who are the actual topic of the conference, because they are the ones who need to be won over to peace, sit nowhere in the windowless hall.

After the Quran recitation, the national anthem is played and everyone jumps up; then a minister greets the conference and gives the floor to the former president Burhanuddin Rabbani, the chairman of the national High Peace Council, who is not considered a friend of the Karzai government, and was probably appointed for that reason. Rabbani, a slightly stooped, white-bearded, slender gentleman with care-filled eyes, is met with reservations as an Uzbek and a leader of the Northern Alliance in the Pashtun south, but his plea for reconciliation is clear and extremely forceful, and couched in an excellent Pashto, as my seat neighbour concedes, who is a local stringer for the BBC's Persian-language broadcasting service. One may, indeed one must, criticize the government for many things, Rabbani says. But now is not the moment for disputes. The Afghan house is on fire, and everyone must do their part to put it out. The applause is loud and long.

After Rabbani, it is General John Allen's turn to speak. He has come to listen and learn, Allen says, having internalized, in his brief term as supreme commander of the international peacekeeping force, the tone with which one achieves the most in Afghanistan. All decisions must be made by Afghans themselves; ISAF merely supports the legitimate representatives of the people, Allen declares time and again, assuring the listeners equally often that the international community will not abandon Afghanistan after 2014. The Taliban continue to lose ground, he says; their attacks are an expression of their weakness. While the sturdily built general speaks in an emphatically modest tone of voice, as if he were humbled by the privilege of standing before this august assembly, his thin interpreter transforms his address into an ardent appeal. 'Let me speak from my heart,' says the general, at which the interpreter puts his hand on his chest: the war has already gone on much too long; everyone has experienced so much suffering; everyone in the country is tired. On the other side

too, many fighters have no greater wish than to return to
their families. Now is the time for them to come home. Not
all the fighters will be persuaded, Allen says. But to those
who are ready to play a part in peacefully guiding the fate of
their country, we extend our hand today.

'I wish you and your families God's rich blessing,' the general closes, and thanks his listeners in Pashto. The applause
lasts no more than one or two seconds. I ask my neighbour
if the speech was as bad as all that. 'No, no,' he answers, 'the
NATO generals always used to sound so warlike; they've
never heard one as modest as this Mr Allen before.'

'Why was the applause so short, then?' I ask.

'No tribal leader likes to be seen applauding a NATO
general. The Taliban have their snitches everywhere.'

Burhanuddin Rabbani's speech at the Kandahar conference was his last. Immediately upon his return to Kabul, on
20 September 2011, the chairman of the High Peace Council
was murdered in his highly secured house. The attacker,
hiding a bomb under his turban, pretended to be a representative of the Taliban on a mission of reconciliation. No
one ever sowed cynicism more perfidiously.

TRIBAL LEADERS 1

The street leading to the house of Haji Agha Lalai, a member
of the Provincial Council and leader of the Alkozay tribe, is
blockaded; there are guards with machine guns in front of his
door. Of the almost five hundred tribal leaders in Kandahar
province who chose to cooperate with the government, Lalai
is the only one the Taliban have not yet assassinated. The
loop of his black turban hangs neatly on his chest; he greets
me with a silent, ceremonious embrace and leads me into
the reception room, which contains the only chairs in the

house. Lalai too explains that the situation is now somewhat better; the enemy has been driven out of large parts of the province because NATO has finally begun to fight. Until a few months ago, the people in the region had the impression that the military strategies of some of NATO's member countries were dictated more by their political situation at home than by the situation on the battlefield.

'Does that mean you object not to the harshness, but to the reticence of some of the foreign troops?'

'Put it this way: what's going on here is not an exercise.'

Yes, there have been casualties, a great many innocent casualties, but that cannot be prevented in a dirty war in which one side has a preference for hiding in the houses of ordinary villagers and the other avoids infantry engagements for fear of losses. The villagers have no other choice but to quarter the Taliban because they kill anyone who doesn't cooperate, he says; and if the villagers, under coercion, do cooperate, death often finds them from the sky. Neither the government nor NATO, with all their soldiers, tanks and reconnaissance aircraft, has been able to protect the people from the Taliban; that is a great failure. Just today he heard from one of his villages that Taliban had gained admittance to the houses by threats. A short time later, heavily armed American troops stormed into the village and arrested not only the enemy fighters but also many of the male villagers. He has been on the telephone the whole day trying to get his own people released. In his tribe's territory alone, eighteen schools and five clinics have been built in recent years – but now all of them are abandoned because the people are afraid to enter a classroom or see a doctor; all the development work has been in vain. Does the government offer him sufficient protection as a tribal leader who opposes the Taliban? Haji Agha Lalai trusts in God and his own guards. He has survived two assassination attempts so far.

KANDAHAR

Founded by Alexander the Great, Kandahar today is the centre of the area settled by the Pashtuns and hence, in principle, the capital of the Taliban; this is where they first took over in 1996; this is where they held out the longest in 2001. This is where Mullah Omar held aloft the mantle of the Prophet, which is kept in a shrine, and proclaimed himself the Amir ol-Momenin, the commander of all Muslims worldwide. This is the city the Taliban hope to reconquer first. Accordingly Kandahar still seems to be in a state of siege, with Afghan army checkpoints every hundred yards on the roads leading into town, NATO armoured cars at every major junction in the city centre, reconnaissance blimps and helicopters in the sky. My fellow journalist from the BBC's Persian-language service, who drives me back and forth across the city in his compact car, knows exactly which bridge or traffic sign on the outbound arteries marks the point where he has to turn around. For the local employee of a foreign broadcasting network, and even for members of the local media, the risk of kidnapping becomes too great just a few kilometres outside Kandahar.

In the centre itself, there is hardly a city block that does not have a war story to tell: a suicide bomber blew himself up at this police recruiting office; hostages were taken at that school; on that lot there used to be a building where Taliban were hiding. In contrast to the north, everyone in Kandahar seems to have a friend or a relative who has had an unpleasant experience with the foreign soldiers, whether a traffic stop, a house search, an air strike on their native village. Only the Canadians, who were stationed here for a time, are often excepted from the criticism; and Canada also donated the solar-powered streetlamps that the whole city is glad of.

And the Taliban? Many of the answers are evasive. The fear of saying something that a snitch could pass on is tangible.

When you are invited to drink tea, which no longer happens as readily in Kandahar as in the rest of the country, or when you talk a little longer in the bazaar, superficially disguised by local dress, with a merchant or an artisan, you rarely hear anything good, neither about the Taliban nor about the state. Instead, you hear conspiracy theories: the war is only a pretext to continue the American occupation – don't the Taliban have their bases in Pakistan? And isn't Pakistan a vassal of America? And should we really believe the greatest military power in the world can't defeat a few thousand fighters in pickup trucks? Whatever you think of the suspicions that almost every inhabitant of Kandahar seems to have, perhaps ISAF should use their host of press officers for something besides supervising Western journalists. The Afghans too have lots of questions.

TRIBAL LEADERS 2

Moulavi Abdolaziz of the Nurzai tribe awaits me with his men in the evening on a blanket spread out in the middle of the wide, unlighted street. Recently the Taliban's supreme judge in Helmand province, he is one of the highest-ranking resistance fighters to have joined the peace process. Abdolaziz apologizes, saying the house the government has provided for him and his family has no separate area for the women; that is why he has to come outside to receive visitors. But is it not too risky, I ask, to drink tea here in the middle of the road, and I'm not talking about the danger of being run over in the dark. He knows that ten suicide bombers have been assigned to him, Abdolaziz answers, but the house that the government has provided is too small; he can't receive guests in it, and he actually has sixty, seventy visitors a day. Apparently the government doesn't care whether he lives in dignity, whether he is assassinated. And what about the sanctimonious talk of receiving Taliban desirous of peace with open arms? Abdolaziz asks. He believed it, but now he sees that it was all just talk; the government is not interested in peace.

Moulavi Abdolaziz has a seductively smooth voice. His torso sways back and forth as if in slow motion, while his gaze rests gently on his listener. All the men's tone, in fact, is so friendly, tender even, that my preconceived notion of the evil Talib evaporates in the first few minutes. An older gentleman ironically calls the tribe's chief 'President' and asks, with a hint of mockery, whether we couldn't continue the discussion over dinner. While Abdolaziz listens with a smile to my obligatory objections that I'm not hungry, have to get home, don't want to cause any trouble, and so on, the plastic tablecloth is spread out on the rug and the food laid on it: salad, bread, yoghurt, herbs and an irresistibly spiced curry; grapes and melons for dessert.

After the meal, Moulavi Abdolaziz tells his story, which I can only take down unverified, my notebook illuminated by an electric torch that one of the men holds for me. He joined the Taliban in his youth, in the early 1990s, to put an end to robbery, rape and murder in the country. Their regime was strict, it's true, but absolutely fair; no one was above the law; murder, adultery, rape, theft, pederasty, hunger, corruption – none of these existed under the Taliban. With time, though, more and more foreigners took charge, mainly Pakistanis and Arabs, and by the late 1990s the first conflicts in the movement arose. The Taliban's principal mistake was the pact with Osama bin Laden. The disaster began with al-Qaeda, Moulavi recounts, and many commanders foresaw it; some even thought Osama bin Laden was an American agent. But Mullah Omar dismissed all their objections. They are our brothers, he said; our guests.

After the expulsion of the Taliban in 2001, Moulavi Abdolaziz surrendered to the authorities and received an amnesty; he still has the document with him. After that, he says, he earned his money dealing in weapons. The crucial experience that led him to take up the struggle again was a scene on the Musa Qala River. From a distance he saw foreign soldiers searching an Afghan woman, patting down her body. Without thinking, he took his rifle and shot at the soldiers – without hitting them, Moulavi Abdolaziz adds regretfully. He fled, but was soon arrested, and mistreated in prison. When he was free again, he gathered a following of men and joined the Taliban once more.

The Taliban too are exhausted and demoralized by internal conflicts, says Moulavi Abdolaziz, who estimates his age at thirty-two. The Afghans, who make up only a quarter of the fighters to begin with, are frustrated because Pakistani Punjabis have long been in charge, but they are not the only ones: Arabs too, Central Asians, even Chinese. The foreigners are not only extremely brutal; they also embezzle money, kill anyone who doesn't cooperate with them, destroy the schools, especially the girls' schools. He himself, Moulavi recounts, was detained for two days in Quetta, Pakistan, because he had criticized the foreign Taliban too harshly. Later he heard that the Americans had announced they would leave the country. He still considers Mullah Omar as Amir ol-Momenin, the Commander of the Faithful, even today. But the Taliban are no longer what they were; sadly, they are controlled by foreigners who have no interest in Afghanistan and do not hesitate to risk its destruction. If the government would only make the Afghan fighters a definite offer, many would join the peace process. For his part, he is still in contact with his old comrades, but what argument does he have to persuade them of peace if he can't even receive guests fittingly?

I ask Moulavi Abdolaziz specifically what he expects of the government. A bigger house, he answers immediately, a job for his men and an official function for himself. What kind of function? Chairman of the municipal Council of Scholars, for example, Abdolaziz suggests; the previous chairman was recently murdered. But he could also head a theological school or something of that sort. And political demands? The prisoners must be released, Abdolaziz says, and only after a further question adds that, after a peace agreement, sharia law must be reinstated, of course. After all, the country is Islamic, but many women are not veiled, or not correctly, as they are in the south. It doesn't have to be the burqa; the face can be exposed. No, the Taliban have nothing against girls' schools, Abdolaziz affirms, or at least not the true Taliban, not Mullah Omar, who is completely different from the idea many people have of him, a modest, quiet man who loves children and compassion. How often has he himself seen Mullah Omar pardon someone who had shaved his beard, for example; the Amir ol-Momenin always thought of the sinner's family.

What does Moulavi think of suicide bombings? I ask. If a person attacks the enemy, and dies in the process, that is a heroic act, Moulavi Abdolaziz explains. But it is a great sin on the contrary to blow yourself up among innocent people, in the bazaar, in a mosque or in the street.

'Aren't suicide bombings one of the Taliban's methods, then?'

'No!' Moulavi Abdolaziz cries. 'We never wanted that; that was introduced by the Arabs.'

'And the attacks of 11 September 2001?'

'I don't want to speak of that.'

'Why?'

'Because the attacks did not take place in Afghanistan and were not carried out by Afghans.'

'But in principle – do you consider Western civilians to be legitimate targets?'

'Only if they fight against Islam.'

'Not the unbelievers as such, then?'

'Haven't we given you a friendly reception?'

'I am a Muslim.'

'We would have received you just as warmly if you had been a Christian or a Jew. You don't want to attack us, don't want to destroy our culture, so it is our duty and our honour to show you hospitality.'

Does he regret his decision to join the peace process? And how he regrets it! answers Moulavi Abdolaziz without hesitation. But he can't go back either; the Taliban are already drinking his blood.

THE LIMITS OF REPORTING

A sheet over his belly, his upper body thin as a stick, and his legs dotted with wounds drying in the fresh air, 'God's Mercy', to translate his name Rahmatullah literally, lies in the courtyard of Mirwais Hospital. His forearms, still yellow with iodine, are pointed upwards, his elbows bent in a right angle, as if to show everyone the stumps where his hands were a few days ago. His hair is standing on end, but that is just from the dust, and Rahmatullah's face is as peaceful as you can imagine. He is twenty years old, he says, a shepherd, and he was out with the flock when he found something metal on the ground, a round disc. Yes, he picked it up, and the mine exploded right away. He had suspected it could be something dangerous, but he was curious and didn't take time to think about it. Then Rahmatullah laughs, because there's no one you can complain to about something so stupid; he laughs so heartily and freely that I can see his upper molars. Even his relatives standing around the bed, a child and men of various ages, the oldest of whom caresses him, have to smile now at Rahmatullah's stupidity, or perhaps only because they too find his laughter so moving. Aghast, I ask whether the people in the countryside still haven't been informed about the danger of mines. Yes, says Rahmatullah, they heard something once, but, still, they don't know exactly what these things are like. What will he do when he goes back to his village? Will someone help him? A state agency or an aid organization? God helps, Rahmatullah answers, and starts laughing again.

'Your laughter makes me weep,' I say, apologizing for my tears.

Seven hundred to eight hundred patients come to Mirwais Hospital every day, the chief physician Mohammad Qasim reports, his face deeply furrowed between his dense beard and his weary eyes. Plus the families, who camp in the garden or in the corridors. The other cities in southern Afghanistan have clinics at most. They have to admit about a hundred patients a day, of whom perhaps twenty are war casualties: victims of mines, bombings, air strikes; wounded Taliban among them, for whom the hospital has negoti-ated a kind of immunity – after all, a doctor must treat every patient the same. Caring for the victims of both sides brings with it the incidental advantage that no one threatens them. Many patients are here who didn't know how to interpret the signals of the foreign soldiers: they approached a convoy instead of stopping, and so they were fired upon. Is it not a crime to bombard a whole village because an enemy might be hiding in one single house? And, finally, the war also explains the high numbers of traffic injuries: people drive so fast on the main roads for fear of ambushes. To say nothing of the many psychological illnesses: forty, fifty patients every day with severe disorders, aggression, insomnia, delusions of persecution and the like. After thirty-four years of war, 80 per cent of Afghans are psychologically disturbed, Dr Qasim estimates, and the traditional value system – honesty, trust, respect for the law, respect for authorities – has deteriorated. I ask whether he believes the war will ever end. Nonsense, Dr Qasim answers, it gets worse day after day; this talk of peace negotiations, of protecting civilians, these high-security conferences – all lies. Everyone knows that the country's fate is decided not by Afghans but by the foreign powers: Pakistan, the United States, Iran, China, Russia, India, Saudi Arabia; everyone is involved. 'Why don't they fight their wars among themselves? Why don't they leave Afghanistan in peace for once?'

Dr Qasim leads me through the hospital, where several European doctors and nurses work, like their Afghan colleagues, at least ten hours a day, six days a week. Children with burns lying naked on a bed, sometimes two to a bed, and whimpering, fathers beside them in utter desperation. But I finally reach the limits of the territory I am able to report on at the bedside of a twelve-year-old who got caught yesterday between the lines of a firefight in the village of Panjabad. Dr Qasim has already lifted the sheet to show me his shredded abdomen. Then he stops, and carefully lays the boy's sheet back down, preferring to spare me the sight. 'We have enough traumatized people here already,' Dr Qasim explains.

CEMETERY 2

After taking a photograph of Nur Agha and his sheep, I continue my walk through the Kabul cemetery. I talk to one inhabitant after another, and they answer my question, saying sometimes four, sometimes eight, sometimes twelve. Four martyrs, eight martyrs, twelve martyrs. At a cistern, children are filling big canisters with water. Their dirty faces, their tangled hair and the rags on their skinny bodies save me the question whether they go to school. The boys and girls pose joyfully for a photo – yes, go ahead, waves a tall, older gentleman wearing somewhat better clothes – and afterwards they can hardly believe it when they look at my camera's little display. The gentleman introduces himself: Haji Niaz Mohammad is his name, cemetery caretaker his occupation, sixty years old – and in two minutes he has talked himself into a frenzy: a dog's life they lead here, poor and respected by no one.

'Look at these children, look at their faces. Look at the tents: Why do people have to live in the cemetery?'

'Does anyone help? The state perhaps?'

'Of course not.'

'Or one of the international organizations, the United Nations for example?'

'The United Nations' – the haji smiles bitterly – 'the United Nations exist only on television.'

Three thousand afghanis he earns in a month, the equivalent of fifty euros, with no old-age provision or insurance. Some days he has so little money that he can't give any to the begging children.

'No, not a dog's life: we live much worse than dogs. Dogs at least are not ashamed.' Then he points at the notebook I have in my hand: 'I'll write you twelve of your books full: that's how great our grief is.'

'The eleventh of September, 2001?'

'I don't know who does such a thing or why,' the haji sighs, 'I only know that we Afghans must suffer for it, all the Afghans. You know, we are not a people with no history. We

had upstanding leaders, we had poets, we had some prestige in the world. There were times when we made trade
agreements with Germany; we had Mercedes-Benzes built
in Germany. But today we are Germany's beggars. Today
a suicide bomber kills a German commander, and all the
Germans think we are terrorists.'

I ask whether it was better under the Taliban. At least
under the Taliban there were no thieves, no rapists, no murderers, says the haji after long reflection. The Kabulis were
able to leave their doors open at night, or leave the alms
box for the care of the inhabitants unlocked in the cemetery
mosque. Today the Ministry of Religious Affairs empties the
box, so not a single afghani reaches the cemetery.

Haji Niaz Mohammad leads me into the courtyard of the
mosque, where he lives. In a flash, a carpet has been spread
out, a plastic sheet laid in the middle, a teapot, glasses, bread
and yoghurt placed on it.

'For its hospitality, though, Afghanistan is still world-
famous,' I contend.

Later I notice the haji discreetly turning my shoes around,
putting their heels towards the carpet. That is an Afghan
custom, to make it easier for the guests to slip into their
shoes as they leave. The world should heed this gesture too
in Afghanistan.

THE UPRISING

TEHRAN, JUNE 2009

CHANCE COMPANIONS

Once more, a door opens at the last minute, this time a
roll-up shutter, to be exact, in front of the narrow shop of
a plumbing business facing a six-lane street along which a
unit of the volunteer militia is approaching – the Basij, about
a hundred men with helmets, shields, clubs and protective
vests over their civilian clothes. The owner of the shop, a
small, slightly bowed man with grey hair and a white moustache, pulls the shutter back down behind us. We being four
people of different ages, strangers to each other, three men
and one woman. Hastily we introduce ourselves, although
there is no hurry since we will share these few square yards
for an undetermined period, as if our lift had got stuck: one
an engineer, another a student, the third a teacher, the fourth
actually just a reporter. From abroad? the teacher asks, as if
that alone was already good news.

'We have to hide!' the engineer cries. 'If the militia find
us, they'll set the shop on fire.'

But the volunteer militia don't get as far as the shop. Many
of the demonstrators have turned around and are throwing
stones at them. Once again, rubbish bins are wheeled out
into the street and set on fire. Stones fly from other directions as well; not two yards from us, two older, clean-shaven
gentlemen join in the fight; across the road, women. Some of
the militiamen want to continue advancing and are throwing
stones themselves; others are retreating. Through the bars
we see the militiamen debating among themselves; we see
their leader shouting, when suddenly the demonstrators call
out, 'God is greater!' and storm forward.

The cheers that break out as the volunteer militia run
away don't last five minutes: an anti-riot squad is already
approaching, the *zede shuresh*. The plumbing retailer closes

the glass door and takes us with him into his storeroom. From there we hear gunshots, screams, sirens. Another five minutes later, as if at the push of a button, there is silence. When the shopkeeper opens the glass door for us and rolls up the shutter, we step out onto a deserted battlefield: billows of smoke, the ground strewn with stones and shards of automobile glass, fires here and there. Out of the houses next door and across the road come too many people to be the residents, all of them rubbing their eyes. The smell of tear gas hangs in the air. It is Saturday, 20 June 2009. What looks like war was a silent protest march when I arrived in Tehran three days ago.

ARRIVAL

The driver who takes me from the airport to the city centre didn't even go to the polls on Friday. Did he see anything of the demonstrations that broke out after the obviously fraudulent election results were announced?

'Sir,' he says, 'I would have had to lock myself in the house and not talk to anyone not to notice the demonstrations.'

'And the reasons, the background?' The driver supplies me with details and dispels rumours. No, the anti-riot troops are not foreigners. Yes, there are enough Iranians who are willing, under circumstances that the state is able to bring about, to club their own mother over the head. He himself was a soldier for many years. The requirements for a military career are complex. It is not enough to have a big, athletic body. You have to have many skills, comprehensive training and enough brains to respond correctly in situations that can't be simulated in training. But there is one task for which a soldier needs only a big, athletic body and as little brain as possible. The anti-riot troops, the driver says, are selected precisely by these criteria – size and stupidity – and are so indoctrinated that they don't even try to think in situations that can't be simulated in training.

WEDNESDAY

The work day ends at 3:30 in my friend's engineering office so that all the employees can go to the demonstration. The qualification match for the football World Cup keeps them busy until a quarter past four, however – a goal for Iran, cheering. The names of the players wearing green armbands go round and round the open-plan office. Then the equalizer: if Saudi Arabia and North Korea draw tonight, Iran won't even make the runner-up playoffs for qualification – but hurry now to the protest march which has already started in Revolution Street, not ten minutes away.

Because the first lives have been lost and because all protests have been prohibited, the people march silently through the centre of Tehran, shouting no slogans, carrying no posters or banners. Even from the bridge, which will later be visible in dozens of videos on YouTube, I can see neither the beginning nor the end of the column. Most of the marchers are holding up A4-sized sheets of paper that they have printed themselves with a slogan or with the photo of one of those who have been clubbed to death. The most popular messages are sarcastic allusions to the president's claim that only a few hooligans are on the streets in Tehran, as if their side had lost a football match. Never has a crowd looked so individual to me: everyone formulates the protest in their own way. There are no identifiable marshals; only here and there someone standing on a crash barrier announcing a message, which then spreads like wildfire. Tomorrow at two in front of the United Nations. No, tomorrow at four in

Freedom Square. Everyone put your hands up! Please break up before nightfall.

It is not clear whether these marshals have climbed up on the crash barriers spontaneously or whether they are members of an organization that is otherwise invisible. Since their campaign offices have been destroyed, the opposition leaders who haven't been arrested are sitting at home talking on the telephone. The presumptive winner of the election, Mir-Hossein Mousavi, turns up at demonstrations unannounced – the only safe way – and has only a megaphone to make himself heard. Mobile phones work only in the morning, text messages not at all; the Internet is so slow that you're lucky if email goes through. Western television programmes and cultural supplements cultivate the myth of the first political mass movement that communicates by Facebook, Twitter, texting and Google groups, but, in fact, the demonstrators are dependent on word of mouth. They are scrupulously careful not to give the anti-riot troops, who may be at the ready in this or that side street, any pretext for action. At the major junctions, the demonstration stops at red lights to let the traffic by. When the lights turn green they rush to close the gap that has opened up. A hundred yards further on, a marshal tells them to walk slower again so that those behind can catch up.

Because any political demand can be dangerous to life and limb, the opposition concentrates on demanding the observance of existing laws, which seems to be exceedingly provocative. It is curious for that matter to see how the movement has stolen the regime's symbols. While the supporters of President Mahmoud Ahmadinejad wave the state's flag nationalistically to cast off their religious image, the opposition, who don't want to go on living in a theocracy, wear the Islamic green – each in his or her own way, as a shawl, a headscarf, an armband or a string between the fingers.

The green headbands recall the volunteers who walked into the minefields in the war against Iraq, or the Lebanese Hezbollah. Now they are worn with chic hairstyles, ideally complementing the narrow sideburns that run right across the men's cheeks. Every evening at ten, people shout 'God is greater' from the rooftops and balconies all over the city, even the Zoroastrian who drives me home later. The Islamic Republic has brought us to this, he rants: desperately shouting *Allahu akbar* like Muslims. The cry that God is greater surpasses every slogan in substance: greater than you who act as if you were gods.

In the night, against all reason, my friend the engineer and I watch the football match that must have a winner in order for Iran to qualify for the World Cup. As if in a pinball machine, the Saudis shoot the ball up to the North Koreans' penalty area, where it bounces randomly from one leg to another before rolling back to the Saudi half of the pitch. Because both sides have refused to compete, the referee punishes us with eight minutes of extra time.

THURSDAY

Among all the ugly squares in Tehran, Artillery Barracks Square, now named after Ayatollah Khomeini, holds a rank all its own. Towering over it is a sky-scraping rectangle of dirty concrete which houses the telephone office; surrounding it are smaller buildings of similar texture; in the middle are an eight-lane one-way street and an equally wide asphalt area that may once have been a car park but is now an undefined open space in front of the underground station. Those who live or have their business here, in what was once the sumptuous centre of Tehran, later became an amusement boulevard and is now a poor neighbourhood, may find it plausible that Mahmoud Ahmadinejad received two-thirds of the votes in the presidential elections.

The young mobile phone dealer who quickly sells me an Iranian SIM in spite of the protest march scornfully shows me his middle finger when I ask why he is not demonstrating. He is impressed by the president, he says: his fearlessness, his patriotism and, most of all, the fact that he is one of us and fighting the bigwigs of the Islamic Republic. He personally is not so keen on religion; he is interested in football and cinema. The walls are hung with posters of American action heroes; his hair shines with gel. To my objection that the president has critics arrested, he replies drily, 'They all do.'

And the censorship? No novels get published at all!

'Sir, I don't read novels; and the newspapers don't have anything to say anyway.'

Holocaust?

'I have no idea what's true and what's not, but in any case all the president did was ask a question.'

Economically, the pros and cons balance out: what his family receives in cash or vouchers is eaten up by inflation, the mobile phone dealer admits. He doesn't follow anyone blindly: he thinks the president should be given a second term, like his predecessor, in which he can learn from his mistakes, bring inflation under control and not antagonize everybody.

'Have fun demonstrating,' he calls after me as I rejoin the march.

'I'm just going to get an impression,' I shout back, and only now do I groan about the weather, although it has been just as hot for the past few days, over forty degrees in the sun, I'm sure. Unlike the first mass rally on Monday, which, according to the mayor, a conservative, brought together 3 million people from all age groups, it is mostly young people who still dare to take to the streets, many of them students, but some white-collar workers, stewardesses in uniform, girls in chadors, a high proportion of women in fact, more than half it seems, and by no means just the youth of Tehran's affluent north side; the whole student body of Iran is represented here, I deduce from the conversations around me, many people from the provinces especially, who live in the halls of residence and have time to demonstrate now that their exams have been cancelled. The division is not between the haves and the have-nots, between the urban and the rural population, between the north and the south of the city, but rather between the generations, and perhaps between different leaving certificates as well. Many of the demonstrators are the children of those who were willing to give their lives for an Islamic state, and who voted once again for the Leader's candidate without a second thought last Friday. The grammar schools and universities that the children attend were won by the parents and their revolution.

On the fifth afternoon of protests in a row, the demonstrators' adrenalin, produced by their surprise at their own strength and their dismay at the deaths, seems to be exhausted. Because the government is pretending to ignore the resistance and is abstaining from further spectacular abuses, not even sending police to direct traffic, yet at the same time is prohibiting all reporting under threat of imprisonment, the protests are slipping downwards in the international news. The information blockade is working: not only are the daily silent marches too indistinguishable in the poor-quality images taken with mobile phones, but the pictures get out too late and too sparsely to make the evening news. All you have to do, evidently, to pull the plug on globalization is to slow down the Internet depending on the day's events, shut down the mobile phone network and stop issuing visas to journalists. I too will have to go back to Germany, as if I was living in the pre-telegraph age, to deliver the news. Ayatollah Khamenei has announced that he will give the Friday sermon tomorrow. Because the signs he gave this week pointed first one way, then another, conversations revolve around the momentous question whether the Leader of the Revolution will see his way clear to a compromise, or whether tomorrow he will give the signal for the assault.

FRIDAY

It's the mobile phones that keep thousands from entering the university campus. For fear of an attack, people are supposed to check them in one of the buses parked in front of the entrance, but, in spite of all the admonitions to leave them at home, there are so many that great clusters of people have formed in front of the buses trying to hand their phones, in little plastic bags that are being distributed free, to one of the marshals leaning out of a bus window. Identified by my clothes, glasses and movements as a son of the middle class, I plead that I've come a long way to attend the Friday prayers, and after half an hour I actually reach the bus window, just as they run out of numbered paper tickets. Only in the past three days, but all the more energetically for the short notice, have the state television channels been drumming, the newspapers advertising, the associations organizing, the sports clubs arranging, the soldiers, militias and civil servants mobilizing for the historic day on which the Leader and the people will 'renew their pledge', as the immutable phrase goes, an allusion to the alliance with the Prophet in Medina. The demonstration is an impressive success, from the looks of it, and an the evening the photos taken from helicopters confirm it.

I have attended the Friday prayers in Tehran three times

before, participating in a tired ritual in which tens of thousands of officials and soldiers and the last stalwarts dutifully
celebrate the revolution and chant, as prompted, the customary wishes of death – death to America, death to Israel, death
to the enemies of the Governance of the Jurists, death to
the immodest, the necktie wearers, or whatever is currently
on the agenda. As soon as the camera panned away, the fists
fell again as if connected to one pulley. But, today, not only
the giant hall is full, not only the campus of the University
of Tehran is packed, but so are the surrounding streets and
squares. The faces show the joyful expectation of football
fans whose team is about to win a historic match. Those who
have not yet secured a place on the pavement hurry at the
moment of the ritual ablutions, for which water trucks have
been deployed – as if it made any difference whether they listened to the sermon a block or two away – the men unshaven
or bearded, in plastic slippers or in shoes bent down at the
back so that they can slip their feet out easily. The only variation in the women's fashions is that some hold their black
chador up over their nose, some wear a black headscarf as
well under the black chador, and some do both. The average age is perhaps thirty years more than that of the silent
marchers: those who come here are defending the revolution
they once fought for, went to war for, defending their fallen
sons and brothers, defending their own biography. For the
civil servants, immediately recognizable by their monotonous
suits, beards, glasses and haircuts, material values may be at
stake; for the older men, who are neither rich nor in danger
of poverty should there be a change of government, what is
at stake are the spiritual values that the Leader incessantly
invokes, because the West lost them, he says, two hundred
years ago. The Islamic Revolution gave these men dignity,
the self-assurance never to cower before anyone again. Their
children, however, are not here. Perhaps they are apolitical,

like the mobile phone dealer, who is merely impressed with the president; but it's just as likely that they are among the students who are rebelling against him.

When the programme begins, with a chorus leader shouting variations on the usual slogans for ten full minutes, I am the only one who doesn't raise a fist. Although no one seems to notice me, it is frightening enough to be standing in a crowd of, let's say, a million people and be the only one, let's say, who is not joining in. The Quran reciter who follows the chorus leader gives me an opportunity to talk quietly with my neighbour. The old gentleman explains to me in a kind voice to what incomprehensible lies the so-called green movement has stooped to discredit the overwhelming winner of the election. If you accept the basic premise that there was nothing improper about the vote counting, everything else sounds as logical as any conspiracy theory. Later the Leader will even mourn the murdered students as martyrs beaten to death by counter-revolutionaries in stolen uniforms. The perfidy of these enemies is so boundless, the state will say, that they even shouted quotations from the Leader.

After the liturgical singer, a boys' choir performs, dressed in patriotic white, followed by a man singing elegies in the traditional style, although his verses do not mourn the martyrdom of Imam Hussein but stylize the conflict of today as Hussein's drama. Never again will an imam succumb to the superior numbers of his enemies, because the faithful will never again abandon him – a song of joy, actually, and yet the old men round about weep as if at the push of a button: the passion of Hussein and the deceit of the British, Americans, Zionists and hypocrites are so familiar to all the listeners, in every phase of history down to the present, that one allusion suffices to call up all the images.

When the men have grown sentimental enough, Ayatollah

Khamenei appears. The dialectical sequence of his arguments and the subtlety of the nuances reveal his long training; the Shiite seminaries are the only centres of learning in the world whose curriculum has been based, from the Middle Ages until today without interruption, on Aristotelian rhetoric, grammar and logic. In a forceful contrast to the previous speakers, and to the drama of the state of emergency in which the nation currently stands, the Leader begins with the composure of one who knows that his listeners are hanging on his every word. He addresses them with the directness and the warm voice of a paternal friend, almost like my neighbour explaining the worldwide conspiracy a moment ago. Like any good rhetorician, the Leader leaves the audience unsure what he is driving at, expresses comprehension for the other side, presents himself as an impartial judge, so that his judgement will be all the more effective when he delivers it at last after the suspense of his extended exposition. He has made his decision: for the listeners and against the silent marchers. The men round about no longer need a chorus leader to scream Death! every few minutes, death to America, Israel, the hypocrites, and so on. Even at those points where the confession of faith is called for, they append to it the arsenal of maledictions.

For his finale, Ayatollah Khamenei suddenly falls silent, and by his silence again is able to heat the emotions of his listeners, which have long since reached the melting point. His control, lowering his voice at the climax to reach yet another pinnacle, is brilliant; as a writer there's nothing else I can call it. The Leader of the Revolution addresses his predecessor, as if Imam Hussein would speak to the Prophet: 'O our lord, O our guardian!' To judge by the weeping, everyone knows what must follow: 'What I had to do, I have done; what I had to say, I have said.' Imam Hussein goes into battle at Karbala: 'I have a worthless life.' My neighbour

too sobs at such humility. 'I have a broken body,' the Leader
says, whipping the compassion of those around me to the
point of hysteria by alluding to his arm, paralysed since he
survived a bomb attack. 'I have some honour, thanks to you.
I possess nothing more, and I will sacrifice that in the path
of this Islam and the Revolution. What I possess is yours. O
our lord, O our guardian! Say your prayers for us! You are
our sovereign, you are the sovereign of this country, you are
the sovereign of this revolution; you are our pillar. We will
go forward with might on this path. Support us with your
prayers and admonitions on this path.' Then the Leader
recites Surah 110, 'When comes the help of God, and victory,' before closing, 'Peace be with you, the mercy of God
and His blessing.'

Some of the older men are wailing outright, their whole
bodies trembling, my neighbour among them. They have
heard what they wanted to hear, and it has not sounded so
clear, so simple, so aggressive for years: the world as a struggle between good and evil, us against them. After prayers
many go chanting through the streets, some in this direction,
some in that, evidently spontaneously, but urged on, even
many blocks away, by the chorus leader, who has returned
to the microphone. From today on, those who demonstrate
will be rebelling not against the government but against the
Leader: in the interpretation of today's Islamic Republic,
that amounts to a 'war against God', a crime deserving of
death.

The students and journalists with whom I spoke just this
morning can no longer be reached in the evening, nor can
the family of the young man who was beaten to death in
the student hall of residence. As of Friday, 19 June 2009,
five hundred spokespersons of the opposition are in cus-
tody, not counting the demonstrators arrested in the course
of this week. I am all the more surprised this evening when

the former home minister Abdollah Nouri returns my call, a cleric with the rank of a Hojatoleslam who spent years in prison, and the only one of the reformist politicians with undisputed credibility outside his own movement.

'What is your prognosis?' he asks first, when I am seated facing him about midnight in the windowless conference room in his house.

'I suspect the silent marchers could only lose an open conflict, not only because of the superior forces on the other side, with their advantages in organization and propaganda, their weapons and their willingness to use them. Those who attended the Friday prayers have their whole history to lose and will therefore stop at nothing; most of the silent marchers on the other hand would not sacrifice themselves for a political goal, an ideology or a leader, which is a sign of progress, actually. And even if the students take to the streets tomorrow, pitting their future against history, the people would not be on their side, the workers, the bazaar.'

Abdollah Nouri is more optimistic: 'Who says the threat would be carried out?' A person who speaks so aggressively and positions himself so unambiguously, without a visible necessity, Nouri says, is either panicking or trying to intimidate the other side. From what he hears, though, the guardians of the Revolution are by no means unanimous in their willingness to resort to force. If enough demonstrators come to Revolution Square tomorrow at four, as he believes they will, the regime will have lost. If it orders the troops to shoot, open rebellion will break out during the funerals at the latest. If the regime holds back, the Leader's threat will have been proved empty.

Before I go, I ask whether he doesn't expect to be arrested.

'My bag is already packed,' Abdollah Nouri laughs.

BACK TO SATURDAY

From Ferdousi Square on, a good two kilometres away, the city is under occupation: every five yards along the pavements stand policemen with helmets, clubs and shields, as well as agents of the secret police, who in Iran are anything but secret. The officers in charge are identifiable by their walkie-talkies. Scattered along Revolution Street and all its side streets are the volunteer militias and the anti-riot troops, waiting in trucks or minibuses. In contrast to the volunteer militias, who, apart from their vests, helmets and clubs, are in civilian clothes, the anti-riot troops look like a swarm of insects in their black plastic body armour. In the street, the militia's mopeds zip past, alternately with the off-road motorcycles of the riot squads, two men sitting on each one – one holding the handlebars, the other a club. Some of the passengers have a length of wooden batten in their hands. Not yet discernible are the *lebas-shakhsi*, the 'plainclothes men', who are the most feared of all because they don't look threatening before they strike. The businesses are open; the traffic in the streets is as usual. The closer I come to Revolution Square, however, the younger the pedestrians get.

'Don't look at the police,' whispers a young man with a rucksack, evidently because I look too curious. 'Act normal and keep walking.'

In spite of the apprehension we both feel, we have to smile when we discover we both have the same first name.

At a quarter past three I reach Revolution Square, which is big and uninviting, like many squares in Tehran, a three-lane roundabout with a building site and a mound of debris in the middle, surrounded by bare concrete buildings several storeys high with little shops in the ground floor, the shop windows dirty. Startled drivers looking out of the passing cars see a military depot: water cannon, buses and off-road bikes with more riot troops and militiamen along the roadside here too, and police on the pavement every two yards. Any pedestrian who stops is brusquely told to move on by a secret police agent. While the volunteer militia act as though they always stood around in Revolution Square, the young people just happen to be walking by. The streets and the shops are supposed to stay open; the mobile phone network is not even shut down as it has been on the previous afternoons. The state is trying to demonstrate confidence, normality. Only the customers are missing, and the shop-keepers are standing not behind their counters but anxiously out in front of their shops.

To kill the time until four o'clock without leaving Revolution Square, I cross the street several times, drink a fresh-pressed pomegranate juice in small sips, and take all the time in the world choosing a pen in a stationery shop. Then I take advantage of a stalled car, hurrying to offer my help push-starting it.

'Get lost!' shouts the commander of an anti-riot company.

'We're trying,' the driver assures him.

After two minutes the commander has had enough and orders four of his men to push the car out of Revolution Square. I look around for the next place I can go to stay in the square.

I don't expect to see much more. Even my friend the engineer is staying home for the first time, like almost everyone in his office: being identified on a secret police video would be enough to ruin not only his own life but his children's future – their education, their chances of going to university. Those of the silent protest marchers who come at all will pretend to be simple pedestrians and cross the square a few times at most. But when I step out of a grocer's with a water bottle at four o'clock sharp, the people come streaming out of several streets into the square and walk in an unending queue along the narrow pavement silently towards Freedom Square, most of them twenty, thirty years old, probably students, but also businessmen and women with briefcases, professors or intellectuals with grey goatees, older women in black chadors, as many women as every day, this time without their printed sheets of paper. The boldest make a V for victory, then gradually others dare too, until every hand points skywards. The visors are now pulled down on the helmets.

The anti-riot troops begin to march. Two of the motorcycles turn onto the narrow pavement: the drivers accelerate; the passengers bring down their clubs or lengths of batten on the people crowding against the fronts of the buildings or jumping into the ditch between the road and the pavement. Shouts, screams, outraged and imploring cries. Another motorcycle squad arrives ahead and blocks the pedestrians' way. The demonstrators flee in all directions, seeking shelter between the cars, run into the side streets or into the traffic, jump over the two fences that separate the bus lane in the middle of the street, and reach the far pavement, the clubs right behind them. Without thinking, I sprint along with a group of perhaps five hundred people around the next corner. Because the next squad is waiting for us there, we split up at the first junction into the alleys left and right. From the next side streets, more demonstrators are joining the march. Soon there are several thousand marching with the V sign again, parallel to the main boulevard. I couldn't be just a reporter now if I wanted to – behind us the clubs, ahead God help us.

Suddenly my eyes are burning and I think I'm going to suffocate, shouts again, cries, as beside us a door opens. Following ten, twelve other demonstrators, I dive into the courtyard of a two-storey building and come to a stop in the passageway of a house. The old woman in the bright-coloured chador going excitedly from one to another must be the landlady. We need fire! someone shouts urgently. Another: No water in the eyes, no water! The old woman brings a stack of old newspapers and sets fire to them on the stone floor of her passageway. Everyone puts a sheet of paper in the fire and holds it in front of their eyes. A girl is sitting on the floor weeping hysterically; another person holds their head out of the door and vomits. The smoke helps: except for the girl, who goes on weeping, everyone else calms down; then everyone comforts the girl. Someone helps the old woman sweep away the ashes; the others go out into the courtyard, where other demonstrators are resting, or back to the empty street – but which way? We should go towards Freedom Square, someone knows, so they go right and I follow, if only because the chances of escaping the clubs are better in a group, since we can scatter in different directions. In a cross street we join a larger column of demonstrators heading towards Revolution Street.

I think, as I flee for the second time through a door that opens unexpectedly, I have seen enough: a plainclothes man striking a man on the back of the neck, in passing, with all his might; the man doubled over on the ground bawling; his friends in tears pulling him away. A car stopped at a junction because there are stones flying; a militiaman shouting at the driver to drive on. The driver, visibly confused, is signalling with his hands that he doesn't know which way when the club smashes his side window. Faces streaming with blood, barricades of burning rubbish bins, a middle-aged woman, resident or dissident, consumed with panic, standing on the pavement screaming, trembling, wailing, as all the people sprint back and forth past her. Again and again the inhabitants open doors and the shopkeepers their shutters for those fleeing, although the district is by no means bourgeois, fairly far south in the city. There are too many demonstrators, dividing up among too many streets and regrouping again and again, for the security forces to bring the situation under control, especially since the resistance is growing more and more furious. The young men throw stones wherever they find any, jump on moving motorcycles and set them on fire, likewise an omnibus of the volunteer militia. Many of the police can be seen trying to avoid the fight, taking care of wounded demonstrators here and there, advising others which way they are most likely to escape. Many of the militiamen are overwhelmed and don't know how to respond when the demonstrators outnumber them, while the anti-riot troops are most efficient at suppressing protest. Only the plainclothes men are more brutal, picking out individual demonstrators and beating them up.

When I am no longer concerned with anything but reaching safety, like many of the demonstrators and many passers-by and drivers who have been caught by chance between the fronts, it takes me two hours to get out of the area. The way back north takes another two hours because the streets are blocked in many places. While the forces of the state circle above in a helicopter, the workers building the underground line beside the urban motorway stand atop their stacked-up housing containers and show the victory sign of the green movement, as do most of the drivers stuck in the traffic jam below. And even here, far from the actual scene of the demonstration, there are altercations. When young people manage to rout a unit of the volunteer militia in the middle of the motorway, the motorists sound their horns; some get out and dance; from the surrounding rooftops and the pedestrian overpass on which I'm standing the people cry, 'Death to the dictator!' Then a motorcycle squad of the anti-riot troops approaches. The demonstrators flee over the crash barrier; some take refuge in cars. I hear someone shout, Everybody honk! and the din of car horns resumes. Volunteer militias are posted at every junction; in the north there are white-bearded men and skinny boys barely fifteen among them. The cries that God is greater are louder this evening and go on longer.

SUNDAY

Just in my own circle of acquaintances, which is not very large in Tehran, eight demonstrators did not come home last night. The police do not know where they are, nor have they been found in any of the hospitals. The state news agency says there are thirteen dead; the rumours mention quite different figures. The city seems quiet; there are police, anti-riot squads or volunteer militias on all the major squares. There is also confusion as to where a demonstration could take place at all: on the grapevine different places are announced and then retracted, some proposals no doubt planted by the secret police to sow confusion; the mobile network is down all day, the Internet doesn't work, the satellite broadcasting is jammed. The wave of arrests continues, rolling ever deeper into the establishment and splashing ever higher in its hierarchy. Several student leaders and journalists whom I found so hopeful this week have been taken away by the secret police – Abdollah Nouri not yet, oddly enough. The state television presents confessed spies, calls the dead protesters terrorists, and accuses the West of having incited and paid for the rebellion. Isolated reformers speak up, including Grand Ayatollah Montazeri, the highest-ranking ayatollah of Qom; a second grand ayatollah says gloomily that he would speak out if there was any point in doing so.

EARLY MONDAY

On the plane I am surprised by the euphoric tone of the
international commentaries celebrating the demonstrators. That may be well meant, but it neglects the fact that
the opposition has no chance against the huge and violent
state security apparatus. And the Revolutionary Guards
haven't even been put into action yet. If the people succeed
– but how? – in continuing the protests, if they could fill
the streets with hundreds of thousands or millions again as
they did before the Leader's sermon, there might also be a
rebellion behind the scenes in Tehran and Qom. If not, Iran
will be governed no longer by the jurists, but by clubs, water
cannon and assault rifles.

WHEN YOU SEE THE BLACK FLAGS

IRAQ, SEPTEMBER 2014

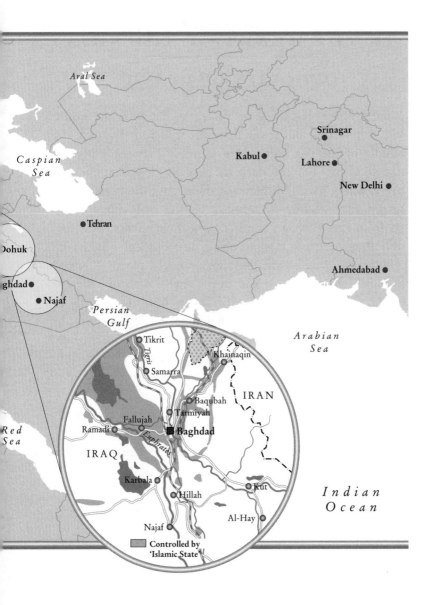

I NAJAF:
IN THE HEART OF THE SHIA

UBIQUITY OF DEATH

Najaf probably has the most central cemetery in the world. Just step out of the covered bazaar that runs through the middle of the city and you're standing between graves, if not on them. For the dead lie here so close that there is barely a foot's breadth between them. And the landscape of brown, clayey stone stretches so far that you take a car to go from one grave to another. The fundamental principle of both ancient and modern urban development – life in the middle, the dead on the periphery – is completely reversed in Najaf: all roads here lead to the shrine of Imam Ali and to the millions who are buried beside him. As recently as the eighteenth century, the inhabitants made a business of selling gravesites to foreigners. The city itself, meanwhile, is demonstratively unadorned and sombre – as if no earthly splendour might compete with the golden dome that glitters, when the air is clear, from fifty miles away in the desert. And then the funerary mosque itself: the courtyard, its walls completely covered with mosaics in bright yellow and blue colours, conjures up images of a paradise garden. Giant fans create a cool breeze while spraying rose water.

A moving dirge is heard in many places, and the faithful join in singing its refrain. Mourners following plywood coffins mumble a long, melodious litany. When the prayer for the dead is finished, they carry the coffins on their shoulders into the mosque, whose vault is lined all around with tiny mirrors. The stark light of the fluorescent lamps, reflected in a thousand fragments, transports the faithful bodily into Surah 24, verse 35, in which God is the light of Heaven and Earth:

'The likeness of His Light is as a niche wherein is a lamp, the lamp in a glass, and the glass as it were a glittering star.' The men and, separated from them by a curtain, the women, whose heads lean against the metal grille around the casket, are immersed as if in silent dialogue. From time to time someone sobs aloud or weeps like a child. Some coffins are draped with the Iraqi flag to signify that the deceased fell in battle against the 'Islamic State'. Then the chant *Lā 'ilāha 'illāllāh* that is heard from the processions at rhythmic intervals – 'There is no god but God' – takes on a militant tone.

You have to have heard, seen, this ubiquity of death, preferably measured it with your own steps and travelled it in your car, to understand the Shiite concept of the world. The 'party' of Ali, as Shia is literally translated, is a religion of lamentation and penitence and was also, well into the twentieth century, a religion of inner contemplation and withdrawal from the world. All its imams, the direct successors of Muhammad that is, except the twelfth and last, 'the hidden imam', are supposed to have been murdered, cruelly, treacherously, ignominiously – and not by the unbelievers, but by Muslims themselves. For the Shiites it is this betrayal of the Prophet's family and message that has been repeated over and over for one thousand four hundred years. The dominance of the Sunnis under which they suffered in Iraq for centuries, the hundreds of thousands of Shiites, including nine thousand clerics, whom the dictator Saddam Hussein had killed in the 1990s alone, the rise of the Wahhabis throughout the Islamic world and now the terror of the 'Islamic State' – every new menace is added to the edifice of betrayal out of their own ranks that the faithful have suffered from the beginning.

'Are you afraid for the shrine?' I ask a watchman with whom I have struck up a conversation after Friday prayers, an elderly, clean-shaven gentleman in a battered suit.

'No,' the watchman answers firmly, 'IS will never advance this deep into Shiite territory. They would be fought by every single inhabitant, even the women and children.'

Life here is better in general since the fall of Saddam Hussein, he says; the people feel truly released. A prayer like today's, with thousands of worshippers – that never happened under the dictatorship; back then Shiites were arrested every Friday. 'And if a thousand people came to Friday prayers, five hundred of them were Saddam's spies.'

'Was the American invasion a good thing, then, all in all?'

'Yes!' says the watchman.

'And are you grateful to the Americans?'

'The Americans didn't do it for us. But we did benefit.'

The pilgrims staying away could become a problem for Najaf. The mosque, the streets and, accordingly, the hotels, restaurants and souvenir shops are much emptier than before the advances of IS because Iran has stopped its pilgrimage tours for safety reasons. The Islamic Republic sees the trip to Najaf, shopping included, as a bonus it can offer to its poorest and most loyal citizens. In some alleys in the old city centre, which has been made into one big pedestrian area with security gates at the entrances, I feel as if in a Shiite Vatican: almost everyone walking around belongs to one of the many theological seminaries. Although they wear the same ankle-length robe as in Iran, a voluminous mantle on their shoulders, a white or black turban on their heads, they look to me quite different here: not only self-assured, but relaxed and friendly, striding more than walking, chatting with a shopkeeper, stopping a devout person from kissing their hand, patting the children's heads. In a big Iranian city, it's hard for mullahs to hail a taxi, so great is the mistrust, indeed the contempt, that they are met with. But here, in the old centre of Shiite spirituality which is beginning to flourish again since the fall of Saddam, they are evidently trusted.

And, yes, they laugh, the mullahs, something I hardly ever see any more in Iran; they wear fine fabrics, elegant rings; the beards of at least the younger ones are carefully trimmed, while the old men lean on finely carved walking sticks.

A DANGEROUS TOPIC

In the evening of my first day here, I visit Sheikh Nasih Muhyiddin, an advisor to the Marjayyat, the council of the four highest clerics in Najaf. At their head is the old Grand Ayatollah Ali al-Sistani, who never speaks in public and doesn't receive journalists. Thus Sheikh Nasih is a sort of unofficial speaker of the Marjayyat who gives interviews and travels abroad to conferences. In his white evening robes, white too his turban, beard and plastic clogs, Sheikh Nasih receives me seated on chairs, the presence of which is in itself something unusual in the house of a cleric. To get the discussion going, I tell him about the fear of Islam among more and more people in the West.

The Western image of Islam is made by enemies of Islam, the sheikh counters; naturally, their image of Islam is bad.

I ask whether, in these days in particular, when the news of the 'Islamic State' is creating a negative image, it is not time for an intra-Islamic debate on the reasons for the violence.

'Every nation has its criminals and extremists. Our problem is that the criminals and extremists receive massive support from abroad: even al-Qaeda was de facto a Western product.'

Isn't that explanation too simple? I ask: after all, the West is fighting al-Qaeda, just as it is now fighting IS.

'Yes, the West first creates terror, then fights it. It was the same with the Taliban.'

Sheikh Nasih is visibly enjoying the ping-pong game of arguments and counter-arguments. Casually leaning on his left elbow, he thrusts his right hand forward at the end of every statement as if delivering a smash. Again and again, the temple of the reading glasses he is holding between three fingers swings on its hinge with the jerking movement.

I ask him whether he seriously asserts that the terror has nothing to do with Islam.

'Of course there have always been terrorists, from the beginning. Just think of the murderers of Imam Ali, the murderers of Imam Hussein. They were terrorists too. And, yes, there have been radical schools in Islam from the earliest times. But what IS is doing – these beheadings, these rapes, this barbarity – that is unprecedented; that goes against everything Islam stands for, including what the most radical schools teach. That has nothing to do with Islam, not even Sunni Islam. Nothing!'

But now the terrorists pretend to be devout Muslims and shout at the beheadings *Lā 'ilāha 'illāllāh* – it's not enough simply to say Islam is a peaceful religion.

'Even Hillary Clinton has said the Americans created IS!' the sheikh persists.

'When did she say that?'

'In Congress. I saw it myself on YouTube.'

While I rack my brain to think of which statement by Hillary Clinton the sheikh could mean, or more likely could have misunderstood, I pre-empt the argument that is sure to come next: 'But Edward Snowden never revealed documents that say the leader of IS is an Israeli agent.'

'I read that he did reveal it,' the sheikh says, surprised that I brought up Snowden myself, whose alleged revelation has been circulating in Arabic media for some time. 'They say al-Baghdadi is a Jew.'

'Snowden never confirmed that statement. They are only repeating the unverified claim that he said it. Or have you heard him say it himself?'

'No, I have only read it,' the sheikh admits, after stopping to think a moment.

Then it occurs to me what statement by Hillary Clinton he was referring to: 'Ms Clinton self-critically admitted to Congress that the lack of support for the peaceful demonstrators and the secular opposition in Syria played into the hands of the extremist groups. That is something completely different from your quotation.'

'In the Arabic translation she said the Americans created IS,' says Sheikh Nasih defensively, 'but I admit I have not verified the translation.'

'You said the image of Islam in the West is created by the enemies of Islam. Couldn't it be that the image the Arab world has of the West is much more one-sided? People will believe anything if it makes the West look bad.'

'No doubt you're right; we accept what we hear much too often without verification if it fits our preconceptions,' the sheikh concedes. 'But, on the other hand, we know from the terrorists' biographers – and these are facts – that they are a bunch of uncultured criminals from all over the world.'

'But ten or twenty thousand terrorists could never conquer such an enormous territory if they didn't have support in the local population.'

'That is a dangerous topic.'

'Why?'

'I can say only this much,' the sheikh says, lowering his voice: 'If IS hadn't been supported by certain circles within the government and the army, they could never have captured a city like Mosul. The Marjayyat has intelligence documents which show that the conquest of Mosul was a concerted action coordinated with parts of the government. Shortly before IS marched in, numerous weapons were transported to Mosul. And yet IS took Mosul without a shot being fired. And the army left the weapons behind, along with the defenceless Shiite recruits who were massacred by IS. That was no coincidence.'

If we are to believe Sheikh Nasih, the old elites, the generals and the supporters of the Baath party in general, who are still numerous, are behind the advance of IS. The jihadists played out their gruesome fantasies, but, in fact, cities such as Mosul are back under Baathist rule.

'And al-Baghdadi may not be an Israeli spy,' the sheikh continues, coming back to the leader of IS, 'but you know that he worked at a Baath party university under Saddam Hussein.'

'You say the government of Prime Minister al-Maliki in Baghdad bears a share of the responsibility for, or actively helped, the advance of IS. But that is a Shiite government. How could that be?'

'Nonsense,' the sheikh grumbles, 'that's not a Shiite government. Maliki may be a Shiite, but he doesn't act as a Shiite. He is only interested in power. We in the Marjayyat know for a fact that the advance of IS is all a ploy to ruin the country. Who stands to gain if Iraq descends into chaos? The head of government benefits because he can declare a state of emergency. That was his plan in any case: he wanted to stay in power, wanted to be a new Saddam. In his power-mad hubris he has destroyed Iraq, just as Hitler destroyed Germany. The whole country is kaput; it's falling apart. If the Marjayyat had not forced Maliki to resign, an open civil war would have broken out.'

'The Marjayyat made Maliki resign?'

'Yes, we sent a delegation to Tehran to explain that Iraq can't possibly go on with Maliki. Only then did Tehran withdraw its support for him.'

'Then Iran made a mistake in supporting Maliki as long as it did,' I say, smelling a chance to elicit from the sheikh a self-critical word about the Shia, 'and Iran is definitely a Shiite government, a Shiite state in fact, is it not?'

'Iran pursues its national interests, like any other state. That has nothing to do with Shia. The Shia is careful to keep its distance from politics.'

That the clergy sullies itself whenever it intervenes in politics has always been the quietists' main argument. Now I realize how Sheikh Nasih not only declares the Shia apolitical but also, conversely, defines politics itself as un-Shiite. It is the time-honoured effort of the clergy to preserve their own purity. By declaring themselves not competent, they also fend off all criticism.

'And what do you say to the Americans' air strikes against IS positions?' I ask.

'Everyone is talking now about the Peshmerga and the American air strikes, but if Grand Ayatollah Sistani had not called on the people to fight against IS, Baghdad would have been overrun. Three million men volunteered within two days. I ask you: what state can mobilize three million volunteers in two days? Only a word from Sistani can do that.'

To Sheikh Nasih, the prestige of the clergy is the source of great power, but that power must be used only in cases of extreme necessity. The day-to-day duty of the scholars is, quite similarly to that of the Christian clergy, to give the people an example of compassion and charity. In these days, most of all, the clergy devote their attention to caring for the refugees in the south, regardless of their denomination, whether Shiite or Sunni, Christian or Yazidi.

'We are not afraid of anyone; we survived the years under Saddam Hussein, the torture, the murders, the massacres,' says Sheikh Nasih. 'For we are utterly convinced that love prevails.'

It has grown late, almost one o'clock. The sheikh says he is not tired.

'But I am,' I admit. 'I just landed in Najaf this morning.'

As a juror might announce his verdict, Sheikh Nasih Muhyiddin announces that tomorrow I can meet Grand Ayatollah Najafi, one of the four members of the Marjayyat: 'Only don't talk to him so much about politics.'

A DIFFERENT SHIA

I do not stay in Najaf long enough to measure the sheikh's words against the real actions of the clergy. From Iran I know the religious case for separation from the state only as argued by oppositional ayatollahs. At the same time, though, I know that in other parts of the country, especially among secular intellectuals in Baghdad, and still more among exiles, people accuse the clergy of arguing for the separation of state and religion only because they form a state of their own within the state. But, even in Najaf, I have my doubts whether the money brought here by pilgrims, and the *khums*, a kind of tithe that the Shiites pay in addition to *sakāt*, the tax for the poor – whether these huge revenues actually benefit the needy. The charity of the clergy is not apparent in the streets and in the surrounding villages, where great poverty still prevails. And the gigantic 400-metre-long, 150-metre-wide, five-storey complex that is currently under construction beside the shrine of Imam Ali is not exactly a gesture of humility. It will offer space for 200,000 people to pray, and also house restaurants, hotels, an ultramodern administrative wing and a library of 3 million volumes: the more hostile the Saudis are towards the Shiites, the more important the mullahs seem to find it to have their own alternative Mecca.

At least the clergy really are taking care of the refugees, as I find on the second day of my journey: 80,000 of them are in Najaf. That is a big task for a city of 600,000 inhabitants, but small compared with the millions who have fled to Kurdistan. I strike up a conversation with two Turkmen women whose families initially sought shelter in the north but then moved on by bus to Najaf, where refugees are better provided for. I also meet a few Christian families who have ended up in southern Iraq. In the distribution centres for food, money and household necessities, seminary students make sure that all the refugees get their share, intervening the moment there is any dispute with an official. Because the money comes from the clergy, the future mullahs are visibly in charge in spite of their youth. Not aggressively, but self-assuredly, Najaf champions a different Shia from that which has held sway in Tehran since the Islamic Revolution. Not only in the West, but in Iran too, and especially in the Iranian state media, it is often forgotten that Ayatollah Khomeini, when he was living in exile in Najaf, was considered a dangerous innovator by the older grand ayatollahs and, by some, a heretic who would politicize Islam. The American invasion gave back to the Shiite orthodoxy a place beyond the Islamic Republic's constricting grasp. Naturally Tehran is present in Najaf with a great deal of money and theologians of its own, most visibly Ayatollah Khamenei himself. But when, after the death of Grand Ayatollah Araki, the leader of the revolution wanted to be declared the 'source of emulation' (*marja' at-taqlid*), the supreme theological authority of the Shia, the scholars in Najaf gave him nothing but a tired smile. Khamenei is not even recognized as an ayatollah here because he has never submitted a theological treatise. When I don't identify myself as a Western reporter, the clerics make no bones about their disdain for Iranian state Islam. Publicly, however, hardly anyone would oppose the Islamic Republic: Iran's influence is too strong, and so are the clergy's traditional efforts to close ranks against criticism from outside. The other side of the Shiite *esprit de corps*, of course, is that internal struggles in Najaf have sometimes been fought with weapons.

WITH SWORDLIKE INDEX FINGER

Like most clerics, Grand Ayatollah Bashir al-Najafi doesn't receive individual visitors until evening. Until then, a Shiite cleric's day is full up with prayers, teaching, public audiences and reading, and the impression I get is that this routine is the more strict and withdrawn the higher the cleric is in the hierarchy. This is not simply a consequence of the asceticism that seems to be written in the face of the grand ayatollah, who is originally from India. The fear of assassination is another reason why the four members of the Marjayyat almost never leave their heavily guarded houses. Even the street that leads to his house is cordoned off; access is by appointment only. The abundance of watchmen, weapons, security gates and armoured SUVs contrasts with the old, indeed humble building the cleric lives in, the bare interior walls peeling, brown carpeting without furniture, not a single decoration anywhere, only a flat cushion to sit on. As a chorus of boys leave the house after singing religious songs for the grand ayatollah, a delegation of Pakistani Shiites take their seats on the floor of the waiting room. Mullahs of various ages and ranks go in and out. An attendant brings tea.

Among the four members of the Marjayyat, the 72-year-old Najafi is the one most inclined to make public statements, and he publicly championed Grand Ayatollah Sistani's recent appeal on television. He speaks to me and at the same time into a microphone that carries his words to loudspeakers throughout the house.

A video camera is also running. Following Sheikh Nasih's recommendation I talk at first about theological matters; I

give the grand ayatollah my own books about Islam; and then
I turn towards politics after all by way of Shiite dogma. How
does he as a theologian consider the *velayat-e faqih*, the 'governance of the jurists', which the Leader of the Revolution
Khomeini has made a doctrine of the state in Iran, I ask. My
innocent expression notwithstanding, the grand ayatollah
immediately realizes what I am driving at and brushes me off
with a platitude: '*Velayat-e faqih* is an old legal question on
which there are different views.'

'But in Iran it is not an old legal question, it is the law of
the land. Surely you must have an opinion on that.'

'Different circumstances can lead to different answers.'

'Very well, but what is the answer of the Marjayyat in
Najaf?'

'We have different circumstances in Iraq than those in
Iran.'

'Does that mean you are against the unity of state and
religion?'

When I refuse to give in, the gentle grand ayatollah
changes his rhetorical strategy from one sentence to the
next: he leans his slender torso towards me; his erect index
finger darts upwards; he looks me straight in the eye from a
few centimetres away.

'Did the Prophet found a state or did he not?!' he asks in
a strident voice.

It's a rhetorical question, of course, intended to draw me
onto thin ice. The Shiite seminaries are the only centres
of learning in the world whose curriculum has been based
without interruption from the Middle Ages until today on
Aristotelian rhetoric, grammar and logic. A theologian
attains a high rank only after proving his mastery in many
argumentative fencing matches.

'I am not here to give answers but to receive your instruc-
tion,' I say in an effort to dodge his thrust. But the grand

ayatollah does not lower his swordlike index finger and continues to hold my gaze with flashing eyes.

'Did the Prophet found a state, or did he not?!'

Twice more I try to escape; twice more the grand ayatollah asks the same question.

'Certainly the Prophet founded a state,' I admit at last.

'So, there you have it!' the grand ayatollah says triumphantly, and leans back. 'How can something be wrong for which we have the Prophet's example?'

I point out that there are no more prophets today, report on the conditions in Iran, which are far from exemplary, and argue that the clergy in Najaf is generally known for its separation of politics and religion – but the grand ayatollah wants no part of dissent against the Iranian theocracy: 'Did the Prophet found a state, or did he not?!'

I am fairly bewildered by the time I leave the house of Grand Ayatollah Najafi. Certainly, reasons can be found in Shiite dogma to support the Islamic Republic's model of the state. The relation between clergy and state was a central point of controversy in theology even before Ayatollah Khomeini. But to fend off questions by referring in a constant refrain to the early history of Islam with a strident voice and a raised index finger looks like a trick to me. I understand a little better the secular intellectuals in Baghdad who mistrust the clergy.

GRAND AYATOLLAH SISTANI'S MESSAGE

Before I travel on to Baghdad, I want to try at least to meet Grand Ayatollah Sistani, who gives no interviews but has an audience for his followers every morning at nine. Sistani, who spent many years under house arrest in the days of

Saddam Hussein, has always been a voice of moderation in the political controversies since the American invasion and, for that reason, was proposed as a recipient of the Nobel Peace Prize by the *New York Times*. In moral questions, on the other hand, he is considered an arch-conservative. In 2006 he withdrew a fatwa declaring homosexuality a crime worthy of death.

At half past eight, when I arrive at the alley in the old city centre that leads to Sistani's house, the faithful already form a long queue, all men, most of them evidently poor. If I join the queue, I risk not being admitted before the end of the grand ayatollah's audience. So I take out my books again and go up to the barrier: Might I humbly offer the fruit of my labour, insignificant though it is, to His Reverence?

In the two hours that follow I meet the entire hierarchy of the attending staff in succession, culminating in Sistani's son Muhammad Reza. From their questions I gather that they have quickly googled my name – but what is someone like me doing in Iraq, and why now?

'I visited the shrine of the imam,' I answer time and again – the easiest answer in Najaf.

I'm well aware there is no chance I'll be admitted if I identify myself as a reporter. And I quickly feel that the higher-level attendants at least are too polite to turn away a Muslim who has come from so far away. And evidently the titles and the contents of my books, *God Is Beautiful* and *The Terror of God*, arouse some interest. Perhaps it also helps that, as an Iranian, I also speak Sistani's mother tongue. Would I come back after the end of the audience? Then His Reverence will receive me for a greeting.

When I finally enter the alley, I have to surrender my bag, my valuables, my ID, my mobile and of course my camera. Because there has been no current photo of him for years, quite a few Iraqis – certainly not his followers – believe the

84-year-old grand ayatollah is severely ill or senile, no longer makes his own decisions, and is manipulated by his sons and advisors.

When I leave Sistani's house almost an hour later, I am in a dilemma. If I publish what I have heard, I will be abusing the trust that Sistani's son in particular placed in me when he admitted me. But, on the other hand, as short and impromptu as my visit was, I feel an obligation to bear witness to the highest cleric of the Shiite world, and probably the most influential man in Iraq. Therefore, without going into the details of the conversations I had first with Sistani's son and then with the grand ayatollah himself, I would like to describe my general impression: Sistani seems healthy in spite of his great age; he is absolutely lucid, highly intelligent, and knows exactly what he's doing. The gaze that Sistani fixed on me was earnest and razor-sharp, yet not unfriendly, but positively interested. He spoke slowly, calmly and articulately, without rhetorical flourishes. He was completely unpretentious, and at the same time conscious of a duty to which he can devote only the few years remaining to him. He spoke without illusions and without mincing words about the conditions in Iran. He wanted to hear from a foreign visitor more than to speak himself; he asked questions about Germans' relation to their history and the specific relation between church and state in Germany; he was up to date on the establishment of departments of Islamic studies at German universities – the Germans are doing that to keep their young Muslims away from extremism, Sistani explained to an equally old cleric who sat next to him, and said it was a clever thing to do.

When I was surprised how well informed Sistani is about the current developments in Germany, he said I shouldn't think he doesn't know what's happening just because he doesn't leave the house: he watches very carefully, he said, what goes on in the world. There is no doubt at all – and his son Muhammad Reza, with whom I talked longer, was still more explicit – that this house has a very clear view of the disastrous situation in which the Islamic world, and definitely Islam as a religion too, is today. The political analyses were knowledgeable and nuanced. When Sistani asked me about my preceding discussions, I admitted my annoyance at the fact that everyone only wants to blame others, preferably the West, for their own plight. That is only an escape, said Mohammad Reza Sistani, pointing to the lack of public spirit, the corruption, the lawlessness, the lack of freedom and the selfishness that predominate in most Islamic countries. Why, he asked, did a young woman such as the mathematician Maryam Mirzakhani, for example, the winner of the Fields Medal, not have the opportunity in Iran to develop her genius for the good of the society? 'In truth, the foundation of our own societies is broken.'

Mohammad Reza Sistani sang the praises of the European Union, in which once hostile peoples with different languages, cultures and political traditions have defused nationalism to the point that they have become friends and partners. In the Islamic world, not even the little Gulf emirates, who have their language, culture and religion in common, are able to join together just in a common market. As if that were not enough of disunity, people now want to divide up the existing states by ethnicity and denomination.

I asked Grand Ayatollah Sistani, his father, about the expulsion of Christians from Iraq. Sistani called it a catastrophe of historic dimensions; the Christians are part of the core of oriental culture, and Iraqi culture in particular. Theologically, Christianity is particularly close to Shia, Sistani said, probably alluding to the images, the processions, the veneration of the Virgin Mary, the intercessions and the concept of redemption in the Catholic Church, which are familiar to Shiite Islam.

Why did he not proclaim his solidarity with the Christians publicly? I asked. The Marjayyat did declare, Sistani pointed out, that the Christians must be received just like the other persecuted minorities. And, after all, it is the Muslims themselves, the Kurds and the Shiites, who are on the front lines of the fight against IS. I answered that the Christians predominantly had the impression that their expulsion was silently tolerated, if not welcomed, by the majority of Muslims. Sistani answered that the Marjayyat, and himself personally, were in constant contact with the representatives of the various churches; they visit him often. The Church knows that the Marjayyat is on its side in Iraq. Perhaps the representatives of the Church know it, I insisted, but his voice does not reach to the West. What would I propose? Sistani asked.

'Why don't you address a message to the Christians of the world?'

Sistani was silent for two, three seconds, without looking away from me. 'I don't believe in public declarations,' he said at last. 'Every day someone announces something, whether it's the United Nations, the pope or the Organization of Islamic Cooperation. I don't believe in it. Those are just words. I am deeply convinced that works count. And if our works are good, if they help humanity, then their message will spread.'

I hope I have done right in spreading the message of Grand Ayatollah Sistani.

II BAGHDAD:
THE FUTURE IS PAST

A THIRTY YEARS' WAR AND MORE

No signposts are necessary to mark the distance remaining on the drive to Baghdad. The closer you get, the denser the succession of roadblocks and the stricter the inspections. After each checkpoint, the cars accelerate as if they wanted to make up the time lost. The driver, who travels this route daily, says, no, it's not for fear of bombs or snipers that he drives so fast. The main roads are safe south of Baghdad, day and night. His reason for wanting to avoid driving in the dark is only that so many trucks have no lights. But then why does he, why do practically all the cars, drive so fast – 90, 100 miles per hour – over a road on which blown-out tyres, abandoned bumpers, even dismantled engines are not the only obstacles? Mopeds, donkeys, pedestrians too use the motorway in Iraq to avoid quieter and hence more danger-ous secondary roads; once I see a complete football team in matching, professional-looking jerseys jogging along the hard shoulder with their trainer. The driver says he doesn't even notice any more that he drives so fast. A few years ago it really was dangerous to take the motorway; perhaps the country has just become used to speeding.

Baghdad, meanwhile, has grown used to standing still. At first I think it is the sheer number of cars, because there is no public transport, and no traffic lights either. But then I notice that many streets have almost no traffic. Finally I realize that the cars all crowd into a few thoroughfares. That means you can get from place to place fast within a district, but, if you want to get from one district to another, you have to go and squeeze through individual checkpoints. Once a diverse mix-ture, Baghdad today is largely divided up by denominations. Those who want to visit their former neighbours find them hours away during rush hour. In the day and a half I spend driving back and forth across the city, I see no playgrounds, parks, places to rest, sidewalk cafés or tea houses, only rub-bish piled in heaps at many junctions or simply dumped on the pavement. I see very few children – do people keep them at home? – and not a single person laughing. No one seems to take the trouble to renovate their house, or even just to paint a façade; all architecture seems to be reduced to mere function.

Except in two, three wealthy neighbourhoods and the closed-off Green Zone, which most politicians and diplomats leave only to travel abroad, public life comes to a standstill when darkness falls. Shops and restaurants close early, against all oriental tradition; the pavements look deserted in the evening, very few streets have lighting, and power cuts are frequent. It has been this way not just since the advance of the 'Islamic State', which has now approached within thirty kilometres of Baghdad. It has been this way for ten years, at times with several bomb attacks a day; and before the third Gulf War, the embargo that cost hundreds of thousands of children their lives; and with the embargo, the second Gulf War; and before the second Gulf War, the first war against Iran with up to a million dead – taken all together, a thirty years' war and more. To say nothing of the dictatorship, with its spies, torture chambers, forced resettlements and genocides against Shiites and Kurds. Perhaps it is the case that a country eventually abandons itself, and most of all its capital, which cannot withdraw into an isolated, regional identity. The city continues to exist, the people go to the shops, to school, to the office or to work. They celebrate weddings, the Feast of the Sacrifice, birthdays. But everything superfluous deteriorates, every beautiful yet useless detail; joy and public spirit decay.

A HOOKAH WITH GOETHE
AND HÖLDERLIN

'Wie geht's?' I ask the German scholar Muthanna al-Bazzaz, who visits me at my hotel the evening of my arrival.

'If a Baghdadi says he is well, you know he's a liar.'

I ask Muthanna whether we can't leave the hotel, whose approximately five guests are being guarded by armoured cars, barbed wire atop high walls, and a team of muscle-bound security guards in beige polo shirts. No problem, says Muthanna, the districts around the international hotels are safe in the evening too. 'I just didn't want you to have to take a taxi through the city by yourself.'

A few minutes later we're sitting in front of a restaurant with fluorescent lighting on a well-travelled main street, and we each order a half chicken because there isn't anything else; since we remain the only guests over the course of the evening, a menu would be too much to ask for. Muthanna, in his early sixties by my estimation, teaches German literature at the University of Baghdad and translates visa applications and medical files on the side, since his professor's salary is not enough to live on. He speaks German with no accent and with flawless grammar – old East German school; only the melody of his language, if anything, sounds unusual, every sentence ending on a low note, perhaps Mediterranean, in any case very sad.

'Why don't you go back to Germany?' I ask.

'I am too old,' Muthanna answers. 'And I didn't get on with Germany either. Everything is better there, absolutely everything, but the people, they seem so lonely to me, especially in old age. I saw the old people living in their little flats with no children or grandchildren; I saw them with their dog or their cat, talking to it as if it was a person, and I longed for family, for a bond that lasts a lifetime.'

Muthanna returned to Iraq before German reunification, married, and now has four almost grown-up daughters whose education he has to finance. Because lessons are cancelled in the schools, the students have to take private lessons from their own teachers, whose salaries are likewise not enough to live on. Only rich parents can afford the private lessons, so the poorer children haven't got a chance. The good money that Muthanna earns with his translation service is almost all spent on his daughters. Now he's stuck on this treadmill, and by the time the youngest has finally finished her studies it will be too late to transplant an old tree like him again.

'And your daughters, do they want to go away later?'

'What young person doesn't want to get away from Baghdad?'

It's not just the politics, he says, which are corrupt through and through. The society has been demolished, has suffered too much, has been disappointed too many times, has lost not only too many people but also its ideals. By now, everyone mistrusts everyone else; there is practically no value system any more that goes beyond one's own family, one's own clan. A gang of murderers like the 'Islamic State', whose core is just a few thousand fighters, could not have conquered a third of the country within days, or a metropolis like Mosul, if the Iraqis' spirit, their resistance, hadn't been exhausted. Yes, of course, IS is being fought now, but by the Shiites and Kurds, whose very existence is at stake, not by a national army.

Muthanna, who is himself Sunni, does not accept the argument that the Shiites have marginalized the Sunnis since the overthrow of Saddam Hussein as a reason for the fall of the Sunni territories. Of course the Sunni city of Mosul was neglected under the Shiite government, but so was the Shiite city of Basra, which at least produces the country's oil – and does Baghdad look well cared for? The only difference is that, in Mosul, people can blame the Shiites for their plight, but in Basra they can only blame the government. No, Iraq as a commonwealth has simply become so fragile that it collapses in the first strong breeze.

In his free time, Muthanna is working on a specialized

German–Arabic dictionary. The university's budget doesn't permit ordering books from Germany; even the teaching materials date from Saddam Hussein's time. He follows events in Germany on the Internet, reads the online editions of *Der Spiegel*, the *Frankfurter Allgemeine Zeitung*, and so on, every day. Muthanna gets exasperated over the deterioration of the German language, over the grammatical mistakes he discovers even in the most respected newspapers, the careless use of the language of Goethe and Hölderlin. And the Anglicisms! He has published an article of his own about 'Germish', which he abhors – in German. It is one of the oddest places on Earth to be exalting Goethe and Hölderlin, over tea and hookahs now on a Baghdad thoroughfare at night, an Iraqi Sunni and a somehow-still-Iranian Shiite.

'What language are you speaking?' the waiter asks.

'The most beautiful one there is!' Muthanna answers.

FOG OF MELANCHOLY

The next day I prowl through the city with the Kurdish photographer Ali Arkady. We start in Mutanabbi Street, whose name alone evokes the intellectual horizons of ages past. For al-Mutanabbi, meaning 'the one who comports himself like a prophet', is the epithet of a heretical poet of the tenth century who is nonetheless one of the most revered poets of Arabic literature. Accordingly, Mutanabbi is the booksellers' street in the centre of old Baghdad, a long, narrow, car-free zone in which the entire book production of the Arabic-speaking world used to be on display left and right, all the classics alongside contemporary literature and whole stands devoted to literature in foreign languages, including, yes, Goethe and Hölderlin. Today most of the stands have switched to school materials, DVDs and CD-ROMs. I buy a state-published travel guide from the early 1980s that praises the harmonious coexistence of ethnic groups, languages and denominations under Saddam Hussein; photos show young women in bikinis by an idyllic lake, smiling mullahs in the Shiite shrines, European-looking business streets in Baghdad, and Kurds in quaint traditional costumes. The book was printed in Yugoslavia, another defunct state.

At the end of Mutanabbi, Ali takes me into the most beautiful – perhaps also the only – remaining coffee house in Baghdad. It used to be called Maqha Shabandar, and the owner has renamed it Maqha al-Shuhada, 'Café of the Martyrs', because his five brothers died in a bomb attack against coffee-drinkers. It is a rambling hall whose high ceilings are borne by slender pillars. The older gentlemen – all the guests are men – playing cards, talking or, in many cases, staring wearily into space, are visibly members of a middle class that must once have existed: old-fashioned lounge suits, clean-shaven cheeks, some with moustaches, others with hats. The sunshine seeping in through the narrow windows makes the smoke of their cigarettes and hookahs glow. The walls are completely covered with wood-framed black-and-white photographs: famous Iraqi actors, singers, poets, politicians; the men mostly in evening dress, their shining black hair combed back or rakishly parted, the women in elegant gowns. Yes, there was once a genuine Arab modernism, there was an artistic production and intellectualism in film, in music, in literature that seemed to combine the best of two worlds, that welcomed the progressive, wherever it came from, while remaining rooted in indigenous tradition. There was also hope for an independent and free society; there were politicians who were looked up to. There were years when Baghdad must have been culturally more exciting, and definitely more diverse, than Berlin. Perhaps that is the source of the melancholy that lies like a fog on the Café of the Martyrs like the smoke of the cigarettes and hookahs: that the future is already past.

RIGHT OUT OF ALI BABA

A block away, the sad ending has already begun. We ask a soldier to let us see the old governor's palace of Baghdad, seat of first the Ottoman and then the British viceroys.

'What do you want to see?' the soldier asks.

In spring of 2003, looters raided one district after another. People say the American occupation not only tolerated the looting but started it, breaking down doors, according to countless eyewitness accounts, and lining the streets with tanks like an honour guard for the looters. The operation, which is remembered in Baghdad as 'Ali Baba', was not the most brutal crime of the American occupation, but certainly the most perfidious. It gets its name from a GI who shouted to one of the looters, 'Go on in, Ali Baba, it's yours.' In spite of the selfless defence of many museum guards, a large part of Iraq's 5,000-year-old heritage was destroyed in a few days, the museums, libraries, cultural centres, palaces, universities and even embassies, galleries and all the ministries stripped bare – except the Ministry of Oil.

The soldier who has nothing left to show seems none-theless glad of the diversion offered by two visitors. But his superior hurries out of a room in his undershirt to take over guiding the tour. At least the clock tower has been restored, he points out.

It's true, the clock tower from the nineteenth century, reminiscent of Big Ben, shines in its old splendour once more and tells more or less the correct time. The halls, however, are empty, down to the bare walls, the stucco flaking off the exterior too, whole rooms collapsed in the Ottoman wing of the palace. Desk and chair still stand in the museum director's office, the dust on them a finger thick, in the corner a bedstead with no mattress, an empty coat rack beside it. Across a brownish field that was once an English lawn, we walk to the garden terrace and stand overlooking the Tigris, which flows by the palace – what a majestic view this must have been! Today we look down at a rowing clubhouse, whose windows are boarded up, and at floating restaurants rotting away. The wild bushes in strips to the left and right of the bank may once have lined promenades.

Things happen here, says the officer, who has put his jacket on over his undershirt, that really are right out of Ali Baba: once he brought his soldiers a sheep and let it graze in the courtyard. When he wanted to fetch the sheep to slaughter, he found – he swears! – a snake forty feet long busy swallowing it alive.

'Forty feet?'

'Yes, forty feet.'

And, if we don't believe it, we can ask the soldier on watch at the entrance.

THE LAST CHRISTIAN

We meet a friend of Ali Arkady's who lives in the neighbourhood around Rashid Street. This is where Baghdad's early and promising modernism had its centre, where the well-to-do Jews and Christians lived side by side with Muslims. The façades are so sooty that for a long time I don't notice their beauty; perhaps I no longer expect to find beauty in Baghdad: porticos borne by elegant columns turning the pavement into a shady arcade; the artistic, sun-screening bars in front of the upper windows, fantastically ornamented balconies and bay windows. All Jewish craftsmanship, says Ali's friend; the Jews in Baghdad were the artists and artisans. Who knows today that, as late as the 1940s, it was not the Sunnis or the Shiites but the Jews who were the biggest and culturally the most influential group among the population of Baghdad? The people who inhabit this quarter today, judging by their dark skin colour, are mostly from southern Iraq, hence Shiites. The Shiite–Sunni conflict is not purely one between denominations but has an ethnic-chauvinistic element: here the Arab Sunnis, often light-skinned, who dominated the country for centuries, there the Sunni Kurds and Arab Shiites, who owe their new-found power and autonomy to the overthrow of Saddam.

In one place after another, individual houses have been torn down and replaced with six-storey rectangular blocks, their façades often of red plastic, which, fortunately, is also covered with soot. In a little stall, more a kiosk than a shop, stand huge linen sacks full of coffee beans and an antique mill. Iraq's best mocha, which, tradition holds, has been brewed here for a hundred years, is served today in little plastic cups, like medicine in a hospital. But the mocha is still delectable – and its aroma still follows us two blocks away. A covered market of bare concrete, for which a block of sumptuous old buildings was sacrificed in a frenzy of socialist development, is apparently inhabited only by snakes; the merchants fill the streets, however, selling fruit from their carts. 'Like Rashid Street' is what the people of Baghdad used to say when traffic was thick, because Rashid Street was already jammed with cars when most Iraqis rode horses or camels. People ride donkeys along Rashid Street again today. When Ali's friend leads us into an alley to show us where he used to play, a man whispers to us that we had better go back to the street; it's *shwaya taʿbān* here, which formally means 'a little tired', but in Baghdad is understood as 'a little dangerous'.

We enter the 'Mother of Sorrow Chotolics', as the church, built in 1843, is labelled in idiosyncratic English. The light and dark blue paint that doesn't quite embellish the bare stone of the interior is peeling in many places. No one seems to care much about the moisture damage either. In the nave, which has ample room for eight hundred worshippers, ten pews are placed at generous intervals. In a corner, red lights blink around a picture of the Virgin Mary ornamented with plastic flowers. A soldier of perhaps forty, who has heard us looking around, switches on one of the three rows of chandeliers and the fans. It's a long time since a Mass was celebrated here; at most a Christian with business at the market stops in from time to time and says a rosary. Otherwise, the cleaning woman comes once a week and, occasionally, nostalgic Muslims who attended the convent school in childhood. Christians no longer live in the area, the soldier says; he is the last one far and wide.

'Ah, you're a Christian?'

'Certainly I'm a Christian,' the soldier answers. 'Alaa is my name.'

I ask whether we can visit the convent. The convent no longer exists, says Alaa; in the late 1990s an investor got his hands on it, for a lot of money and a little pressure, to convert it into a shopping mall. The last Christians moved away then to the better parts of Baghdad, to the Kurdish part of Iraq, and abroad of course. The mall never opened; since the Americans invaded in 2003, it's just not safe enough here.

'Was it better, then, under Saddam Hussein?'

'Of course it was better under Saddam,' says Alaa. 'We didn't use to think about whether someone is a Kurd or an Arab, a Sunni, a Shiite or a Christian. Often we didn't even know.'

'Don't you think it's strange', I ask Alaa, 'that a Christian country's war so dramatically worsened the situation of Iraqi Christians?'

'Those were no Christians,' says Alaa.

'But Bush definitely argued as a Christian when he announced they would liberate Iraq; he even called it a crusade.'

'It wasn't about religion,' Alaa answers, saying the same thing I hear constantly from Muslims about the present war. 'The Americans were only interested in business.'

I ask whether there aren't problems with extremists: after all, the church door is wide open. None so far, Alaa answers. But then, Mass is not held here any more, otherwise a bomb might go off, as one did in 2010 in the more comfortable district of Karrada, killing over sixty churchgoers. It doesn't take much to terrorize people who can't defend themselves. It was the same in the 1940s: a few attacks and no support from any side, to say nothing of protection, and the Jews all emigrated. What the 'Farhud', the 1941 pogrom in which 150 people died, was to the Baghdad Jews, that was the Karrada attack to the Christians: it confronted even the most patriotic of them with the question whether there was any future left for them in Iraq.

'And is there a future left for Christians in Iraq?' I ask.

Alaa gives a negative click of his tongue and jerks his head upwards.

'And why have you decided to stay on?'

'You're not going to believe me,' says Alaa with a bitter grin. 'I have my appointment at the embassy tomorrow at ten.'

'Tomorrow?'

'Yes, with the Jordanians.'

'And from there?'

'To Europe.'

I ask whether he doesn't at least get something like sympathy from the Muslims. The politicians and the religious leaders definitely declare their solidarity with the Christians,

Alaa reports, but, among the population, sympathy is shown only very rarely – it's rare enough that a neighbour stops by even just to ask how it's going. Although the church door is standing open, as we no doubt noticed.

'Are there Muslims among your friends?' I ask.

'Yes, of course,' Alaa answers.

'And don't they try to persuade you to stay?'

'No, they say too I'll be better off going.'

Because I still don't want to believe it, I ask whether there's anything that could be done, or a miracle that could happen to make the Iraqi Christians stay. Alaa clicks his tongue again and jerks his head upwards.

A WARRIOR

As we're leaving the church, Ali's friend suggests we meet a fighter from the Mahdi Brigade, the militia of the radical Shiite preacher Muqtada al-Sadr, saying he knows someone who knows someone who … After a few phone calls, Ali's friend leads us through alleys that look *shwaya ta'bān* to me. Another couple of phone calls in front of a house that is a century or two old, and suddenly a young, athletic but not muscular-looking man in the light-blue football jersey of the Slovenian team steps out onto the street, shower slides on his feet. His shiny black hair is combed back; his beard is narrow and neatly trimmed as a pop star's. In the back of the waistband of his knee-length sports trousers he carries a shiny silver-coloured pistol. Haydar is his name; he shakes our hands without smiling. The day before yesterday he got back from a mission in Amirli, a town liberated by Shiite militias; the 13,000 inhabitants, most of them Turkmens, had been besieged and starved for more than eighty days, yet did not surrender to IS.

Haydar invites us into the house where he lives with his parents and four siblings. In a narrow, windowless front room, made smaller still by a partition, we sit on a couch. There is no light; the power frequently goes off; they don't have enough petrol for the generator. Haydar pulls up a white plastic chair in the doorway; now he has the pistol on the chair seat between his thighs. Then he tells us his story.

He was seventeen, still in school, when he joined Muqtada al-Sadr in 2005 to drive the Americans out of his neighbourhood; he was immediately arrested, was in a military prison for four years – no, not in Abu Ghraib; he was in the US camp at Baghdad Airport.

'Were you mistreated?'

'No, only beaten a little during interrogations. Other than that, it was okay.'

When Haydar was released at the age of twenty-one, he had no school certificate and no trade. He joined the Mahdi militia again, which was practically the government in this neighbourhood, providing security, supplying the poorest inhabitants and settling disputes. When Grand Ayatollah Sistani called for mobilization against IS, most men volunteered right away, Sunnis included.

'You have Sunnis in your ranks?'

'Yes,' says Haydar, and on his phone he shows us photos that he took after the liberation of Amirli, exhausted but happy men of all ages in improvised uniforms, machine guns on their backs or in their raised fists. With his finger Haydar points out the Sunnis among his comrades. He confirms that Iranian Revolutionary Guards participated in the liberation of Amirli – about a thousand men, he estimates – naming the unit and the Iranian commander; the Iranians' expertise and materiel was helpful, he says, because IS is well equipped.

The gravity Haydar radiates is unsettling in such a young person. He speaks calmly, almost without emotion, with pauses between his sentences, looking me straight in the eye. He has hardly experienced anything else besides war, fighting; perhaps he wouldn't be able to adapt to civilian life any more. He makes no secret of his keenness to play a man's part, a heroic part, in his world of discipline and weapons. What he despises most about IS is their malevolence – the rapes, the crucifixions, the slaughter of the children, the beheading of the foreign journalists. IS can't even fight, he says; they retreat every time they encounter real resistance, fire their modern rockets from a distance, mingle among the civilian population, set off bombs, kill worshippers at prayer. 'Those are no Muslims we were fighting, neither Shiites nor Sunnis. They're monsters.'

I interject that the Mahdi militia too is accused of bomb attacks, on Sunni mosques or on shops that sell alcohol, bars and places with dancing. Those are lies, Haydar explains: the Mahdi militia would never kill underhandedly. Then he asks me whether I know the story of Imam Ali who spared an enemy. Certainly I know the story; it is prototypical of the Shiite ideal of heroism: just as the imam was about to kill the attacker with his dagger, having pinned him to the ground after a long struggle, his enemy spat in his face. Then the imam lowered his dagger and let his enemy live. 'Why are you sparing my life?' the attacker asked in surprise. 'You spat on me,' the imam answered. 'If I killed you now, it would be in anger because you insulted me, and not in battle.'

I have no idea whether Haydar is ignorant of the Mahdi militia's attacks and abuses, or whether he knowingly denies them. But I see that he is a warrior, nothing else, a warrior such as there has not been in Europe since two world wars ago perhaps, seeking only to win honour in battle. But what if such honour was suddenly valued less than a school certificate or a trade?

When Haydar has put his pistol back in the waistband of his trousers and we are standing outside his house again, I ask him whether he knows the history of his neighbourhood. Haydar looks somewhat puzzled, so I tell him that, a few decades ago, it was mainly Jews and Christians who lived here, probably in this house, a rich one back then.

'Didn't you know that?'

Just as Alaa the Christian soldier did, Haydar gives a negative click of his tongue and jerks his head upwards. Tonight he will return to Amirli to continue the fight against the 'Islamic State'.

III KURDISTAN: THE WAR FOR OUR WORLD TOO

LITERALLY OVERNIGHT

The problem is still the heat; over forty degrees Celsius even now in September; in high summer it gets to over fifty degrees in the sun, with no trees and no walls to offer shade. The white tents are simply pumped full of heat. The most bearable place is the strip of shadow that the tents cast beside them, only it disappears at midday. Then the refugees doze listlessly on the ground or wait on the other side of the tent for the shadow to reappear there. Again, the problem is still the heat, and the more so since it increases the stench that lies over the tents because the first latrines are just being built, and of course no one has a refrigerator where there isn't even electricity. But soon the refugees will be tormented by the cold coming into the tents through finger-wide slits; by the time this report appears, it will be only another two, three weeks at the most before autumn descends on Kurdistan like a deluge. Even more than the wind, the refugees fear the rain. Because the plain is slightly sloping, the bare earth that many of them sleep on will be transformed into mud. There are not even enough blankets, to say nothing of warm jackets, sturdy shoes, gloves and hats. Instead the bodies will have to be kept warm by each other, with ten to fifteen people in the twelve square metres that each tent encloses.

The American photographer Sebastian Meyer and I are in Khanke, an already poor town in Dohuk district, where some 750,000 people came in early August fleeing the 'Islamic State' – 750,000 refugees in a district of 1.2 million inhabitants. Here in Khanke, the numbers indicate a drama of still greater, practically biblical proportions: 67,000 refugees to 24,000 inhabitants. The refugees are everywhere, not only in the 750 tents along the main road, but in garages and warehouses, in schools and unfinished buildings, in living rooms, nurseries and corridors. They are Yazidis who held out for days in the Sinjar Mountains until American aircraft bombed clear an escape corridor for them and Kurdish PKK fighters rushed to their aid in pickups. The stories they tell are similar: the explosions that shook them awake, the fearful waiting in the dark while listening to the fighting going on outside, finally the sudden silence at dawn as a signal to flee at once, the panic, the exhaustion, often to the point of fainting, during the climb, then survival in the mountains and, more cruel than hunger and thirst, the uncertainty; finally another forced march, rescue, and since then the stark misery of a Yazidi refugee's existence in Iraq. After more than thirty days, they still haven't seen a doctor, and they are being provided for almost exclusively by the population of Khanke, whose eagerness to help is gradually reaching its limits – and the population here are themselves Yazidi. In the neighbouring Muslim town of Kamura, which is caring for refugees with similar dedication, there has already been a dispute because the local people want at least the schools to be vacated; the holidays are long past, and where are their own children to go in the daytime? The refugees, afraid of the approaching autumn weather, refuse to move into the tents and insist that they need accommodation that offers shelter against rain and cold. But, of the fourteen big camps that are to be built in Dohuk district alone, only one is finished.

'We're working twenty-four hours a day,' says the director of the Dohuk health authority, Nazim Ismet, and you don't need to see the rings under his eyes to believe him. 'My staff have been waiting for their salaries for two months because our budget is exhausted, and they have given up even counting their overtime. We have formed seventy-six mobile teams, but we simply can't catch up. There are too many refugees, and we have too few employees, especially medical staff. We buy the medicines from local businesses that give us credit out of pity.'

'And what about international aid?' I ask, still aghast because I have seen no foreign organizations in Khanke.

Dr Ismet shrugs his shoulders, as if he would like to know the same thing: 'With the help of UNICEF and WHO, we'll probably manage in the foreseeable future to provide basic medical care and enough food. We'll also manage to vaccinate the children at least against polio. But as far as accommodation is concerned, I'm not optimistic. There's not enough time left before summer ends, and we haven't nearly enough funds to build whole refugee cities in a hurry.'

Dr Ismet is afraid of epidemics that could break out because of the general exhaustion and the desperate hygienic conditions, especially cholera. Practically all the children are already suffering from diarrhoea. Five hundred million dollars for refugee aid have been promised by the Saudis, who, through their support for IS, are chiefly responsible for the refugee crisis. The churches are active of course, but they are helping only Christian refugees. The Shiites have mostly fled to the south. But the situation of the Yazidis, who have suffered the most, is appalling.

For the unvarying stories they tell us in the tents and schools, factory halls and unfinished buildings always include the Sunni neighbours who lived side by side with them, peacefully, fraternally, until those neighbours began associating with the terrorists. The stories include the old, the sick and the disabled who had to be left behind or who died along the way. The stories include the nightmares that haunt many refugees, the behavioural disorders, not only in the children, intermittent fits of aggression or obdurate silence. And, most of all, the stories include the women and girls kidnapped by IS. Some told us about telephone calls from their daughters who were apparently encouraged by their kidnappers to report their rapes in order to inscribe the terror deep in the hearts and spirits of all Yazidis. And they are not only stories – they are also faces, many if not most of them faces in which horror is written.

In a tent city on the outskirts of Zakho – 110,000 refugees to 200,000 inhabitants – we talk to Jane Hirto Hamo. She gives her age as twenty-nine yet looks at least ten years older, her gaze expressionless, the skin of her forehead and around her eyes full of wrinkles. She was fleeing with her husband and two children when IS fighters blocked their path. She was immediately separated from her husband, who managed to escape in the chaos. Jane and the children, on the other hand, ended up with hundreds of other Yazidi women and children in a school in Tal Afar. From there, all the girls who were older than twelve or thirteen were taken away and sold; the average price was $600. I ask how she knows the figure: the IS fighters said it themselves. She saw two girls, thirteen and sixteen, who were brought back to the school to say good-bye to their mother. 'We have been married, Mama,' the girls said, and under their veils they showed where their arms had been beaten black and blue. Jane and her children got away when they were about to be taken to another city after an escape attempt. It was a normal car, not a pickup as usual, and they begged the driver, who didn't have a long beard, to help them. The driver didn't respond at all, but then suddenly he stopped and pointed to a spot in the distance. There are the Kurds, the driver said, and he let them out of the car.

We have no way of verifying this and similar accounts of systematic rape by IS. But there are too many, and they are too similar, for us to think they are all invented. And whatever the truth may look like on the other side of the front – for the Yazidis it is this truth that will define their lives from now on: their existence in Iraq was annihilated literally overnight. It is a completely traumatized population that we encounter, people who say unanimously that they will return to their villages only under the protection of international troops, if at all, and who at the same time have no outlook for the future whatsoever. The Shiites have their brothers and sisters in faith in the south, and fled to them; the Christians for the most part will want to find their footing in the Christian villages and cities of Kurdistan, or emigrate to the West. The Yazidis, however, who lived in mountain villages, who only rarely have any higher education, assets or relatives abroad, who are also very conservative people with centuries-old customs and a strict code of honour – where are they supposed to go? And what will happen when the first girls return with swollen bellies? They say they only want to receive their daughters with love and tenderness and don't want to harbour any hatred against the Muslims, because the Shiites too were persecuted, or hatred of the Sunnis, because the Kurds who are helping them are themselves Sunni;

indeed, the refugees look remarkably meek as they tell of the horror they have been through, and the hopelessness that lies before them. They only say very clearly, each one says firmly: they can never again live without fear alongside Sunni Arabs. IS has already achieved its principal goal.

WHAT FOR?

Of course we wonder constantly, as we learn of terror in ever new extremes, what motivates the jihadists, how they justify their excesses of violence to themselves, what theological arguments they appropriate. With the possible exception of certain violent criminals and sadists, no one is purely and simply evil. Those whom we perceive as evil – only from a historic distance, often enough – almost always see themselves as the agents of a higher moral necessity and give their brutality a rationalization that we must not simply dismiss as insane if we want to combat it. But, on this trip, I can't figure it out, because, for one thing, I don't meet a single Iraqi in these eight days who can muster any understanding for the jihadists – after all, I am not travelling in the zones they have conquered. I can therefore only conjecture that the elimination of inhibition which, by all accounts, has taken place in the ranks of IS is intended not only to terrorize their enemies but also, as in other ethnic-religious conflicts, to close ranks and make supporters into accomplices: those who have participated in mass murders, beheadings, torture and systematic rape cannot so easily go back to a civilian life organized along conventional ethical lines. And certainly we must not underestimate the attraction of unrestricted power, weapons and testosterone surges on young men once the abolition of civilization can be subjectively portrayed as heroic. I realize I am letting myself get caught up in speculation; I am writing it down nonetheless to describe what is going on in our own minds, and more tormentingly in the minds of the Iraqis, and in the minds of the victims most of all: the inevitable search for an explanation. In the tent cities and schools, factory halls and unfinished buildings around Dohuk, the question of the political, historic and religious reasons for the rise of IS is overshadowed by a more general question: What do people do that for?

TO THE FRONT

Hence it is not so much in anticipation of new knowledge that we drive to the front lines in a Peshmerga pickup truck; we are drawn rather by the irrational desire to see for ourselves the jihadists we have heard so much about, to see their black flag, if only from a distance of a few hundred yards, with our own eyes. On the road south, we drive through deserted, mainly Christian villages before we get out in the town of Telskuf, thirty kilometres from Mosul. Since 21 August, the cross has stood once more atop the clay-brown dome of the church, although the inhabitants have not yet returned; we see only scattered people who have probably come to get something out of their houses and are loading their cars. Otherwise only the Peshmerga are now at home in the houses along the main road.

Western and adventure readers imagine Kurdistan as a wild mountainous country, and large parts of it are exactly that, successively rising ridges of green, brown, stone and even snow-covered peaks. But, along the front, Kurdistan is a wide, desolate plain crossed by roads running in straight lines. You don't have to be a military expert to realize that rifles and machine guns, the only weapons we see among the Peshmerga, cannot have much effect against the tanks, mortars and rockets of IS. The commander, whom I take to be the legendary General Wahid Kovli because of his dapper uniform and elegant appearance, is all the prouder of having recaptured Telskuf. They feigned a night attack from the north to approach IS unnoticed from the west and east. When the jihadists realized that they were firing their rockets in the wrong direction, they retreated headlong to the next village, Batnay, three kilometres to the south. Yes, there are many Baathists among the jihadists, former officers of Saddam Hussein's army who simply stopped shaving. Sitting on a living room sofa, the commander swings his arms wide to illustrate the movements of the various units. On the silent television set is the press conference of the new Iraqi prime minister, Abadi, with the terribly resolute-looking François Hollande. What does the commander think of the plan Barack Obama announced this week of supporting Kurdish ground troops with weapons and air strikes, sending military advisors to the Iraqi army and forming an international alliance against IS that would include Sunni Arab states?

'Those are beautiful words,' the commander answers, 'but so far only words.' About the American announcements he is sceptical; as to the weapons the Germans have promised, he seriously doubts they will be delivered in time before the war is over. 'We fought wars against Saddam alone in the past; we'll beat the Baathists this time too.' Of course, the commander sees himself as responsible only for the Kurdish territory, which will, sooner or later, 'naturally' be declared its own state. In central Iraq, the Arabs will have to drive IS out themselves; the Peshmerga can cover their flank if Kurdistan is completely liberated first.

'And the front?'

Yes, we can have a look, but no photographs: restricted military zone; he's sure we'll understand. The enemy must be denied all information.

THE GENERAL

I realize that the commander in the dapper uniform is not Kovli at all only after a squad of young Peshmerga have driven us to an unfinished building in a solitary spot two kilometres south. On the floor of room with no other furniture besides a thin mattress and a refrigerator, its window openings covered with blankets, sits a small, bearded man. Instead of a uniform, he is wearing a long shirt over traditional Kurdish trousers. We notice by our escort's repeated bows and humble salutations that the man is most highly esteemed. Yes, this is Wahid Kovli, the legendary general, who of course spends his days not in a safe living room, but in this darkened, unfurnished cubicle twenty yards from the front. The general's voice is at least as deep and rough as that of Joe Cocker, with whom – once the similarity occurs to me – he also has his stocky stature and his sparse hair in common. He curses in every sentence, without exception, laughing at the same time so drily that his vocal cords sound like bass drums. He smokes four packs a day, he admits drummingly as he lights up a first cigarette. Sebastian asks whether he might take photographs after all, and offers to submit all his pictures for inspection.

'Take all the photos you want, my boy, but first we're going to drink tea.'

So this is the man who is on the front lines, spearheading a war for the world of Barack Obama and François Hollande, and hence for our world too. Our escort reverently show us on their smartphones short videos posted on Facebook: the general with the bloody corpses of bearded fighters, the general in a crossfire, the general triumphant amid his men. In battle he always leads the charge, and he has been known to jump like James Bond onto the pickup of a fleeing enemy.

So naturally General Wahid Kovli, who else, liberated the Mosul dam.

When it gets dangerous, they send me first, the general drums on his vocal cords so credibly that you would very much like to have him as your defender, and never as your enemy. A Peshmerga since his youth, he will remain one as long as he lives. Home – ah, he can't even remember the last time he was home. He would rather tell us about the training camps he has been through, including ones in America and Israel, and he thinks the Israelis are at least better than the damned Arabs. Our escorts take turns photographing each other with the general.

'Have you a rough estimate of how many enemies you have killed over the years?'

'No idea,' the general growls good-naturedly, but seems surprised at the question.

'And how many battles you have fought?'

'Beats me.'

'Do you know at least how many wars you've been in?'

'Hell, I'd have to think about it.'

What makes this war different from the others is the deviousness of the enemy, who avoids open battle at all costs, relies on his modern weapons and commits every conceivable war crime, not only against captured soldiers but also against defenceless civilians. Until yesterday, it was raining rockets here that the sons of bitches were firing from a safe distance. Besides being cowards, the sons of bitches lie every chance they get; you can't count on the simplest agreements.

'You make agreements with IS?'

'Yeah, of course we ring each other,' the general confirms, and tells us about a four-minute phone call that he had just yesterday with the IS commander on the opposite front line, a son of a bitch named Faid who's not a jihadist but one of Saddam Hussein's former officers, like many of IS's military leaders. This Faid had noticed that he had a Peshmerga spy in his ranks.

'And did he know who the spy is?'

'The hell he did; he was just saying that.'

Finally General Wahid Kovli gets up to take us to the front line. In spite of the rockets, he leaves his helmet and his armoured vest, putting only a black kerchief on his head and tying it at the back like a pirate. I imagine I can hear not only my own heart beating but those of the young Peshmerga who drove us here. But the sight we are offered outside drives away all fear from one second to the next: in front of a wall of earth piled up chest high and shored up with sandbags, an officer in a starched uniform silently lip-synchs and dances to a pop song issuing at moderate volume from a loudspeaker. Facing him is a row of seven Peshmerga rocking their assault rifles to the rhythm. Then I spy the video cameras: they're shooting a patriotic music video. 'O Peshmerga, O Peshmerga,' goes the refrain, and each time the officer spreads his arms, leans to the side and smiles dreamily. It soon becomes obvious that he is not a professional but a real officer: try as he may, he can't manage to move his lips in synch with the sound track. But then singing isn't what the free world needs the Peshmerga for.

What looks more alarming to me is that hardly any of them look like fighters; they look like civilians of all ages who have picked out different uniforms from a costume hire. Many of their bellies are round, more than a few heads are grey, and their smiles are so friendly that you would very much like to have them as your friends, but not necessarily as your defenders. In conversation, most of the front soldiers confirm that they volunteered only recently to defend the homeland. Two of them returned expressly from England, where they have been living for twenty, thirty years; they talk in British accents about Arsenal FC and what's the matter with Özil. Their giving up the comforts of a Western European life does credit to their patriotism but not to their combat experience. My admiration is all the greater that they have been able to repel IS with nothing but rifles and their general. Thirty, forty yards in front of the earthworks, they have buried explosives which they will detonate if the enemy approaches again.

General Wahid Kovli passes me his binoculars. I see the road that leads out into the wilderness, a row of buildings flickering on the horizon, a pickup truck, and above the pickup truck a spot that must be the black flag of the Islamic State. No, the net gain in knowledge is not zero. According to a tradition that is widely held in Islam to be authentic, the Prophet's son-in-law, Ali ibn Abi Talib, whom the Shiites revere as their first imam and the Sunnis as the last of the four rightly guided caliphs, said:

> When you see the black flags, stay where you are and move not your hands nor your feet. Then you shall see a miserable, insignificant band. Their hearts shall be as pieces of iron. They shall have a state. They shall keep no treaty or pact. They shall appeal to the truth, but they shall not be the people of truth. They shall name themselves after their children and their cities. Their hair shall hang down long like that of a woman. This condition shall last until they quarrel among themselves. Then God shall bring forth the truth through whomever He will.

To those who do not speak Arabic, it only remains to be explained that Abu Bakr al-Baghdadi translates as 'Father of Bakr of Baghdad', and the seventh-century prophecy is sufficiently clear. Most of the other commanders of the 'Islamic State', such as Abu Musab al-Zarqawi, Abu Muhammad al-Adnani and Abu Omar al-Shishani, are also called by the names of their children and their cities. I always wondered why their fighters grew their hair long.

Four hours later – long after we have left the front – rockets are fired again from behind the black flag. Three of the Peshmerga we met die, and General Wahid Kovli is wounded so severely that he has to be taken to a hospital. I hear he has returned to the front in the meantime. God shall bring forth the truth through whomever He will.

THE ENTRANCE
TO HELL

SYRIA, SEPTEMBER 2012

THE CENTRE AND THE MARGINS

In the centre of the city and in the prosperous quarters, the war can only be heard, at intervals of an hour or half an hour, sometimes every ten minutes, less often in the daytime than at night, an isolated mortar shell or endless salvos. The people no longer even raise their heads, walking through the new shopping malls and the much bigger bazaar, waiting at the counters in the shops or in traffic jams, sitting in the cafés and restaurants, going on with their work or their talk. The shells are fired from Mount Qasioun, from whose foot the city extends far into the desert, ordinarily a favourite destination for outings, especially in summer because the air up there is one, two degrees cooler, and also cleaner. But no one goes on outings any more in Damascus. On Fridays, when the shops and offices are closed – so that no one has to go anywhere – the streets and pavements are empty, and the city looks deserted, especially at night. On the other days of the week, on the other hand, the first impression is one of dizzying normality. The people have long since grown accustomed to the checkpoints that interrupt the flow of traffic everywhere, accustomed to the refugees camping under bridges and in parks because they have no relatives in the centre of the city and in the prosperous quarters. Doesn't anyone wonder where the shells land?

Yes, everyone seems to wonder, at least everyone I ask, and many have answers too, very concrete descriptions of the war, because they live at the margins and in the poorer quarters of the city, but now they cannot go back to their homes after work, except to salvage their property, if it hasn't been looted. That is the second thing, after the appearance of normality, that surprises me about the city: the people talk. They speak for or against the state, speak fearfully or hopefully about the rebels – but they speak. Those who knew Syria before the uprising will remember how impossible it was to discuss politics among strangers or in public. Now almost every taxi driver talks about freedom and democracy; some don't want to let me get out when they discover I'm reporting on Syria abroad; they drive around the corner here and around the block there, explaining to me how they see the situation, their distress, their rage, their vision of what the country should be.

Where do the shells land? I ask a young cobbler on the first day. He has got his family lodged with relatives in the old city centre, and he makes a date with me on the spot to show me his district, Midan, where the rich people never went even before the war. In the minibus, the cobbler tells me to keep quiet so that I don't attract attention as a foreigner, and he silently points out the destroyed buildings, especially the mosques, the burnt-out petrol stations, the tracks the tanks made on the concrete. The poorer the rows of buildings look, the more shrapnel holes they have. Unlike those in Egypt or Tunisia, where the revolution took place in the centres of the big cities, the Syrian protests started in the rural regions and the margins and poorer quarters of the cities, where the liberal economic reforms under Bashar al-Assad did more than just aggravate the hardship, for at the same time the people saw the sudden wealth of the few, unusually conspicuous for the formerly socialist Syria, the Western saloon cars and SUVs, the new boutiques and posh restaurants, the lighted advertising panels everywhere. Those panels, advertising Internet access or built-in kitchens, still stand along the thoroughfares on their iron pillars as high as houses, only there no longer seems to be anyone changing the posters or cleaning the glass. The cobbler tells me with a look where to get out, and leads me into a dusty alley where the neighbours are playing backgammon on the pavement. We enter one of the four-storey buildings that are bare masonry outside and in; in the hallway several cats come to meet us; we mount the stairs, dust-covered shoes before the door of every flat, and reach the roof, which in summer is both dormitory and lumber room: 'You see the war?' the cobbler asks.

Yes, I see four black columns of smoke rising into the air, not five hundred yards away, I estimate, and I hear the shots of assault rifles.

The sequence of events is always the same: the rebels take up a position in a district in which they can count on the support of the inhabitants – these are, in Damascus and other cities, the poorer suburbs and quarters inhabited predominantly by Sunnis. Then the government's artillery moves in, lately supported by air strikes and rockets, to 'liberate' the people, as it is invariably called on state television.

'But the state lies!' the cobbler declares, and points to the smoke plumes: no one is ever warned; the inhabitants flee, he says, only when the roofs are caving in over their heads. 'Talk to the people while you're in Syria! Every single person here will tell you a thousand truths.'

Back on the pavement, we sit down with the men in their traditional djellabas playing backgammon. Their hope in the revolution, the hope of all the people, or at least all the Sunnis, in the quarter seems to be taken so much for granted that they specifically point out the one neighbour who still supports the government. Every one of them tells of monstrosities committed by the security forces, executions in the street that they have seen with their own eyes, tortures, bombings. I hear about the grocer on the corner who was arrested just a few days ago.

'Aren't you afraid?' I ask.

'The Syrian people have strong hearts,' they answer.

Yes, they have, I think, and I am surprised in this

conversation as in so many others I will have this week at the absence of one thing: hate.

These people, all of them so-called simple people, many of the men bearded, their wives all with headscarves, demonstrated peacefully for nine months, got clubbed, shot at, and finally dragged into a war that is raging at this moment not five hundred yards from here. They have seen the pictures of the massacres, most recently in the Damascene suburb of Darayya just a few kilometres away, supposedly four hundred dead, including many women and children – four hundred Sunnis, we have to add, because the terror is aimed specifically at the majority group. And yet they do not talk of reprisals but extol their city as the oldest in the world that has never belonged to a single ethnic group or religion; they sympathize with the rebels but criticize their strategy of house-to-house fighting; they rail against the Gulf states, which support only the radical groups among the armed resistance; they emphasize that their anger is directed against the ruling family, not against the Alawites per se. Is that plausible when the elite in both government and military consists almost exclusively of Alawites and Alawite militias are purposely assigned to carry out the massacres, as the men also mention? They do not want to exclude the possibility that there may be acts of retaliation here and there, and they start inveighing against the Gulf states and the Salafists again. But the Syrian people are smart enough to know that the government is inciting a denominational war to discredit the opposition as religious fanatics. The only man in this street who still supports the system is also an Alawite, and yet he still plays backgammon with the others. Perhaps the Syrian people will oblige the government by taking part in a holy war, but the cobbler and his game-playing neighbours won't, that much I believe.

I recount only this first chance acquaintance at such

length, but the pattern repeats itself, and I could report most of my encounters very similarly: when asked where I'm from, I introduce myself as a foreign reporter, and immediately we are in the middle of a conversation or I am taken along to those parts of the city that the Ministry of Information advises against visiting, probably not just for reasons of safety. I am surprised myself that I can move around so freely. After entering the country with a journalist's visa, I submit a list of the politicians I would like to interview on the first morning – that's all. Maybe I'm being shadowed, maybe my phone is tapped, but I suspect rather that the security forces have other problems to worry about at the moment. The artists and intellectuals too, who introduce themselves by the number of years they have spent in prison, and the opposition activists, whose meetings are recogniz-able by the collection of switched-off phones on the sofa in the anteroom – they too confirm that, since the peaceful mass demonstrations changed into an armed uprising, they are hardly bothered any more. I can go ahead and quote them by name, they say; the state is focused on the military conflict.

ARTISTS OF THE REVOLUTION

Mouneer al-Shaarani says it's as if he was under a curse: all his calligraphies turn into political statements. Although the uprising has been going on so long, eighteenth months already, he still feels as if on alert and can't think of much else. A soft-spoken, very polite gentleman with a white beard whose impassioned words do not spill over into gestures and facial expressions, al-Shaarani receives me in his studio, in which mostly older – which in Syria now means pre-revolutionary – works are on display, extremely formalized, sometimes completely abstract-looking inscriptions that are nonetheless based on a perfect mastery of the calligraphic styles. He is one of the best-known calligraphers in the Islamic world; his large-format works fetch top prices at auctions in London and Dubai. And yet today he is more interested in showing me on his laptop the little slogans and logos he has designed for the demonstrators: 'No to Fear', 'No to Poverty', 'No to Silence'.

It was inevitable, in view of the violence of the state, that a part of the movement would take up weapons in the end, and yet it was – al-Shaarani hesitates because he doesn't want to say the word 'mistake' – it wasn't right, because it was exactly what the government wanted to provoke so that it could declare the revolutionaries terrorists and come down on them even harder. The peaceful mass demonstrations, which beset the government more, have no longer been possible since then – only decentralized protest assemblies, which are smaller because they are organized at short notice and rarely appear in the international broadcast news any more. It was a mistake – now al-Shaarani uses the word – that the weapons are no longer used only in defence, as they were in the beginning, but more and more often offensively too. The Free Army is hardly able to hold the districts and cities that it occupies if the government troops advance without regard for the civilian population. Furthermore, he says, it has become practically impossible to control who is involved, especially since the government has released hundreds, thousands of criminals from the prisons. Add to that the religious extremists infiltrating from abroad. 'No to Foreign Interference' was another slogan of the movement, al-Shaarani explains, and shows me the calligraphy on his laptop.

'And what do you hope for from the West?' I ask.

'I hope for nothing from the West,' says al-Shaarani.

'Nothing?'

'Yes. It would be a significant gain if the West did nothing at all, instead of reinforcing the Muslim Brotherhood, which dominates the National Council, and setting up opposition figures in exile who know little about the situation in Syria. And don't Saudi Arabia and Qatar form part of the West? Can Saudi Arabia or Qatar do anything without the approval of the West?'

'Do you mean the West is intentionally abandoning the secular forces so that the religious factions gain the upper hand?'

'Intentionally or unintentionally; in any case the Western international community is supporting only Islamists, both in the armed resistance and in the exile opposition.'

Later I meet al-Shaarani again in the studio of his friend Youssef Abdelke, which is situated in a densely populated lower-middle-class neighbourhood near the now dangerous Baghdad Avenue. I don't need the exact address; I have only to ask in one of the shops and the shopkeeper leads me to the door, taking the opportunity himself to wish the famous artist a good evening. Tall, with a white pigtail and a dense moustache, Abdelke stands out in his neighbourhood by his appearance too. The two friends seat me on a sofa and pull up two wooden chairs to my left and right. They are both about the same age, somewhat over sixty; their French has the velvety accent of the Levant; two companions, two long-time political activists, Abdelke having spent many years in prison, al-Shaarani in exile; two former communists too – 'I still am a communist!' Abdelke interjects – and both full of hope that in their old age they will yet see the freedom they have fought for all their lives.

'The people have lost their fear,' says Abdelke, 'that is the critical point: forty years of fear are now over.'

The regime could hold on a while by force of arms, but in the long run it can no longer govern against a whole people, especially as the paralysis of the country has now gone on so long, the oppression has become so brutal that the regime's own clientele is increasingly turning away: 'We are approaching the point where the regime's survival no longer benefits anyone.'

Youssef Abdelke says not all of his pictures have become political. Nonetheless, as he spreads out his most recent works on the floor of his studio – including still-lifes and drawings of animals – his friend al-Shaarani detects the urgency and the suspense of the current situation in every subject.

TWO VIEWS

There may be yet another reason why the Ministry of Information is not shadowing me: my hotel is in the Christian part of the old city centre, where not a breath of revolutionary wind is blowing, and a foreigner who can pass the checkpoints without complications moves in a social stratum in which at least some of the population think the rebels are terrorists and the opposition an ignorant hoi polloi stirred up by foreign influences. Again, to describe just one of many similar encounters, I shall mention the amiable engineer who, although he too had to flee one of the suburbs before the war, can afford at least to house himself and his family in the good hotel in which I am staying. His stay has already cost $2,000, he groans in English, $2,000 for a holiday in his home town, and now his factory has had to close as well because the roads have become too unsafe for its employees and its suppliers, so he is also out of a job. He is Sunni; he has neither anything to do with Alawites nor any particular sympathy for the government; in the beginning he even sympathized with the young demonstrators; most of all the corruption makes him angry. But now he has experienced first-hand the chaos that the so-called Free Army is causing; he has seen the bearded fanatics, foreign jihadists among them, heard their foreign languages.

'Were you at home, then, when the rebels took over the neighbourhood?' I ask.

'No,' says the engineer, 'we had already fled, but neighbours told us, and we have seen pictures too.'

'On television?'

'On the Internet too,' says the engineer, and gets out his iPad to show me a video in which long-bearded men with assault rifles run through a street. He shows me other pictures, such as photos of a destroyed hospital, and asks what kind of revolution destroys hospitals.

When I ask whether the hospital couldn't have been destroyed just as well by government troops, the engineer goes into high gear and explains to me, with detailed evidence that I can't entirely dismiss as absurd, the West's and the Gulf states' plan first to destroy Syria and then to rebuild it after their own notions. His wife, sitting beside him in the courtyard of the restored historic hotel, takes her cigar out of her mouth and nods: 'Don't you see they want to make Syria into another Iraq?'

Damascus is telling itself two diametrically opposed narratives these days, each in several variants, and with only one thing in common: every new report, every new image, is easily inserted in the existing interpretation. You have only to watch Al Jazeera and the Syrian news channel side by side, without listening to the sound or reading the crawl text at the bottom: the footage of destroyed cities and weeping mothers is the same, presented by each side as evidence of the opposite camp's barbarity. Sometimes I imagine the two sides sitting at one table – say, the cobbler from Midan and the engineer from my hotel – exchanging their arguments, and then I hear of families, especially in the middle class, in which father and son, brother and sister, husband and wife can't speak a word to each other any more because each sees the other's political views as wrong, and worse: as criminal.

OUTSOURCING TERROR

Strangely, the atmosphere at the checkpoints, where the state and the population meet in day-to-day life, is nonetheless polite, often friendly. The soldiers I talk to in a military hospital in Damascus also seem to me, not sinister fiends, but honestly concerned. Some of them tell touching, politically ambivalent stories that cannot have been prepared by a propaganda machine. The driver who vituperates against the state with great gusto can still joke with the recruit who leans into the car window at a checkpoint. Often enough I have been in countries in which the army is perceived as an occupying force; I know the grim and the timid looks wherever soldiers and civilians meet. Strangely, I see them only rarely in Syria.

Only once do I hear the driver cursing softly as we approach a checkpoint, and I see him look around for a chance to turn back or into a side street without arousing suspicion. But it is not an ordinary inspection, because beyond it is a district in which rebels are entrenched, and the soldiers aiming their assault rifles at the car don't look like the ordinary soldiers but are wearing only black T-shirts above their combat uniform trousers. Their very physique stands out: the commander is almost fat, his soldiers conspicuously large and extremely muscular, and, even before we hear their harsh commands, their dark looks show that they are absolutely in no mood to joke around. I mustn't open my mouth no matter what happens, the driver whispers to me just before the commander bellows his question what we're doing here. The driver stammers something in which I understand only the word for 'wrong turn' or, more exactly, 'lost', and the commander shouts at him that he needs a car. At your service, says the driver, whereupon four body-builders with their rifles squeeze into the back seat of the Iranian make that looks like a toy car and isn't much bigger. At first I'm glad I don't have to make room and stay behind with the commander.

Ten minutes later, when the soldiers have got out, the driver whispers 'Shabiha,' as if it was dangerous even to pronounce the word. 'Did you notice their rifles were loaded?' No, I didn't notice that; I'm not familiar with the different positions of locks and catches on rifles. But the driver doesn't have to add that someone could easily have bumped a trigger accidentally in the press on the tiny back seat.

The government and its supporters, including the engineer in my hotel, vehemently deny that there even exists such a thing as Shabiha militias. Have I found proof? No. But I have noticed, and anyone who goes to the outskirts of the city must notice, that a certain type of Syrian soldier is distinguishable, almost ostentatiously distinct from the regular troops, in clothes, physique and expression. Whether they call themselves Shabiha or not is perhaps not so important. What is more important is that one camp is certain of the existence of a government militia that has no other purpose than to murder and pillage, while the other camp considers the existence of such a band of killers absurd, doesn't even see them in the city centres and the wealthier quarters, and so blames the massacres and lootings on a mysterious, external power. That means that both camps are afraid of an enemy who will stop at nothing, and both receive each new act of violence as evidence to justify their particular fear.

Some will object that the existence, and the crimes, of government-aligned militias is sufficiently documented. Nonetheless, some of the Syrians – many wealthy people, many Druze, many Christians, the vast majority of the Alawites – continue to support the state because they perceive it, in the form of government, civil service or regular army, as corrupt perhaps, but not savage. 'Assad is no Saddam Hussein!' How often I hear that during my stay. No, he is not, because Saddam Hussein's rule, like that of so many other tyrants, was founded on open violence, on publicly announced executions, on torture in the regular prisons, on poison gas attacks that he didn't even try to conceal. The rule of Bashar al-Assad, on the other hand, cannot be understood unless you take into account the human face it has tried to present from the very beginning – in his appearances with his young, pleasant-looking wife in the midst of urban society; in the announcements, which became ritual, of wanting to engage in dialogue with the opposition; in the economic liberalization that gave the country the brave new world of global consumer goods. By outsourcing terror, so to speak, to the militias whose existence it vehemently denies, the state terrifies the oppositional part of the population and at the same time demonstrates daily to its supporters through the evening news how mercilessly the opposition would deal with them if it came to a change of government. In this way the regime draws its legitimacy from the extremism of its opponents – which it therefore fuels systematically. With increasing success: when the wounded soldiers I talk to in the military hospital mention the rebels' brutality, that may or may not have been drilled into them; but, as perfidious as the state propaganda may be, it is hard to imagine, in the morgue, that their dead suffered their crude stab wounds or severed limbs post mortem. The coffins are stacked in the corridors because there is no space left in the cold room.

THE FEAST OF ST ELIAN

With the photographer Kai Wiedenhöfer I drive to the festival of Mar Elian in the town of Al-Qaryatayn, two hours
north of Damascus. Ordinarily, the festival is attended by
Christians from all over the country, but this year only the
local parish has come, all of whom fit in the pews of the little
church that is over a thousand years old, the men in pleated
trousers and short-sleeved shirts, the women in knee-length
skirts, the young people with plenty of gel in their hair, the
children with glitter on their clothes. The Mass consists
almost entirely of songs and sung prayers that sound not
very different from Quran recitations; at the Lord's Prayer,
the congregation spread their hands with palms upwards just
as Muslims do at the Fatiha, and at the Eucharist the long-
bearded monks kneel and bow until their foreheads touch
the floor. For the Bible reading, the priest has chosen – not
by coincidence, I'm sure – the redemption of the people of
Israel from the tyranny of Pharaoh. He is a member of the
monastery of Mar Musa, which is viewed critically by both
the government and the official Church because the order's
Italian founder, Paolo Dall'Oglio, has spoken publicly about
the violence of the government militias and called for dialogue with the opposition. Since the founder's expulsion
from the country, the order has been led by a Syrian, Father
Jacques, who is likewise unsparing with criticism.

After the Mass, Father Jacques takes me with him into his
austere office, which is also where he sleeps. The Catholic
Church in Syria, he says, not mincing words about the situation in his country, is making the same mistake as in Iraq,
where they positioned themselves on the side of the government out of fear of the Islamists. If the Church doesn't want
to talk about the oppression, it should at least remain neutral,

otherwise it will be held responsible later. Unfortunately, in the parishes themselves, especially the rural parishes, the Christians are motivated by the fear that there will be no place for them in a revolutionary Syria. While there are many young Christians who are in prison, many members of the Church, especially in the countryside, don't know their own history, think Islam is a nightmare, and don't notice how fundamentalist they themselves have become.

I ask whether the Syrian Christians aren't right to be afraid when they see what has happened to their co-religionists in Iraq.

'Not only we Christians: all Syrians are standing at the entrance to Hell. Not because the people want to live in freedom, but because their rightful wish is answered with violence.'

'And if Syria does become a second Iraq in the end?'

'Then there would no doubt be an exodus,' says Father Jacques, and immediately adds that the Christians are much more integrated in Syrian society than those in Iraq or in Egypt. Besides, fundamentalism has little influence on Syrian Islam compared with other Arab countries. Here, in any case, the order has better relations with the Muslims than with some Christians. I ask Father Jacques what he thinks of certain European politicians' demand that only Christian refugees should be accepted from Syria.

'These European politicians should do everything they can so that no one has to flee Syria, instead of making irresponsible statements that promote the very denominationalism that endangers us. We Christians belong to this country, although the fundamentalists don't like to hear that, neither here nor in Europe. Arab culture is our culture!' Five times the Mar Musa monastery has been raided – by criminals, note, not by Islamists – five times, although after the first robbery there was hardly anything left to steal. No, says a

nun softly, they don't have the feeling the government wants
to protect them. Their feeling is rather the opposite.

AT THE TOMB OF IBN ARABI

If there is a theology of pluralism in Islam, it was formed in
the thirteenth century by the mystic Ibn Arabi, called even
today the Greatest Master, *ash-shaykh al-akbar*. In one of his
most famous poems, he wrote:

> My heart can take on any form,
> For gazelles a meadow, for monks a cloister,
> A temple for the idols, the Kaaba for pilgrims,
> The tablets of the Torah, the leaves of the Quran.
> I follow the religion of love:
> Wherever its steed turns,
> I go that way.

Ibn Arabi's funerary mosque is in the middle of the old
Salihiyya quarter of Damascus, a dense net of very busy,
unembellished backstreets and alleys where only very few
foreigners strayed even in times of peace. The worshippers,
the sexes separated, are immersed in silent contemplation,
or softly chanting the Quran, which lies open before them
on little wooden stands, or performing their ritual prayers.
Some wear the long hair and colourful rings of the dervishes,
others the long beards, short hair and white robes that
Salafists favour; between them are some men in Western
suits, their cheeks clean-shaven, as well as children playing
among the faithful. I too perform my prayer and, before I
can go over to the wall to linger, a young man addresses me
in broken Persian to ask whether I am Iranian. Apparently
he saw by the position of my hands that I followed the Shiite

rite. I need to be careful, he says softly; Iranians have many enemies in Syria these days. I get this advice often. Because the Islamic Republic supports the Syrian state with money, weapons and military advisors, it's better not to stand out in public as an Iranian.

We withdraw to a corner of the shrine to talk undisturbed. The young man is delighted that I know the works of Ibn Arabi, and at the same time is enthusiastic about Iran; he leaves no doubt that he is on the side of the Syrian government; refers to the rebels only as extremists and terrorists. Does he know that the Islamic Republic persecutes Sufis mercilessly? I ask. At first the young man doesn't understand, and then he asks several times whether he has understood me correctly. Yes, I say again and again, and tell him about the many dervish convents that have been levelled in Iran, and about the mystic sheikhs who have been driven through the streets with their hair shorn off or, in some cases, executed. Unlike their Syrian brothers, the Sufis in Iran can practise their rituals only underground, and at great peril. The young man simply can't believe it, although he doesn't seem to mistrust me otherwise: he sees the Syrian state as a bulwark against Islamism, which is a threat to Sufism, and now he hears that this state's closest partner, its protector, persecutes and murders its own Sufis.

The uprising in Syria mixes up the habitual patterns of our perception. The regime, strictly secular in its whole bearing, has as its chief sponsor an Islamic theocracy, while the West is on the side of an opposition that is, at least in parts, decidedly religious; Syrians speaking perfect English and looking perfectly cosmopolitan defend the authoritarian structures with the argument that the people are not mature enough for freedom, and over whisky they call for the army to sweep the rebels out of the country with an iron broom, while bearded men and scrupulously veiled women place their hope in democracy and appeal to human rights. And in between we hear of commanders of the Free Army who, asked why they have grown their beards long, answer: Give us weapons and we'll shave them off again.

THINKING WITHOUT GRADATIONS

Rashid Darar knows the pious Muslims who strike fear into more hearts than just those of the government's supporters – he knows them up close. He shared a prison cell with them for years. An imam who can no longer preach in any mosque because of his critical stance towards the regime, he founded the 'Islamic-Democratic Movement', which is one of the few opposition parties tolerated by the state. Once, Darar tells me in a café near the train station that is frequented by the most well-known intellectuals – and hence no doubt by agents of the secret police – once an Islamist prisoner asked him in a surly tone whether he does his daily prayers.

'How old are you?' Darar asked him back.

'Thirty-five,' the Islamist answered.

'I've been doing my prayers longer than you've been alive,' said Darar, whereupon the Islamist was silent for a while.

Then he asked Darar whether he believed in democracy. Darar said he did.

'And in human rights?'

'Likewise.'

'Then you're an unbeliever anyway.'

So far, Darar says, this kind of thinking without gradations, dividing the world strictly into believers and unbelievers, permitted and prohibited, is suspect to most Syrians. The reality of people's lives is full of nuances, and especially from the villages he hears again and again that the militant Islamists are not welcome there. But if the state continues to rely on brute force and the bloodshed goes on, the population will gradually grow more radical too.

'I am afraid for my country and afraid for my religion.'

THE INTENSIVE CARE UNIT

Kai and I arrange to meet a driver who promises to smuggle us past all the checkpoints into one of the devastated areas that surround Damascus. We drive along the hard shoulder of a multi-lane road, with demolished buildings visible to the right, then turn off into a rubbish-strewn field. Our taxi is not the only car struggling across the uneven terrain, and it is not dark, but broad daylight. A light commuter traffic between war and peace seems to be tolerated, then.

The city we come to looks deserted at first glance. The walls of the buildings, several storeys high, are dotted with smaller and larger holes from bullets and shells; unbroken windows are rare; the concrete is strewn with broken glass, cartridge cases, tank tracks and scattered rubbish; the shutters of the shops are rolled down, some of them bent aside to allow a look inside, the complete inventory looted. The stray dogs probably had their share too. After the fourth junction, we discover a few inhabitants: first a woman with two shopping bags; a block further on, children. We pass rows of houses that seem to be still inhabited, washing hung on the balcony, a bakery where a little queue has formed, here and there street vendors selling fruit or other provisions. Then complete silence again for several hundred yards. There's something odd about the electricity, too: for the most part it seems to be cut off, but then we drive through a block where the street lamps are lit in the middle of the day.

I walk along the wall of a burnt-out hospital, looking for a way in, and in the side street I find a sign indicating a gynaecological clinic. I go down some stairs and am suddenly facing several men and women in dusty, sooty green smocks who look just as startled as I am. I introduce myself and ask if I may look over the hospital. A doctor hesitates a few seconds and looks at her colleagues before nodding with a very sad expression. May I fetch the photographer? I ask. Again the doctor hesitates and looks round. All right, she says at last, and goes out to the street with me to show the driver where he can park without attracting attention. Then she leads us down the dark hallways where the water is up to our ankles and the electrical wiring hangs from the ceiling. They just came back three days ago to clean up as much as they could, the doctor explains. Evidently the attackers walked through the corridors opening every single office, examining room and bedroom to throw in firebombs or something of the sort, not grenades apparently, since no holes have been torn in the soot-blackened walls. The windows are shattered, all the furnishings are charred to their metal frames, the hospital beds, the wheelchairs, the cots, all burnt to skeletons.

'Who were the attackers?' I ask.

The doctor can't say with certainty, since the entire staff fled with the patients when the army marched into the neighbourhood. But naturally she suspects it was the militias.

'Shabiha?'

'Who else?' the doctor answers.

Then she leads me to the intensive care unit on the top floor. They had three patients who couldn't leave the hospital, two very old men and a boy, and a nurse who refused to abandon them.

We enter the intensive care unit, which once consisted of four beds and the necessary equipment. The bedframes, with their backrests raised, are still here, and so are the cases of the medical instruments. The doctor doesn't need to point it out, we see it ourselves: in three of the raised backrests, exactly at head height, there are holes made by numerous bullets that went through the bedframes and into the wall, from both pistols and rifles, Kalashnikovs to be exact. Under the beds, again at the head end, the pools of blood have dried. There are no other bullet holes in the room; there was no fighting. The only shots were aimed at the three backrests at head height. In one other place we see bullets in the wall and dried blood on the floor: this is where the nurse must have been standing.

Could this scene have been staged? We came to this hospital by chance; no one could have expected our visit in this prohibited area. The doctors and nurses had obviously just begun their clean-up work. And nothing looked more authentic than the shock their faces showed.

'May we report on this? May we take photos of the intensive care unit?' I ask again.

'I'll have to ask the director,' says the doctor, finding in her nervousness no one at whom she can direct an inquiring look.

'He's coming,' she says after a phone call to the director. But the director of the hospital does not come, even after the second call.

After the doctor has called him the third time, she sighs that he won't be coming after all: he has been told that if anyone finds out about the intensive care unit, they're all dead. The doctor consults with her colleagues who have come into the room, and in the end gives Kai permission to take photos, including the raised backrests.

'One day there will be a court that will judge the evidence,' I explain.

'God willing, it will be before Judgement Day,' says the doctor.

Kai has not published the photos, and I have altered some details in the description of the place to make the hospital

hard to identify. We have given the unaltered report, with
the photos, to an appropriate institution. My writing about it
at all may be justified by the fact that human rights organizations have collected numerous reports of hospitals that have
been shelled, stormed and set on fire, and of patients shot
in their hospital beds. But the reader will believe me when I
say there is a difference between reading a report and seeing
those backrests with your own eyes.

THOSE WHO CAN READ,
LET THEM READ

In Homs too we visited two of the neighbourhoods in which
the war raged. But here we were escorted by soldiers and
by staff members of various official agencies – not apparat-
chiks, but three young people in jeans, as curious as they are
friendly, who listened to good Arab and Western music in
the car on the drive from Damascus. Besides the devastation,
which is very similar to what we've seen, we find a big ladder
with a rope that is supposed to have been used by the rebels
as a gallows; and, in a toilet, a cast-iron water basin with a
bare electric cable in it and a cord hanging from the ceiling for attaching bound hands. But nothing during the visit
occurs by chance or unexpectedly and, during discussions
with the so-called population, we are surrounded by soldiers.
The escorts say they will gladly go a little further on with
the soldiers so that I can speak to the people more easily;
they don't understand that the conversation would still be
rather uninformative. Helplessly, I try to visualize the truth:
the gallows and the basin for electric shocks may be fake,
but, if it's all a show, why do the weapons that are supposed
to prove that foreigners are supporting the rebels turn out to
be so puny? A dynamite case that is obviously from regular

Syrian Army supplies, or a home-made catapult with a spiral spring that might have been taken out of a truck or an industrial machine. And the church that we are led to has, to our escorts' surprise, not been desecrated at all, but hit on its roof by a shell; the Bibles stand untouched on the shelves.

We wave down a cyclist to ask him to tell his story amid the ruined houses. All this speaks for itself, he says, visibly less than eager for a conversation. But we would like to hear it from you, my companions quite amiably urge him.

'Those who can read, let them read,' says the cyclist, and rides on.

WE TOO
LOVE LIFE

PALESTINE, APRIL 2005

We too love life wherever we can,
We dance between two martyrs, erect a minaret between
them for the violets, or a palm tree.
We love life wherever we can,
And steal a thread from the silkworm to build a sky and
fence in this journey.
We open the garden gate to let the jasmine out into the
road for a fine day.

Mahmoud Darwish

IN SEARCH OF PALESTINE

I'm flying to Palestine! I emailed a friend before the trip.
Where is that? he asked, half taunting, half sympathizing.
Where is Palestine? I drove back and forth through the
Occupied Territories for five days and didn't find it. Three
years ago, after the breakdown of the peace negotiations and
the outbreak of the second Intifada, there was at least a dream
that united the Palestinians. They were angry, and many of
them found excuses for the violence, even for the violence
against civilians, but all of them had a goal in sight: a state
of their own. And they knew that this state would be limited
to the 1967 borders. No one mentioned Haifa, Jaffa, Acre.
What was at stake was Nablus, Jericho, East Jerusalem. It was
desperation – but at least there was also passion, there was
pain. This time, I saw only apathy. All scepticism towards the
media notwithstanding, I had arrived hoping that the peace
process had actually begun moving again. Ariel Sharon had
announced the withdrawal from Gaza; George W. Bush
had promised to support a Palestinian state; the Palestinians
had elected a president, Mahmoud Abbas, whom even Israel
looked on as a man of peace.

The radicals hadn't perpetrated any attacks in a long time. In return, the Israeli army had lifted some restrictions. That was the story on all the Western channels. Once I get there, it turns out – after the first afternoon, the first checkpoint, the first newspaper, the first conversations – that the good news is a media bubble which someone for some reason is blowing into the air.

WITHOUT HOPE

On Palestinian soil, nothing has changed that would give the people a reason to hope – not the Israeli army's harassment and not the disposition to violence among the Palestinians; not the corruption of the Palestinian National Authority and certainly not Sharon's ambition to permanently annex East Jerusalem and the big blocks of settlements in the West Bank in which 80 per cent of the settlers live. The Palestinians, who will soon make up the majority of people in Eretz Israel, according to demographic predictions, and thus by their existence will challenge Israel's self-image as a 'Jewish and democratic' state, would then be crammed into four non-contiguous and therefore easily controllable enclaves, one in Gaza, the other three in the West Bank. The withdrawal from Gaza allows the Israeli prime minister to present himself as a man of compromise and relieve the international pressure. His actual goal is demonstrated by the unabated expansion of Israeli settlements in the West Bank and was explicitly stated by his advisor Dov Weissglass on 6 October 2004 in the daily *Haaretz*: 'The significance of the disengagement plan is the freezing of the peace process. And when you freeze that process, you prevent the establishment of a Palestinian state, and you prevent a discussion on the refugees, the borders and Jerusalem.' The withdrawal from Gaza, Dov Weissglass continued, is 'the amount of for-maldehyde that is necessary so there will not be a political process with the Palestinians.'

Even now, during a drive from Hebron at the south end of the West Bank to Nablus in the north, there is hardly any stretch where your gaze could wander without meeting a Jewish settlement on one hill or another. And this is supposed to become Palestine one day? The Israeli left supports Sharon's withdrawal from Gaza, not because they overlook his actual intentions, but because they hope that giving up those settle-ments will set in motion a dynamic of peace that could lead to withdrawal from the West Bank too. Sharon, then, would be that Mephistophelian power whose actions do good even though his will is evil. Unfortunately, from the Palestinian point of view, that looks about as realistic as Part Two of *Faust*.

If the Palestinian resistance groups have largely abstained from attacks since the end of the second Intifada in February 2005, it is apparently not because of any new realization, but because of the sheer exhaustion of their society. In the one week I was there, I met hardly a single Palestinian who did not mourn a victim in his family – and none of these victims had blown themselves up. At the same time, the conditions in which they live have continually deteriorated since the first Intifada. The Palestinians rose up with all their strength and have now collapsed all the more wretchedly. Hamas and jihad are husbanding their strength and concentrating for the time being on enlarging their influence day by day. It was not long ago that the Palestinians were considered the most cosmopolitan and democratic society among the Arabs, with the largest proportion of women in leadership posi-tions. Now a religious dogmatism is spreading among them on a scale I have not seen even in Iran. The middle class are sinking into poverty or emigrating. The Christians espe-cially, who have always made their mark on the society, are giving up hope. Secular Palestine has withdrawn into two, three islands, in Ramallah, Bethlehem, East Jerusalem. Even in Nablus and Hebron, Hamas dominates the urban land-scape. And the giant prison that is Gaza, one of the most dismal places on Earth, has already been taken over by the Islamists. Cafés, women without headscarves, alcohol – all prohibited, if not by law then by the pressure of a public sphere that outdoes itself in piety with every passing day.

Who can blame the Palestinians for running into the arms of the Islamists when Hamas, with its charitable network and its ideals of devout brotherhood, offers them at least a minimum of social services which the Palestinian Authority is unable to deliver? The Israeli government has been com-plaining for a long time that it finds no partner for peace on the Palestinian side. Soon the work will be complete that will make that complaint indisputable. The West Bank prob-ably has to deteriorate as far as the Gaza Strip before the situation can be cemented in a so-called peace treaty after the right-wing Israelis' notions: a Greater Israel with a few Palestinian protectorates. Whether they are called a state or not is ultimately not so important. The main thing is that they are walled in. Ariel Sharon has given the Israelis to understand that Palestinians are terrorists who must be locked up like animals. He has treated the Palestinians col-lectively like extremists. Now the Palestinian society is gradually approaching the picture that the Israeli right has been painting of it for years. Its human face threatens to dis-solve, and with it the basis for a peaceful compromise that seemed within reach four, five years ago. In Gaza it is already difficult to talk about the form a reconciliation might one day take. It's no longer possible to discuss anything. The stories of the victims that burn in the hearts of everyone I talk to stifle all discussion and every attempt to awaken understand-ing for the other side, the other victims. I cannot remember

ever returning so depressed from any other country. Was it a
country at all? It wasn't Palestine.

Cynical though it may be, this idea crossed my mind with
increasing frequency during the trip: in comparison with the
present state of affairs, perhaps Eretz Israel wouldn't be such
a bad option. If a uniform Jewish state is the plan, the Israelis
should at least put it into effect quickly so that there is an
end of the terror and the Palestinians can grow accustomed
to their fate, as the Israeli Arabs have done. It is possible
to adapt to being conquered if it offers at least a minimum
of comfort. At least the Israelis treat their own Arabs like
subjects. There are laws for them, courts, jobs. Of course
they don't have equal rights; Israel is a democracy only for
Jews – but do the people in Egypt, Syria or other Arab states
have more rights? And public administration certainly works
better in Israel than in the Arab states, whether they are
organized dictatorially as in Egypt, Islamistically as in Sudan
or democratically as in Lebanon.

It is no wonder that, although most Israeli Arabs would
like to see a free Palestine, they leave no doubt that they
would nonetheless go on living in Israel after a peace accord.
In the West Bank, too, the people lived better while they
were being governed by Israel. There were schools worthy of
the name, roads that were maintained, very little corruption
– and they were able to move freely. The Israelis played the
part of old-school colonists: they wanted to bring civilization to the savages. Since the Palestinians have taken over
the administration of the cities in the West Bank, almost
nothing works any more. Of course, the primary reason for
that is the occupation. How is a state supposed to work if
not even its representatives – to say nothing of the ordinary
citizens – can travel freely from city to city? But, at the same
time, the occupation obscures the fact that the PA, with its
many centres of power, can hardly be expected to organize

life anywhere near as well as the Israeli state does for its own citizens, the Arab ones included.

THE WALL AGAINST EMPATHY

The Israeli government's problem at the moment is not the Palestinians. With the Americans backing it up, it can do whatever it wants with them anyway. The Israeli government's problem will be the Israeli society, which for the most part is not at all interested in the West Bank and the settlements. Most Israelis simply want to live in peace and quiet. The current government has given them quiet, to begin with, and is popular for that reason – not because it espouses the idea of a Greater Israel. But if the right does get serious about annexing the West Bank, it will have more trouble with its own society than with the Palestinians, who by then will be completely devastated.

Hardly anyone notices that Ariel Sharon's policy is like that of Hobbes's God, who first makes the people sick (in this case, violent) and then boasts how well he can heal them (that is, subdue the violence). Very few Israelis want to hear anything at all about the Palestinians. The summary of recent history I hear most often is: We offered them peace; they didn't want it – fine, then they will bear the consequences; only keep those savages away from us. The wall with which Israel is locking up the Palestinians (and, in the process, annexing a part of their land in advance by the wall's path) is a day-to-day reality for the Palestinians: a monstrous swathe of concrete running right across their roads, fields, villages. For the Israelis, who hardly ever see the wall with their own eyes (and earth has been piled up against it on the 'Israeli' side, and plants planted, so that it doesn't look quite so high) – for the Israelis, the wall serves first and foremost a symbolic purpose: it eliminates the Palestinians from their, the Israelis', reality.

Twice I was out in the evening in Israel, in West Jerusalem and in Tel Aviv. It was easy to strike up conversations in the cafés and bars. Where do you come from? You don't say, that's interesting, tell me about it. And what are you doing in Israel? Oh? You weren't in Israel? You were in Gaza today? And yesterday? Ramallah? – Change of subject. Outside the circles in which people continue, in spite of their exhaustion, to work for peace, not a single Israeli I met asked what the situation was like in Gaza, in Ramallah, in Nablus; no one wanted to hear what I had seen there a few hours previously. Why should they? Everyone knows all about it anyway. Better to put up the wall and talk about the Champions League. Have another beer?

The Russians probably treat the Chechens still more brutally than the Israelis treat the Palestinians. There are probably worse forms of occupation than those in the West Bank and in Gaza. In a way, I can understand it when Israelis argue again and again in their defence that other states' crimes are much greater, so why are they always the ones accused? But what it is that leaves one completely baffled in Israel – it is certainly not the return of fascism; if it were, it would be easy to see through and to explain ethno-psychologically, which is why lazy minds and anti-Semites make all their lopsided comparisons with Nazi Germany. Yet those comparisons are more than just lopsided: they are fundamentally mistaken. Israel, taken by itself, over the longest period of its history, is a liberal-minded, civilized, humanitarian country. It is a democracy. And that is why the question is inevitable, and much more painful than in the case of authoritarian regimes: How does that kind of society fit with this occupation? Why do they treat the Palestinians as if they weren't human beings? I write that in general terms, but in my five days there, and likewise during my previous trip, I could give dozens of examples each day of Palestinians being humiliated, violated in their dignity, treated like criminals, locked in cages, herded past the muzzles of loaded assault rifles. These are everyday experiences in the lives of practically all Palestinians. Whenever they want to go from A to B, they have to walk past a loaded assault rifle aimed at them. At the checkpoint to enter Gaza, which is as monstrous as the German–German border crossings used to be, except that the Palestinians do not sit in cars but are sent through the chutes at a run like pigs, an Israeli soldier asked what business I had there. Was I a veterinarian?

MY CAPITULATION

I didn't want to mention that last anecdote. I know exactly what resentment it will be misused to feed in Germany. It did not appear in the earlier drafts of this text. But I saw by the reactions of friends who read the manuscript that they couldn't understand my bitterness. Critical as they were of Israeli government policy, my text seemed to them too one-sided, too polemical, too sweeping. They didn't understand why I, who in my earlier texts had tried to steep myself in the perception of the Israelis, their heroic history and their day-to-day fear of terrorism, just as much as in the perception of the Palestinians – why now I mention only one side's pain and assign guilt so unequivocally. My friends are right. In contrast to my trip three years ago, this time I could not penetrate the Israeli reality. I walked through West Jerusalem and Tel Aviv, saw the people among whom I would be happy to live, a little trying but wonderfully diverse in their origins, friendly to strangers, the women enchantingly beautiful, people whom I found congenial or not, but in any case closer to me in their lifestyles and habits than the people in Hebron or Gaza. Just as last time, I had no end of admiration for what the Israelis have built in their state. But I was stuck on the outside, as if I had run up against plate glass.

I liked the Israeli life just as much as three years ago, but I couldn't enjoy it any more. Something in my reality had collapsed like a cardboard façade. Something in me said, You are guilty; they are the victims. They're not better people than you, but you are the occupiers, not they. And I think I can say, in retrospect, when it was that my perception finally tipped into one-sidedness: at the checkpoint entering Gaza, when I was asked about my profession. I would have liked to scream in the soldier's face: It's you who are beasts! That's something I must not write, nor even tell about, because it blocks out so much else. But now I have to write it to explain why I was no longer able to take everything into account. On this trip I was no longer able to remain an observer and to understand the people I was writing about. And that had always been the premise of my reporting. As much as I sympathized with the people, I forced myself to report on them as accurately as possible. But now I am not reporting; I am judging. I am no longer sympathizing; I have become partial. For that reason, I am finding description difficult – or I don't really want to describe. It's all been said before, I think; who needs the umpteenth story of the Palestinian olive trees that the settlers cut down under the watchful eye of their army? I notice it myself as I read: the whole time, I'm writing down what I thought, not what I saw. Perhaps that too is an observation: that I have lost that sympathetic understanding. For me as an author, it is a capitulation.

THEY ARE HUMAN BEINGS

The question is not why an occupying force is so brutal. Occupying forces usually are. The question is why even such a state as Israel could become so brutalized. I am afraid the answer contains a truth not just about Israel but about our Western civilization of today, including Europe. Once the other is branded a danger, he becomes a wild animal, and we lose all our inhibitions. State of emergency. It is the same question as the one about the pictures from Abu Ghraib: every day, prisoners in many countries suffer similar abuses or worse, especially in the Arab world. What is disturbing about Abu Ghraib is not so much the tortures themselves, but the torturers: citizens of a democratically constituted state. And not only that: they considered their behaviour so normal that they took lots of photographs and emailed them. If we are to believe the statements of the soldiers who later stood trial, they didn't even notice that they were violating the standards of civilization they had grown up with. The prerequisite for humane behaviour is seeing the other as human.

In Ramallah I visited Mahmoud Darwish. If anyone ever earned the epithet 'national poet' in the twentieth century, he did. Darwish was a poet who could still write 'we', not just 'I'. In his poems, and through his poems, Palestine preserved and reinvented its nationhood when it had disappeared from the map. In his last years, Darwish increasingly freed himself from the role he had acquired as the voice of the Palestinians. His themes became more and more intimate and, by the same token, more universal: love and desire, solitude and death. As a Palestinian, he has no chance of escaping into the private sphere, he said, but he feels his political duty today is to preserve what he sees as most endangered by the occupation:

humanity. 'We are human beings,' Darwish said, human beings who love, who quarrel, who are tender and selfish, magnanimous, courageous and anxious. Resistance against the occupation, he says, means remaining human beings, not becoming what the occupiers want to make them. 'They are human beings,' I thought during the next few days whenever a soldier at a checkpoint pointed his machine gun at the Palestinians.

Darwish was deeply pessimistic. Mahmoud Abbas is an honourable man, he said, yet his authority does not even reach as far as his own prime minister. The Palestinian society is crumbling, only to have its debris swept up by the Islamists. The external occupation is exacerbated by increasing internal pressure: censorship, prohibition, attacks. As a young man, he wanted to save the world, Darwish said with a sneer. Later, he would have been content to liberate Palestine. Finally he settled for the West Bank. Today he is happy if he can live halfway unmolested in Ramallah.

The reading by Darwish that I attended two days after our conversation had the atmosphere of a pop concert: barricades all round the big theatre, two giant screens outside for the live projection, the president in the front row, ovations by several thousand people who listened intently for two hours to a poetry that is the opposite of what the fundamentalists on both sides proclaim, the opposite of slogans: humanity down to its finest ramifications.

> We open the garden gate to let the jasmine out into the
>   road for a fine day.
> We love life wherever we can,
> Wherever we settle, we sow quick-growing plants; where
>   we settle, we harvest the slain.

On the flute we blow the colour of far, far away, draw on
    the dust of the path a whinny
And write our name, stone by stone – O lightning, light the
    night for us, light it a little.
We love life wherever we can …

LIFE AS
WHAT IT IS

LAMPEDUSA,
SEPTEMBER 2008

Baltic
Sea

Mediterranean
Sea

Punta
Alàimo

Via Bonfiglio

Refugee camp

Via Greale

Cala
Calandra

Lampedusa

Strada di
Ponente

●Cologne

Harbour

Airport

Cala
Francese

Mediterranean Sea

Damascus ●

Jerusalem ●

Mediterranean
Sea

Lampedusa●

Cairo
●

SUNDAY OUTING

The gate in the iron fence that is supposed to close off the jetty is ajar. The customs officer who wants me to go away because I don't have a permit is satisfied, after a brief exchange, if I retreat two, three yards. There's an official visit today, the officer explains, almost apologetically, and nods in the direction of the two gentlemen in dark suits. The young Arabs squatting on the ground are the first boat refugees to arrive after days of stormy seas, probably the advance party because they were faster than the others. Stole a fishing boat, they say, and sailed yesterday, nine friends, all about twenty, fashionable haircuts, hip-hop-style ankle-length jeans, one pensive with glasses, one pretty boy with long hair, one speaker, pointedly relaxed. A Sunday outing is the term they use here for a boatful of refugees who set out on their own, many of them spontaneously, and against all odds make it across without drifting off course or being intercepted, setting sail in Tunisia and landing on European soil less than twenty-four hours later. The relief is plainly visible in their faces. They don't even look particularly exhausted; they do look like they've been on a Sunday outing, I agree now. Most other refugees are at sea for days because they take wide detours to avoid the patrols of the Frontex agency ('agency' is Europe's euphemism for what is actually an armada), thirty, forty people on an inflatable boat who have literally paid the shirt off their back for a seat in the scorching sun. The staff of Doctors Without Borders waiting in the harbour often experience pure horror when the boats arrive: refugees half dead, or outright dead, of thirst and exhaustion, almost all of them dehydrated, many traumatized, generally with burns, cachexia, severe nausea, starvation, often with broken bones; but these nine friends simply cast off and sail away without stopping to think, encounter no storms,

no engine trouble; they're not even crowded, not even sun-
burned because they all fit under the roof of the cutter; they
slip, unbelieving, through the net of Paradise, as the Schengen
border is known in Africa. There is nothing the Doctors
Without Borders can do for them.

The officials take the young men to the receiving camp; in
two, three weeks they'll be transferred to another camp on
the mainland. There is no repatriation treaty with Tunisia, so
they have a good chance of being let out, after three, four, or
maybe eight more months of dreariness, with a deportation
order that they can toss in the wastepaper basket. Everyone
knows it: the nine Tunisian friends, the officials, the two
gentlemen in dark suits, the reporter. Most refugees go on
northwards anyway, so the state is not troubled about them,
and those who stay on are needed: without the illegal aliens
in Italy who work for two, three euros an hour, Germany
wouldn't have peaches for two, three euros a kilo. The composure with which the nine Tunisian friends are questioned
and then, not even twenty minutes later, led away belies the
fact that their situation is nonetheless a critical one: a break
with everything that has made up their lives up to now; the
beginning of a life whose outlines they can't even imagine – in
Europe, yes, in the promised land, but without rights, without health insurance, without social security, far from their
families, always in fear of the police. Amid the other dramas
that play out on the Mediterranean Sea and on the officially
fenced-off jetty at the port of Lampedusa, their change of luck
seems like a usual case that almost never happens any more.

GHOSTS

Lampedusa is in an uproar. I park my scooter on the square
in front of the church and go to the Internet café, and when

I come out ten minutes later, and want to ride to the hotel, my scooter is surrounded by a procession of the Virgin Mary, for which all 5,000 inhabitants of the island seem to have turned out in their Sunday best. It's a holiday; the town is all dressed up. The story here is that there doesn't seem at first glance to be any other story. The customs officials and the Doctors Without Borders have received 19,820 people in Lampedusa this year, plus the nine Tunisians who arrived today, 19,820 already and it's only September – but the village bears no trace of them. Their camp, one, two kilometres out of town behind a hill, is not shown on any map, not indicated by any signpost, and accessible only by special permit, which you have to apply for a week in advance with a list of all the questions you plan to ask. Only at the harbour are the refugees visible in the short interval between their landing and their transport to the camp, and only from the hill that rises above the town, since the view at the jetty itself is obstructed by concrete blocks. As I said, the gate is ajar; anyone could stroll to the dock, but it is only reporters like me, who imagined Lampedusa as some kind of hell, who do that. As the Doctors Without Borders report, it used to be possible to walk out of the camp; there were several holes in the barbed-wire fences, but what were the refugees supposed to do with no money on an island where they couldn't go into hiding? Once three, four black people had a look round the village and even ordered a beer, without being able to pay for it, and the mayor put out the word that the refugees were hanging around in bars getting drunk at no charge and insulting the tourists. If you believe the mayor, the island is going to ruin. In fact, almost all the people I talk to say they hardly notice the refugees. Those who spend their holidays in Lampedusa are not interested in sightseeing, a charming old town or beautiful landscapes, which the island doesn't have anyway. They come for the sea. They want to sunbathe, swim or dive, especially when it's too cold for that in the rest of Italy. No reality intrudes to stop them from doing so.

For me as a reporter, this is different. Normally I'm overwhelmed with impressions, but here I wait like an angler for refugees to arrive so that I can get any impression at all before they are whisked away, an impression of something besides a seaside resort. All over the world, the rich have refined their methods of blocking out reality: built fences, walls, stereotypes, anything to avoid seeing the misery, but their achievement in Lampedusa – receiving 19,820 refugees this year alone, with a population of 5,000 – puts any gated community to shame. It's not as if no one talks about the refugees. Indeed, it was by talking about them almost exclusively that the mayor won his last election. A new hospital was already not being built, but now it's not being built because only the refugees get health care. Just as the government in Rome sent the army to secure cities that are already among the safest in the world. Just as they declare a state of emergency, not only on Lampedusa – not only in the south for that matter – but throughout the country while they're at it. The emergency being not the state of the refugees, mind you, but that of the country. They're a friendly kind of people here: you feel their ease immediately when you arrive from the capital. Surely no one has anything against the Africans, Arabs and Asians, not even the mayor, who claims to understand their reasons for fleeing their homes. They just don't want them here – at least, not so many that they outnumber the guests, and not outside their own windows – like nuclear reactors. It's not enough that the refugees are invisible. Like ghosts, they haunt people all the more that way.

MIDNIGHT

The big fireworks show is beginning in the harbour. All that
will be visible from the receiving camp is the sky glowing
and flashing. They'll hear the explosions. Those who fled
war will think they're back in it. To those out on the sea, the
rockets in honour of the Blessed Virgin will light the way.
Might it not be a joyful celebration that they have survived
the voyage?

An hour later, as if out of a clear sky, a heavy rainfall
sets in. If there really are any boats at sea now, as the customs officials suspected, and if they still reach the jetty, the
Doctors Without Borders will have their hands full. I can't
sleep; I couldn't be on holiday here; I notice that I don't even
appreciate the magnificent sea. The mayor is right: the island
is stricken by the refugees. The inhabitants can't help it –
it's just the situation that makes inhumane what is no more
humane on the mainland: closing your eyes. Refugee organizations estimate that, for every three refugees who reach the
coast of Europe, one drowns on the way. Even Italy's right-
wing foreign minister, Franco Frattini, estimates that several
thousand die per year. Perhaps not the tourists blinded by
the sun on the beach, but the people who live here, I am
sure, think of them during every storm. Let the churches
take them in, the mayor grumbles, if the Vatican cares so
much about them, the churches and monasteries all over the
country. They should set up floating reception camps off the
coast, his deputy demands. They should shoot them, advises
her party leader, Umberto Bossi of the governing Lega Nord
– literally, he said: 'After the second or third warning, bang,
the cannon fires, without so much talking back and forth.
The cannon shoots somebody down. Otherwise we'll never
see the end of it.'

THE PREVIOUS MAYOR

'No, you're mistaken, the refugees are not a major issue for the people here,' says the former mayor, 'not a topic of conversation in the families, in the bars and restaurants. After all, they're practically invisible.'

'Are they really not a burden?'

'They were in the beginning, in 1993 when first ones arrived. In those days there was no camp, no money to provide for them, no clothes, no food supplies. Back then we had to take care of the refugees ourselves, there was nothing else for it, and we did it. Of course some people grumbled, and security really was a problem; the refugees hung around all day; some slept on the beach. But now?'

'I can imagine that people are somehow concerned about what will become of them.'

'Why? The refugees create jobs: sixty for the locals in the receiving camp alone; then there are investments, more frequent flights, the housing for the staff of the outside organizations.'

'But the news stories are not exactly good publicity for the island.'

'True, our image has taken a blow,' the former mayor admits. 'There are fewer tourists coming – but who's the one broadcasting all over Italy that Lampedusa is going to ruin? My successor! And he's not even interested in the refugees. He's interested in a state of emergency that he can capitalize on.'

'The Berlusconi principle, you mean?'

'Yes, the Berlusconi principle, only on a village scale: my successor wants public works contracts that he can deal to his friends, subsidies that will win him votes. He claims the carabinieri are overtaxed and dramatically demands

barbed wire around the receiving camp. Next, he demands
the establishment of a private police force because there's
no other way to restore security – security on Lampedusa,
where, you have to realize, nobody even needs to lock their
door at night. The only crime the refugees have committed
in all these years was to order three beers they couldn't pay
for. So why does my successor want a private police force?
So he can award new contracts. Just now he gave us a heart-
rending lament about the conditions in the receiving camp.
It's too crowded, he says; it stinks; it's inhumane how the
refugees are treated. And how might we improve their situation? By putting the camp under municipal administration
– more new jobs! Where it benefits him, the refugees are
poor unfortunates, and the next day he says Negroes stink no
matter how often they wash.'

'Is it racism?'

'No, just the usual prejudices, nothing more. People
like him aren't like the fascists used to be. People like him
profit from every refugee boat that lands in Lampedusa.
It costs €12,000 to dispose of the boat as hazardous waste:
the engine, the battery, the metal – you can't just sink it at
sea. They get paid €12,000 and then they pay someone else
€2,000 to throw the parts in the household rubbish or just to
scuttle the whole boat at sea.'

'Didn't the current mayor win the election with anti-
refugee slogans?'

'He won the election because he picked a quarrel with the
carabinieri. They were too strict, he claimed; they harassed
the people here, just like the health inspectors and the building inspectors and every other state agency for that matter:
they should just leave the people alone and let them organize
their own affairs. The people – don't make me laugh! When
they say the people, they mean themselves. They want to pri-
vatize everything. Except things that don't bring in money;

the state can go on providing those – flights to Lampedusa for example: would the state be so kind and subsidize them? To those people, the state is a business unit.'

The former mayor silently stirs his fourth espresso for half a minute as if trying to think what other allegations he can make against his successor. He himself is a leftist of the old Italian school: secretary general of the Communist Party on Lampedusa at thirteen because he could read and write confidently at a time when that was not taken for granted in southern Italy. He has always been an agitator, had his first political victory as an adolescent: the establishment of a turtle preserve on the east side of the island. The photos are hung on the walls. Lampedusa is actually Christian Democrat, he says; his own electoral victory was an exception. But the Christian Democrats were at least political opponents. Oh, how he despises these new types, their ignorance, their lack of principles, their opportunism! They know nothing, he says, of Lampedusa's history – about which he's writing a book; do I know a publisher in Germany who might translate it?

'We are a people of migrants ourselves, of boat refugees if you will; we set sail for Tunisia because there was work in Africa then. Many of us married Arab women; others were born there and later moved to Lampedusa with their parents. Many of us are Arabs, although they don't like to hear it said.'

It's half past nine in the morning; the former mayor is sitting in one of his two hotels wearing a T-shirt and Bermuda shorts, his mid-length hair combed back, a broad face and a smile to match; his voice is deep from the cigar that he probably puts out only when he goes to sleep. You can see that he either enjoys eating too much or gets too little exercise, but in his heart he still has the zeal with which he once fought for the turtles.

THE CAMP

Concrete slabs between rows of shipping containers stacked two storeys high, each so full with six bunk beds there is barely room to stand; the men's section crowded everywhere, in fact, although there have been storms at sea for days and all the bunks aren't even occupied. The whole camp, officially for seven hundred refugees, is less than sixty metres wide, less than two hundred metres long, I estimate; the population density is higher than in any Japanese highrise. Every square metre manifests the authorities' efforts to walk the fine line between potential accusations of treating the refugees inhumanely or of spoiling them. Rough-hewn strips of foam rubber that look like building insulation serve as mattresses; the sheets are paper; all the dishes are disposable plastic. In the men's section a silent throng stands in front of the gate, yet no one is able to explain to me what the men are waiting for. All of them are silent, in fact: the boredom is palpable, as are the inevitable tensions among the refugees. The women have much more space, however, and even a few trees for shade; they have chairs and three pieces of bright-coloured plastic playground equipment for the children. But the men – here the Central Africans, there the Arabs, the Eastern Africans in the corner, a few scattered Tamils, Nepalese and East Asians – sit on the floor or lie on the rectangles of foam rubber that they have brought out of the dormitories. Behind the medical service's container, more mattresses are heaped up, a whole hill of the stained dark yellow foam, for the time when the sea calms down. Eight sweat-soaked football players have taken possession of a pitch and placed four plastic bottles to mark two goals.

The match is contributing to the relaxed atmosphere, says the young director, constantly brushing his hair off his large sunglasses, his shirt open to the fourth button, jeans with a wide designer belt, pointy leather shoes. His company won the contract after the previous camp had to be closed down. A reporter disguised as a refugee had been starved and mistreated for a week, and his report had found its way to the European Parliament. The woman from the United Nations refugee agency, who has been working in the camp since then, confirms that no one is beaten any more.

As much as the director strives to infect me with his enthusiasm, every item on his programme makes me think: God, how bleak. We are standing in the cafeteria, which is much too small, with its four rows of tables, for anyone to sit here, so it's used only to dish up food which the people take outside to eat on the concrete slabs; the menu plan is balanced, all the vitamins are supplied; primi, secondi, dolci, the director exults, and like a circus magician he switches on the conveyor belt between the tables that sticks a plastic film on top of the plates: 'Would you like to try some?'

'No, thank you,' I stammer, thinking at the same time that very few of the refugees had three meals a day before they made the sea crossing.

Compared with Libyan camps, this is a holiday resort, as the Central Africans can attest, and likewise compared with the camps of the illegal aliens and the Roma on the outskirts of many Italian cities. Those are third-world slums in every sense of the word: plywood walls and sheet-metal roofs, no water, no sewers, a bog at the first rainfall. Lampedusa on the other hand is definitely EU-compliant. God Himself couldn't come up with a more wretched implementation. For a day or two they just sleep, says the woman from the United Nations refugee agency. Only after that do they actually realize where they are. Even two weeks later, the dominant feeling for most of them is relief. Only one Arab is complaining that there's nothing but pasta to eat, pasta every day, he can't stand it any more.

No, Lampedusa no longer has any scandals to offer. Instead it's become a showcase in which Europe can display its humanity to reporters and parliamentary commissions. Yes, if humanity is defined not by the minimum standards of any European prison, but as enough to eat, a place to sleep, clothes, no beatings, no verbal abuse, a doctor in emergencies and a psychologist in case of screaming fits, then the camp is humane. A scandal is what's happening on the other side of the showcase, before a refugee gets to Lampedusa at all. The inland camps would appear to be scandalous, but not even the Doctors Without Borders can visit them; reporters are out of the question. Any Western European would also consider the life of an illegal immigrant inhumane, which is what usually follows a refugee's stay in the camp if the authorities fail to grant asylum. The operations of the Frontex agency could also be a scandal – the agency that Europe founded to intercept the refugee boats well before they reach its territorial waters. Without checking whether there are people on deck who have a claim to asylum, Frontex forces the boats to return to the African ports from which they started. Speaking into a German television journalist's microphone, the Italian commander of one mission said he had instructions to board the boats and confiscate food and fuel to prevent the boats from continuing on their way. According to other statements, Frontex soldiers are said to have destroyed inflatable boats on the high seas to prevent them from continuing. Nothing is known with certainty, however, since the agency is not accountable to any government. It rejects inquiries even from the European Parliament on the grounds that its work involves secret intelligence. 'To combat illegal immigration, we need to be not do-gooders, but bad guys,' said, candidly enough, the home minister of the country where humanism was born.

THE NEW MAYOR

Procession of the Virgin Mary again in the evening, this time out of the village and up a hill. In the middle of Mass, the faithful suddenly turn ninety degrees to the left and address Mary, first in chorus, then individually for two, three minutes, with such fervour as if it was not an image standing there, but the Virgin herself. Because the mayor of the town is a head taller than the average, I see him throughout the Mass yawning through his beard. After two hours of brisk walking and a Mass that goes on so long that half the congregation started back before Communion, he is tired; that's understandable; and now the poor man also has to explain to the one thousandth journalist that he has nothing against foreigners. Even his leftist predecessor admitted that the right-wing mayor gets on splendidly with the dark-skinned priest whom the bishop sent to Lampedusa when the parish was short-handed.

'Naturally,' the mayor explains, sitting on his folding chair while beside him the altar is being disassembled, 'naturally the refugees', whose distress he describes in detail, 'must be helped. Unfortunately, the governments in Rome, whether right or left, have failed. The left's demands to open the camps would only drive the miserable refugees into crime, prostitution, drug addiction. And the determination of the right to treat these unfortunates as criminals is unrealistic. You couldn't build enough camps to intern them all.'

'And your solution?'

The mayor was waiting for that question. The whole time he's been pressing on both top corners of my notebook so that I can write better. Each time I ask a question, he points with his index finger at a blank space where I can write his answer, and then he sometimes turns his head around towards mine as if he wanted to read along and verify that my record is correct.

'We as a municipal government have given the matter a great deal of thought and amassed a great deal of experience,' the mayor begins. 'The solution is that these poor people need to be aided in their home countries!'

I notice that the mayor is waiting for acknowledgement, or at least a request for clarification, but nothing occurs to me at the moment. 'There is probably no politician in Europe who would contradict you,' I say, trying to phrase my demur politely.

'But I mean it!' the mayor says excitedly, 'We have to build schools, we have to build democracy, we have to get involved in a big way.'

Then he explains his master plan which, admittedly, would cost a lot of money. With every single item, he points his finger again at the place I should write down his proposal. I bite back the question whether the mayor himself wouldn't be the most suitable candidate to implement the master plan for Africa. Instead, he mentions in passing, as if it were part of his master plan, that Italy needs the refugees to do the dirty work that Italians are above doing.

'Isn't that a contradiction?' I ask, startling him.

'If Italy needs labour,' the mayor says with renewed excitement, 'the government needs to grant visas! We are five thousand inhabitants. We can't solve Europe's problems. We are Christians. We have received the refugees and we will continue to receive them. But we are tired of all the negative stories being written about us. The journalists act as if the island was on the verge of collapse, when it's really marvellous here, a fantastic place for a holiday.'

'Certainly,' I confirm, and ask whether the mayor didn't contribute to the hysteria himself with his interviews.

'That was a malicious attack on me by the left-wing

newspapers,' the mayor retorts, well aware of what I'm alluding to: 'In summer, when the camp was overcrowded with two thousand refugees, I said the people were living like animals there. I didn't say they are animals! Do you understand? And when we had the problems with the water supply, I said the poor black people can't get clean when they wash – because they have no water, you understand? I was the one who took on the Vatican to get them to receive the poor people. I don't have anything against Africans. I don't have anything against Arabs. I don't have anything against Asians. I only have something against lawlessness. A democracy has to be able to keep order and enforce the law.'

'A blockade?'

'Yes, you can call it a blockade. If the government wanted, it could block the sea route tomorrow.'

The mayor sees me writing down the sentence without asking another question. So he points his finger at the paper again: 'I say that in the interest of these unfortunates who will find in Europe nothing but crime, prostitution and drugs. We mustn't lure them into disappointment.'

NIGHT AGAIN

The sheet lightning awakens me. The moment I step out on the terrace, chunks of ice fall from the sky like none I have ever seen or would have thought possible. At first I don't understand and step back under the eaves only to keep from being struck dead, and then I realize it must be hail – hailstones the size of tennis balls – and not an apocalypse. After a few minutes comes the cloudburst. The water floods the terrace so fast that it forms puddles in my hotel room, in spite of the towels I lay along the cracks under the doors.

Two hours later, I drive the motor scooter through

pond-sized puddles up and down the deserted, brightly lit seafront promenade until I discover some people in front of a French warship at the very far end of the old port. It's probably too big to moor at the jetty where the refugees are supposed to arrive. Sixty-five Somalians were rescued during the storm, I overhear, including thirteen women, eighty nautical miles off the Libyan coast, one woman pregnant, fifth month, one injured. That it's a Frontex ship that picked up the refugees, and so close to the Libyan coast, surprises the Doctors Without Borders. No one knows any details, but everyone, including the woman from the United Nations refugee agency, says Frontex is there to keep the refugees away from Europe. Those who work for the Italian state – that is, besides the customs officials and the carabinieri, the staff of the receiving camp – are recognizable by their latex gloves, like the Westerners in Afghanistan. People unload a canister of disinfectant from a van.

'And the refugees,' I ask, 'where are they?'

Because the bus hasn't arrived yet, they're waiting aboard the ship, where it's warmer. I know by now what the word 'Somalians' means here: they probably all belong to a single family or clan; their trek started months ago; they fled the war at home, or perhaps they were expelled; some died on the way, that's certain. The opposite of a Sunday outing. Soldiers pass big red plastic bags, almost empty, from the deck, one for each refugee, I assume: their personal belongings. Everyone on the jetty, with or without latex gloves, speaks in hushed voices, almost in whispers, and sparingly; we just stand there and stare at the lit-up ship with the sixty-five rescued people in its belly as if we were waiting for Father Christmas. If we all took each other's hands now, with and without latex gloves, to sing a Christmas carol, I wouldn't even be surprised, I'm so thankful for the blessing that rescue signifies. Then I remember that I'm the only one here seeing such a landing for the first time – but a Tunisian interpreter also grows sentimental when I speak to him, and his eyes shine. If the word martyr has any meaning today, the interpreter says, the word witness, to use the precise meaning of the Arabic *shahāda*, it is for those waiting in the belly of the ship to step into the light, and for all the other refugees of this night who will not see it: they are the witnesses of our time. The term martyrdom fits too, I add. And then we talk about Jonah, and the refugees in the scriptures, about Mary, Joseph and the baby Jesus, and I say these stories do not belong to a distant past but are taking place here, three hundred yards from the beach where the holiday-makers will go swimming again tomorrow, and back there are the restaurants on the harbour where they will have lunch when the French warship is patrolling off Libya again to stop other refugees.

Before the bus arrives, I feel the restlessness that grips everyone, a silent stir, although only three soldiers seem to have begun to move on deck. They go inside the ship through a hatch and emerge a short time later with the first refugees, whom they support by the arm, an older man first who apparently has an injured leg, then a pregnant woman, just like Joseph and Mary, I think now, two incredibly foreign people, not just because of their dark skin and the wide, exotic robe of the woman with the red headscarf that hangs down, Somali style, over her belly – much more foreign are their eyes, disturbed, timid, anxious and yet grateful to life that they still have it. Following Mary, the procession of the other refugees, first the women, mostly young girls, much more delicate than Europeans or the Central Africans in the camp, then the men, also slight, setting their feet on the ground as carefully as if it was the first time. And it really is as if they were being born again. I want to greet them, to call out in Arabic 'Peace be with you', or at least smile at them, but because no one else is doing so, I am too self-conscious, and so they stagger one after another out of the belly of the ship with no comment from the onlookers, with no greeting or expression of joy; they teeter a few yards across the deck on the French soldiers' arms, and then the Italian soldiers waiting on the jetty lead them down the gangway to land and seat them on the bus which will take them to sleep off their exhaustion on insulating foam mattresses and paper sheets. I tremble, I'm so moved to see life, bare life, as if at a birth or a death, life as what it is: a gift.

WITH OR WITHOUT APPROVAL

When the refugees' bus has driven away, I talk with the captain, who comes on land just for me.

'Congratulations,' is the first thing I say, 'my heartfelt congratulations!'

'What for?' the captain smiles, a tall, athletic man of perhaps forty with a crew cut and a receding hairline, but he knows at once what I mean. His joy, at least, is visible.

I hear how the refugees were discovered, huddled together on a little wooden boat, no, not in the storm – it would have been too late then – but shortly before, when the stars were in the sky.

'How did the refugees react when they saw your ship?'

'They debated when we put the spotlights on them; some were glad and waved to us, others were afraid and seemed to be arguing for flight. We put out our boats and blocked their way. When we told them we wouldn't take them back to Libya, then, yes, they were all glad; then, they cheered. A little later the clouds built up, and they got quiet, and when the thunderstorm broke they realized how narrowly they had escaped death.'

'What about other refugees who were under way in boats tonight?' I ask. 'Is there a chance anyone survived the storm?'

The captain thinks a moment and then says, 'Zero per cent.'

When I ask about Frontex, he almost bursts out, 'When I see sixty-five people in a wooden boat on the open sea, I don't give a damn about Frontex; I don't think about immigration, papers, customs. I save the people, damn it.'

For him as captain, he continues, tacking an explanation onto his little outburst, maritime law takes precedence over any European Union regulations, so he couldn't act otherwise anyway.

'Does every captain see things that way?'

The captain knows at once what statements I'm alluding to. 'I am certain', he says, 'that all French captains at least would have done the same. Besides, I had the approval of my command.'

I am certain this captain would have done the same even without the approval of his command.

CAIRO, OCTOBER 2012

Where have you been for so long? asks the muʿallim – the Teacher, as we all call the head waiter – Where were you all this time? and he doesn't seem to accept residence in Germany as an excuse. Couldn't you have dropped by sometime? He is seventy-eight by now, still works a twenty-four-hour shift when he's on duty in the tea house, then a day off, then another twenty-four hours. At each visit I wonder more anxiously how the Teacher bears up, considering he already looks as if he hasn't slept in twenty-four hours when he starts his shift: his eyelids half closed, his tall, thin body slightly bowed in his blue-grey galabiya, his plastic slippers audibly shuffling across the floor, as if to make sure none of the guests forgets that someone is slogging away so that they can enjoy their hookah and their card game. Or is the shuffling supposed to be just an accompaniment to the great Umm Kulthum, still singing about 'those days' through loudspeakers that sound as if they too are seventy-eight years old? The Teacher can't be exhausted, though, so loud and piercingly he shouts his instructions, even at the end of his shift, as if he had to wake his assistant waiters out of a deep sleep. And his hair, not yet grey at seventy-eight, his almost smooth forehead and his rascally grin when he invites me to his house, where he enjoys life himself between shifts, for spirits and hashish. No, I think the fatigue is part of the Teacher's professional image, and in reality, or at least in the first few hours of his shift, it's not really fatigue but the serenity that's necessary to ignore all the excitement, to resist all the change. There is no institution in Cairo more constant, more even-tempered, less impressed with progress than the tea house. A city with pyramids on its outskirts needs places in the city centre too where everything stays the same as it was in 'those days'.

'And what about the revolution?' I ask.

'Ah, the revolution,' the Teacher mumbles, and raises one of his eyelids, as if to say with a piercing look all there is to say.

'Weren't you in Tahrir?' I persist, pointing to the revolutionary and also anti-Islamist stickers stuck to the windows of the tea house: 'Religion for God, the Fatherland for all.'

'Only the young people were in Tahrir,' says the Teacher, referring to his assistant waiters, who are over thirty.

Of course he's glad the dictator has been overthrown, only he doesn't see the revolution as solving the most urgent problems, especially that of poverty. On the contrary: the economy has more or less collapsed; meanwhile civic life is asleep.

'Cairo can never sleep,' I cry.

'That's true,' the Teacher chuckles, and lets both his eyelids close as if to prove the contrary.

When he opens them again two seconds later, he says these young people – meaning the assistant waiters again, apparently – thought a revolution is something you finish in a day. It's not, of course; he never thought it was. Nonetheless, he says, it is amazing – he never would have thought it possible, he admits – that the president can become a prisoner and a prisoner president. If ever a president refuses to leave office again, he'll have the young people to reckon with now.

'Things won't change unless the people change them,' the Teacher says, quoting a Quran verse, a revelation applicable to all places except the tea house.

Then he stands up again and shouts his instructions loud and piercingly, as if he had to wake his assistant waiters out of a deep sleep.